ALSO BY JOHN BOWE

*Gig: Americans Talk About Their Jobs*
(with Marisa Bowe and Sabin Streeter)

# NOBODIES

# NOBODIES

## MODERN AMERICAN SLAVE LABOR
## AND THE DARK SIDE OF THE NEW GLOBAL ECONOMY

## John Bowe

RANDOM HOUSE / NEW YORK

Published in the United States by Random House, an imprint of
The Random House Publishing Group, a division of Random House, Inc., New York.

RANDOM HOUSE and colophon are registered trademarks of Random House, Inc.

Part of "Florida" was published in a different form in *The New Yorker* (April 21, 2003).

ISBN 978-1-4000-6209-6

LIBRARY OF CONGRESS CATALOGING-IN-PUBLICATION DATA
Bowe, John.
Nobodies : modern American slave labor and the dark side
of the new global economy / John Bowe.
p.  cm.
Includes bibliographical references and index.
1. Slave labor—United States.  2. Equality—United States.
3. Globalization—Social aspects.  I. Title.
HD4865.U6B68 2007
331.11'7340973—dc22      2007012063

Printed in the United States of America on acid-free paper

www.atrandom.com

2 4 6 8 9 7 5 3 1

FIRST EDITION

*Book design by Casey Hampton*

*To Sonia Bowe-Gutman*

*The onetime darling of Seventh Avenue, Isaac Mizrahi, was hired last year by Target to bring style to shoppers in forty-seven states. Critics were nearly unanimous in their celebration of Mr. Mizrahi's belted suede jacket and all-American turtlenecks, praising particularly his ability to accomplish so much at an affordable price.*

*Few stopped to inquire how it was possible to attain Mizrahi chic for as little as $9.99. Mr. Mizrahi's clothes are manufactured at factories around the world, said Lena Klofstad, a Target spokeswoman, who declined to name specific countries. "We have standards for all our vendors and a compliance area that takes care to enforce them," she explained, "so Isaac is freed up to focus on what he enjoys, the design." When asked if he knew where his bargain styles were being manufactured, under what circumstances and by whom, Mr. Mizrahi pleaded ignorance. "I don't know," he said. "And I don't want to know."*

—"I Came, I Bought and I Helped," *The New York Times,* November 18, 2003

Homo homini lupus.

*Man is a wolf to man.*

—Latin proverb

# Contents

# Introduction

A few years ago, I was co-editing a project called *Gig: Americans Talk About Their Jobs*. The book consisted of interviews with people talking about their work, which of course led to discussions about their worries, marriages, sex, Jesus, Satan, and every other subject that interconnects as people pursue a living. To find many of the book's subjects, I drove thousands of miles, meeting hundreds of people all over America. In North Carolina, while looking for a guy who worked in a chicken-processing plant, I met some labor activists. They happened to tell me about a community group that had uncovered a slavery ring in the orange groves of southern Florida. Like most people who hear about the subject for the first time, I thought it sounded . . . *interesting*.

At that time, the case was still under investigation by the FBI. Like many investigations, it might have gone nowhere. But an indictment followed: *The United States of America v. Ramiro Ramos, Juan Ramos, and José Ramos*. The three men would eventually be charged not with labor abuse or nonpayment of wages but with holding people in involuntary servitude—slavery. The same kind of slavery supposedly outlawed 140 years ago by Abraham Lincoln and the passage of the Thirteenth Amendment.

Over the two years it took to write about the case for *The New Yorker,* I spent a lot of time thinking and hearing about others like it. At first, I was outraged. Then I moved past outrage and began to reflect more calmly on the meaning of slavery in a country that (a) long ago outlawed it, and (b) spends an awful lot of energy talking about freedom. After all, it was one thing for people to treat one another wretchedly in screwed-up Third World countries. But what about us, in the land of the free?

The biggest surprise for most people who read my story was that slavery still existed in America. For others, it was the prevalence of such incidents; the Ramos case was just one of *six* successful forced labor prosecutions to come out of South Florida in recent years and dozens of cases that surface each year nationwide.

For me, the biggest shock was grasping the immense indifference it takes for a supposedly free country to allow even a single such case to happen. Ramiro Ramos, it would emerge, had long been known to his workers by the nickname "El Diablo," the Devil. And despite years of evidence, news accounts, and audible murmurings that easily could—and should—have aroused suspicion of rampant labor abuse, this employer, with his ludicrous, cartoon-villain name, remained a welcome player in the network of growers, cooperatives, holding companies, subsidiaries, and corporations responsible for bringing orange juice to my table (including Tropicana, Minute Maid, Taco Bell, Wendy's, Burger King, McDonald's, Kroger, Wal-Mart, and virtually every other large retail food vendor in America).

What did it mean that none of them thought it was weird to be working with a guy named El Diablo? And what did it mean that I was drinking someone else's misery for breakfast?

Free people benefit from slave labor. Not just big corporations, but "regular people"—like you and me. We buy Granny Smiths picked by slaves in New York and Washington State. We buy paper from trees planted by workers in Georgia and Alabama who don't get paid or barely get paid. We buy car parts made of steel fired with charcoal made by slaves in Brazil. We buy binders, cell phone chips, and leather purses manufactured by slaves in China, and shirts from Wal-Mart made by slaves in Burma. Our war in Iraq is conducted to an enormous extent not by Americans, but by foreign migrant workers hired by American companies, several of which have recently been accused of slavery. Our reconstruction efforts in Mississippi and Louisiana after Hurricane Katrina have generated numerous claims of forced labor from the immigrants doing the work.

As the sci-fi writer and sometime futurist Bruce Sterling has written, "People have a marvelous facility for ignoring other people's pain." And he's right. It's not a left-versus-right thing or a rich-versus-poor thing. It's a human thing. Man has always been a wolf to man. The subject of this book, therefore, lies beyond something as simple as "rich people exploiting poor people" or "big, evil corporations taking over the world." It's a life force, a tension that dwells in *all* people. The simple desire to get ahead in life can become a monstrous impulse when fertilized by the right circumstances. Moreover, I would argue, this impulse lurks in a million invisible ways in even the nicest people.

This book is about three recent instances of slavery in the United States. In the first chapter, we'll spend some time with El Diablo and his world, learning about how he was able to harvest oranges in broad daylight using Mexican workers who didn't get paid and who couldn't leave his control. The story is one of corporate and legal chicanery at its baldest. In the following chapter, set in Tulsa, we will see many of the same forces at work, but explore how they play out in the minds of all involved—a psychic biopsy of slavery's guts. Finally, in the last section of the book, we visit Saipan, an island in the U.S. Commonwealth of the Northern Marianos Island where slavery cases pop up with alarming frequency and a society is dependent, much as the United States was for so long, upon the abuse and exploitation of foreigners.

Beyond these cases, however, my real focus is what is now called "globalization." I want to make it absolutely clear that everything in this book is a simple and patent metaphor for the dark potential of this phenomenon. By studying how free and powerful people respond to unfree and less powerful people, my intention is to meditate a bit about the meaning and potential hazards of our current enthusiasm for globalization.

For years, Americans who read or watch the news have been treated to a barrage of stories charting the decline of American manufacturing, the rise of China's economy, and the harsh conditions in which Chinese workers toil. An even longer-running, if slightly less insistent, series of stories has detailed the decline of American wages since 1968 and the widening gap between rich and poor.

Most readers have heard about this, and by the time this book is printed the statistics will have changed a bit, but as of this writing, 20 percent of Americans have a zero or negative net worth. Since 1970, the bottom 40 percent of American households lost an astounding 80 percent of their wealth. Currently, the top one percent of American households has gathered more wealth than the entire bottom 95 percent, and the richest 300,000 Americans pulled in as much income as the poorest 150 million. This is not wacko Internet stuff; these numbers are gleaned from the U.S. Bureau of Labor Statistics and the Census Bureau.

The same trend of growing inequality is spreading all over the world. According to statistics from the World Bank, the number of people living on less than two dollars a day has risen by almost 50 percent since 1980, to 2.8 billion. In fifty-nine countries, average income is lower today than twenty years ago. The gap between the richest fifth of the world's population and the poorest fifth has doubled in the last fifty years. The top fifth has 80 percent of the world's income. The poorest fifth has one percent.

There are different ways of connecting the dots between these combined trends, some more alarming than others. But it doesn't take a Bolshevik to look at this basic picture and wonder, Umm, what happens if these trends simply . . . *continue*?

In the 1920s (the last time the wealth gap in the United States was as wide as it is today), Supreme Court justice Louis D. Brandeis proclaimed, "We can have democracy in this country, or we can have great wealth concentrated in the hands of a few, but we can't have both." The quote resonated with me as I wrote about El Diablo and thought about the enormous transfer of wealth taking place around the world, from poor countries and poor people to richer ones. What would a decline in democracy as predicted by someone like Brandeis look like?

According to the doctrine of free trade in an era of globalization, American workers now compete with foreigners. As we move into a world of decreased trade restrictions, our incomes will perhaps fall—and then fall and fall some more—until all workers around the planet earn similar pay for similar work. If the nostrums of free trade hold fast, the price of everything we buy will go down in equal measure, and everything will be fine. We'll live just as we do today, but without having to feel guilty about those poor foreigners in sweatshops who increasingly seem to manufacture all our stuff. If all people are equal, as Americans profess to believe, it should be considered a positive goal if all the average Joes, Wangs, Nguyens, and Carmelitas around the world one day become equally paid and equally regarded. But what if it's not so simple? What if the "race to the bottom"—as the current loss of American jobs and the global pursuit of ever-cheaper sources of labor has come to be known—radically reshapes our world, and instead of freedom delivers us into a future of barbarism and tyranny?

It may seem like a paranoid thing to wonder. But the fact remains that since human beings have become civilized, we've spent far more time doing things El Diablo's way than, say, living in free, relatively egalitarian democracies. The number of human beings throughout history who have been born into lives that could accurately be described as "free" is nothing but the merest fraction of human experience. Certainly, then, the permanence of our currently free condition should not be taken for granted.

In the United States, most modern slavery involves the coercion of recent or trafficked immigrants. Such cases are incredibly hard to detect, because much of the time the perpetrators don't rely on chains, guns, or even the use of force. All they require is some method of coercion: threats of beating, deportation, death, or, perhaps most effective, harm to the victim's family back home should he or she ever speak up.

These cases occur in out-of-the-way places that are, to quote one activist I met, beyond most Americans' "cognitive map." They're hidden down country roads and in culturally remote immigrant communities, where law enforcement is lax and modern ideas of "human rights" are sketchy. The victims of modern servitude often come from countries where legal authorities are corrupt and unhelpful, if not outright threats. These victims are usually either unable or unlikely to flag down a stranger, cop, native-born American, official, reporter, or social worker to protest their conditions or to ask for help.

Modern slavery cases tend to follow a limited number of patterns. Sexual trafficking rings turn up every year, with women—from Russia, Mexico, Honduras—smuggled under false pretenses into the United States and sexually exploited for profit. Domestic workers—nannies, maids, cooks, anyone who works in a home—are frequently coerced into working for free, threatened with violence, sexually abused, and held against their will for years. Then there are the out-and-out weirdos, the only category of modern slavery that does not rely almost exclusively on immigrant victims. This group includes the husband-and-wife owners of a group home for the mentally ill in Kansas, convicted in 2005 of enslaving their charges, forcing them to work naked on the compound farm and perform sex acts on video as "therapy." Other examples might include the psychos who kidnap women and keep them chained up for years because they "love" them.

The focus of this book is what I somewhat ineptly call "labor slavery" within the contemporary United States. The term is my attempt to differentiate from all other forms the enslavement of workers making ordinary goods intended for consumption by the general public. In Los Angeles in 1995, in what became known as the El Monte case, seventy-two Thai women were found held in a squalid garment factory. Some had been enslaved as long as seventeen years. In Oklahoma, the owner of a welding factory was recently accused of defrauding and abusing fifty-four East Indians, forcing them to live inside a cavernous factory under threat while feeding them paltry rations of food they found disgusting. And then there are the agricultural cases, with El Diablos popping up not just in Florida but in Maine, New York, Washington,

Georgia, North Carolina—virtually everywhere food is grown. Each of these cases would be examples of labor slavery.

I don't suggest that the work performed by other victims of slavery is not also labor, or that one form of forced labor is more abusive than any other. But I wish to separate those varieties as cases that, sadly, very well might always take place on the fringes of even the most just society, akin to drug abuse or domestic violence. Given the moral and legal habits of the United States, and for that matter the habits of virtually every First and Second World country on earth, it's hard for me to imagine that the beneficiaries of these forms of slavery could ever pose as "legitimate" enterprises. It's far easier for me to imagine the American (or European or Japanese) public ignoring or accepting Mizrahi casual wear fabricated under conditions of slavery or rampant labor abuse—because that's what we already do.

It's important to realize that from the vantage point of today's world, for most of human history the idea of freedom, as we know it, didn't exist. As Harvard slavery historian Orlando Patterson notes, in ancient societies, "man had no moral view that would make him see something wrong in the fact that some men were masters while others were slaves." Another of slavery's most eminent scholars, Cambridge's M. I. Finley, weighed in after a lifetime of scholarship with the same conclusion. It was simply impossible for most people in most societies to have any idea that slavery was wrong, or that there was a different and more just way to arrange society.

Then along came the Enlightenment, in which the idea was put forth that "all men are created equal." And yet, even after that, the founding of America took place upon a bedrock of slave labor. Was it because the American colonists woke up one morning and said, "Gee, let's enslave millions of Africans! And let's talk a whole bunch about freedom just to *really* rub it in?"

I very much doubt that many free citizens of the American colonies had any objective view or collective understanding of what was happening to their society. To read Winthrop D. Jordan's excellent *White Over*

*Black: American Attitudes Toward the Negro, 1550–1812* is to learn how pernicious, subtle, and sneaky a thing slavery really is. In the same way that it took a million small victories and understandings, transformations and laws, to carve out the more-or-less modern world, the imposition of slavery upon the colonies was a piecemeal, gradual process requiring a million ignorances and lazinesses.

It is helpful to think of slavery in the modern world as something like a resistant disease, refusing to die off, constantly metamorphosing into new guises. During World War II, even before the Nazis came along, Stalin sent millions of Russians to forced industrial labor camps. As Hitler marched millions of Jews to their deaths in concentration camps (where forced labor was a central fact of life, prior to death by exhaustion or the gas chamber), the Nazis also enslaved seven million gentile workers from conquered territories, millions of whom also perished from overwork, malnutrition, brutality, and disease. After the war, China imprisoned millions of citizens to labor in "re-education camps."

Today, an estimated 27 million people are enslaved around the world. Brazilians and Peruvians are lured to the Amazon rainforest and forced to burn wood into charcoal and mine for gold. "Political prisoners" are held in North Korea and China and forced to atone for their crimes with unpaid labor. In Nepal, Pakistan, and India, millions of bonded workers toil for entire lifetimes—weaving rugs, making bricks, and working on farms—perpetually indebted to their employers and unfree to leave their employ. In Mauritania, an estimated ninety thousand *harratines* keep house, raise children, and tend livestock. In Thailand and Eastern Europe, tens of thousands of girls are sold by their families each year into sex slavery. In the desert hinterlands of wealthy Persian Gulf states, thousands of boys are imported from Bangladesh, Pakistan, and India and sold as camel jockeys.

If slavery is a disease and the disease still exists among us, what, one might wonder, is the cure? It's hard to say, and probably silly to reduce any solution to one tactic or another. But one thing I've come to believe regarding slavery and all of its attached and related subjects (freedom, globalization, democracy, and inequality, for example) is that it depends far less upon economics and far more upon how we think and view other people than anything else.

It's a more demonstrable assertion than one might think. In 1944, for example, 21 percent of white Americans answered yes to the question "Do you feel that Negroes in the United States have just as good a chance as white people to get any kind of job?" Twenty-four years later, 97 percent responded to the same question with a yes. The United States still suffers from racial and economic inequality. But it's impossible not to correlate the shift in attitude with actual economic reality; the period from World War II to the 1960s was one of marked economic advancement for black Americans. It was as if a great swath of society said at once, "Let us be equal," a magic wand was waved, and *voilà,* a large swath of society suddenly became a lot more equal.

A more recent example would be the following: in 1970, 79 percent of American college freshmen said their primary goal in life was to develop a meaningful philosophy of life. In 2005, 75 percent said their primary objective was to be financially very well off. It is a mind-blowing shift of perspective—and, I would hazard, an amazing indicator of how uncool it became among American college students to think of other people.

The current period of rising inequality in the United States began in 1974. Prior to that, working-class wages were rising and society was becoming more equal. So one question to ask is whether college-aged Americans got selfish. Did that selfishness and lack of regard for others result in social or legal changes that caused greater inequality? Or did the inequality come first? Maybe the world started to become a less fair place and, as a result, college-aged Americans and the rest of us have simply gotten more fearful about our lot in life.

I don't know. But I do suspect that as tedious and politically correct as it sometimes seems, the obsession with "human rights" and the just, equal application of them to all human beings is the one thing that staves off a mass societal regression from "civilization" to a world of bloodshed and mayhem. Because a world where in theory everybody is a *somebody* is a radically different place from a world divided into somebodies and nobodies. As you will see in this book, even a garden-variety case of forced labor—call it "extreme nobodyism"—opens up a dark, dark can of worms indeed.

I have always walked around with the notion that people in the world today must somehow be more valuable than people in ancient times. No one told me this; it was just an assumption I always made, imagining modern people as free and productive, sensitive and thoughtful, and so on, while ancient people were enslaved, miserable, ignorant, and short-lived. Writing this book gave me occasion to do some research to see, albeit somewhat unscientifically, if I was even remotely correct. What I learned was that if money were the sole arbiter of our worth or place in the world, most of us would still be enslaved.

In Greece in Homer's day, the ninth century B.C., an average-looking slave woman was worth four oxen. A highly attractive one was worth twenty. Around 200–300 A.D. in Roman Palestine, a healthy young farm slave was worth one healthy young cow. Across the empire, in Rome itself, a slave trained in medicine was worth fifty cows. In early medieval Ireland, a female slave was worth as many as sixty-four cows. In Iceland, she'd only trade for eight. Five hundred years later, in West Africa, slaves were exchanged for three to six cows. Slaves purchased by Europeans on the African coast went for eighteen English pounds apiece in 1740. In 1794, they could be bought in the United States for $500 apiece. In 1825, their price had tripled, to $1,500. The average slave in the American South in 1850 would be fetching the equivalent of $40,000 in today's money.

Fast-forward. There are now seven billion human beings glutting the market. A slave in Mauritania is worth about one camel. An eight-year-old camel jockey in the Middle East goes for a mere $300. In Mali, a young adult male laborer can be purchased for only $40. In Thailand, a young, HIV-free girl suitable for prostitution can be purchased for $1,000. In the American South, an illegal Mexican farmworker can be bought for as little as $600—more or less the cost of an old pony.

# FLORIDA

On April 20, 1997, at around 10 P.M., the Highlands County, Florida, Sheriff's Office received a 911 call; something strange had happened out in the migrant-worker ghetto near Highlands Boulevard. The "neighborhood," a mishmash of rotting trailer homes and plywood shacks, was hidden outside the town of Lake Placid, a mile or two back from the main road. By day, the place was forbidding and cheerless, silent, its forlorn dwellings perched awry, in seeming danger of oozing into the swamp. By night, it was downright menacing, humid and thick with mosquitoes.

When the sheriff's officers arrived, they found an empty van parked beside a lonely, narrow lane. The doors were closed, the lights were still on, and a few feet away, in the steamy hiss of night, a man lay facedown in a pool of blood. He had been shot once in the back of the head, execution-style. Beyond his body stood a pay phone, mounted on a pole.

The 911 caller had offered a description of a truck the sheriff's officers recognized as belonging to a local labor contractor named Ramiro Ramos. At 1:30 A.M., officers were dispatched to Ramos's house.

It's unclear how much the officers knew about the relationship be-

tween Ramos and his employees. Migrant farmworkers—nearly all undocumented Mexican and Central Americans, in this case—usually arrive in this country with little comprehension of English or of American
culture. Since they frequently come with little money and few connec-
tions, the contractor, or crew boss, as he's often called, often provides
food, housing, and transportation to and from work. As a result, many
farmworkers labor under the near-total control of their employers.
Whether the sheriff's officers were or weren't clued in to the fraught im-
plications of this dynamic, they would undoubtedly have gained insight
into Ramos's temperament if they'd known the nickname for him used
by his crew of seven hundred orange pickers. They called him "El Diablo."

At Ramos's house, police found a truck fitting the caller's description.
When a quick search of the vehicle yielded a .45-caliber bullet, police decided to bring in Ramos, his son, and a cousin for questioning. Interro-
gated at the station house, Ramos admitted that the night before, he had
gone driving around the dirt roads outside town, collecting rent from
his workers and looking, he said, "for one of his people." But when the
police asked him if his search had any connection with the shooting, he
said he didn't know anything about it. According to the sheriff's report,
Ramos at this point became "upset" and said he wished to leave. He and
his relatives were released.

The deputies went into the night, looking for migrant workers who
might be willing to offer additional testimony. Witness by witness, a story
began to take shape. The dead *chofer,* or van driver, was a Guatemalan
named Ariosto Roblero. The van had belonged to a *servicio de transporte,*
a sort of informal bus company used by migrants. The van and its passengers had been heading from South Florida, where orange season was
ending, to North Carolina, where cucumber season was getting under
way. Everything seemed fine until they hit the migrant ghetto outside
Lake Placid. Roblero had stopped to to make a pickup. And then, as the
van waited, a car and a pickup truck raced up, screeched to a halt behind
and in front of it, and blocked it off. An unknown number of men
jumped out, yanked the *chofer* from his seat, and shot him. The other
driver and the terrified passengers scattered into the night.

With each new detail, an increasingly disturbing picture of Ramos's operation began to emerge. El Diablo, it seemed, had been lending money to his workers, then overcharging them for substandard "barracks-style" housing, gouging them with miscellaneous fees, and encouraging them to shop at a high-priced grocery store, conveniently owned by his wife. By the time El Diablo had deducted for this, that, and the other thing, workers said, they were barely breaking even.

Worse, they were trapped. El Diablo's labor camp was in a tiny, isolated country town. He and his family, a network of cousins and in-laws, many of whom also worked as labor contractors, patrolled the area in their massive Ford F-250 pickup trucks, communicating with one another through Nextel walkie-talkie phones. For foreigners unfamiliar with the area, escape was almost unthinkable. But just to make matters crystal clear, El Diablo told his workers that anyone indebted caught trying to run away would be killed.

The previous night's murder, the witnesses alleged, had taken place when an indebted employee had left. The murder was meant to send a signal to local workers and to *chofers* thinking about aiding their departure from El Diablo's territory.

If the case sounds like a slam dunk, what happened next was, unfortunately, all too common in cases involving undocumented workers. After spilling most of the beans off the record, all the informants but one declined to name Ramos or his accomplices as the perpetrators, or even to offer their own names. One of the passengers in the murder victim's van told detectives that he couldn't remember a single thing about the incident. He managed not to see the color, the model, or the make of either assailant's vehicle, nor did he see who shot whom, or whether, in fact, anyone had even been shot. He only said that he was leaving for Mexico the next day, never to return.

Another witness acknowledged seeing the murder but, according to the sheriff's report, refused to name the shooter, stating his belief that "if he told, he would be killed by the Ramos family." The Ramoses knew where his family lived in Mexico, he said; if they didn't kill him personally, they would kill one of his relatives. He, too, was leaving town and wouldn't tell where he could be reached.

The sheriff's office was stumped. There wasn't much they could do without firmer testimony. However, they contacted federal authorities, and a few weeks later, at dawn on May 1, 1997, local law enforcement agents, backed by the Border Patrol and the U.S. Department of Labor, returned to Ramiro Ramos's house armed with a search warrant. The house and office yielded an arsenal of weapons not generally considered essential to labor management, including a Savage 7-millimeter rifle, a Marlin .22 rifle, an AK-47, a semiautomatic rifle, a Browning 9-millimeter semiautomatic pistol, and a Remington 700 7-millimeter Magnum rifle. The agents arrested Ramos and charged him with immigration violations.

One would think, perhaps, that authorities would have enough evidence to halt a clearly and alarmingly exploitive situation. Here were seven hundred workers on U.S. soil working under threat of death, for low pay or possibly no money at all.

Five days later, Ramos was released on $20,000 bail. The labor charges were dropped. Weapons charges were never brought. Business went on as usual. And the murder of Ariosto Roblero remains, to this day, "unsolved."


The collective image of the South Florida interior is usually conjured by a single word: swamp. Beyond a smattering of self-described "crackers" and a few thousand American Indians sweating it out on sleepy reservations, the area has traditionally been reluctantly populated. The reasons for this are easy enough to understand: the landscape is unremittingly flat; summer temperatures are stultifying. Even in winter, the air hangs heavy, dank, and still—except, of course, during the frequent thunderstorms and devastating hurricanes for which the area is known.

"I've got swampland in Florida I'd like to sell you" has long been a way of teasing a person for being gullible. The joke refers to the Florida land boom of the 1920s, which began when the increasing popularity of bona fide boomtowns like Miami and Palm Beach caused parcels elsewhere in the state to be gobbled up, usually sight unseen, by speculation-crazed northerners. Tracts billed as "oceanfront" were often situated dozens of miles away from open water or roads and chopped into ridiculous proportions, most famously by a Mr. Charles Ponzi, to as many as twenty-three lots per acre. The fact that few buyers had ever dreamt of actually moving to the "Riviera of America" didn't deter Florida land prices from rising as much as 1,000 percent annually—that is, until the fall of 1926, when the famous Miami hurricane battered the area, crashing the market and causing the overpriced deeds to become as worthless as the muck they represented.

In the last eighty years or so, the area has been tamed, drained, canaled, paved, built upon, planted over, covered with ethylene plastic, injected with pesticides and fertilizers, and thereby induced into yielding a more predictably handsome return on investment. The steamy lowlands have become an outdoor food factory, a hydroponic stew of gook and chemicals capable of producing year-round. Florida now churns out more fruits and vegetables than any state but California, reaping an average of about $7 billion per year.

Almost anything can be grown on Florida's 44,000 farms: some 280 different crops, including tobacco, potatoes, peanuts, escarole, pecans, okra, peppers, cucumbers, snap peas, radishes, sweet corn, and even normally cold-weather-loving blueberries. But the principal commodities are juice oranges (1.2 billion gallons from 103 million trees), tomatoes (1.5 billion pounds a year), and sugarcane (about a half billion dollars a year).

Some forty miles inland from Fort Myers Beach and Sanibel Island is the town of Immokalee. A few towns down from Lake Placid, it sits at the bottom of a cluster of remote agricultural outposts dotting the South Florida interior. Three stoplights long, Immokalee (which rhymes with *broccoli* and means "my home" in Seminole) is bordered on the south by the Big Cypress Swamp and surrounded on all other sides by citrus groves and tomato fields. Outside town, there are pretty-enough sights to be seen: stands of cypress, southern pine draped with Spanish moss, canals lined with cattails, and wading pink flamingoes. Inside the town limits, however, the place looks more like a work camp or factory than an American community.

Municipal authorities in Immokalee bother little with public services; for several days when I was there in 2002, a visitor turning onto Main Street would pass a decapitated black dog, left to rot on the median strip across from a new-looking Walgreens. In 2001, a county sheriff's deputy was sentenced to fourteen years in prison for dealing crack and shaking down local drug dealers.

The town's official population is about twenty thousand, but during the growing season, between November and May, it increases to nearly twice that. The year-to-year population reflects the current wave of migrants and the detritus of previous ones: forty years ago, the town consisted largely of poor whites, African Americans, and Puerto Ricans. In the 1980s, Haitians arrived. A little later, the Mexicans and Guatemalans trickled in. Today, some Haitians, whites, and African Americans remain, but the bulk of the population consists of Mexican and Central American migrants.

The arduousness of farm labor has been well documented. The average migrant has a life expectancy of just forty-nine years. Twenty thousand farmworkers require medical treatment for acute pesticide poisoning each year; at least that many more cases go unreported. Nationally, 50 percent of migrants—up from 12 percent in 1990—are without legal work papers. Their median annual income is somewhere around $7,500.

Florida farmworkers have it even worse. No one knows for sure how many there are. The most reliable guess is about three hundred thousand. An estimated 80 percent of them have no work papers, and at last count, in 1998, their average yearly pay was an estimated $6,574. Adjusted for inflation, these income levels have fallen by as much as 60 percent in the last twenty years.

According to the Florida Tomato Committee, during the 2005–2006 growing season, Florida farmers were paid $10.27 per twenty-five-pound box of tomatoes. The migrants who pick the tomatoes, however, are paid an average of 45 cents per bucket, a rate that has remained unchanged for thirty years.

To earn $50 in a day, an Immokalee picker must harvest two tons of tomatoes, or 125 buckets. Each bucket weighs about thirty-two pounds. Once a worker has picked enough tomatoes to fill it—about fifty, depending on the size—he must then hoist the bucket onto his shoulder and walk/run across soft, spongy, lumpy soil to the *dumpeador,* an overseer who checks each bucket for ripeness. The worker then raises his bucket, dumps its contents into a central bin, and runs back to the tomato plant, anywhere from a few yards to a hundred yards away.

Orange and grapefruit picking pay slightly better, but the hours are longer. To get to the fruit, pickers must climb twelve- to eighteen-foot-high ladders, shakily propped on soggy soil against shifty boughs, then reach deep into thorny branches, thrusting both hands among pesticide-coated leaves before twisting the fruit from its stem and rapidly stuffing it into a shoulder-slung *moral,* or pick sack. A full sack weighs about a hundred pounds; it takes ten sacks—about two thousand oranges—to fill a *baño,* a bin the size of a large wading pool. Each bin earns the worker a *ficha,* or token, redeemable for about seven dollars. An average worker in a typical field under decent conditions can fill six, seven, maybe eight bins a day. After a rain, though, or in an aging field with overgrown trees, the same picker might work an entire day and fill only three bins.

Most Americans have by now heard about the dangers of illegal migration. For starters, there are the perils of crossing the border, which include running out of food and water and dying in the desert heat. Between 1995 and 2004, more than 3,000 Mexicans died while trying to enter the United States. According to the U.S. Border Patrol, the death rate is rising; in a recent twelve-month period, a record 460 migrants died crossing the border.

Moreover, gangs and police on the Mexican side of the border prey on migrants, knowing that they are seldom armed and frequently carrying cash. (The term used by *coyotes,* the notorious professionals who guide or smuggle migrants across the border, to describe their clients is *pollos*—chickens, vulnerable and ripe for plucking.) On the American side of the border, migrants lucky enough to survive the crossing face armed Border Patrol guards, canines, choppers, and, most recently, self-styled vigilante groups like the Arizona-based Minuteman Project, which, since April 2005, has chartered at least twenty chapters across the country.

Although farmwork has never been a lark, it's possible to find fairly recent accounts of farmworkers who were happy with their profession. In Daniel Rothenberg's *With These Hands,* published in 2000, numerous farmworkers in the United States recount their experiences. One, a former Vietnam veteran named Gino Mancini, recalled:

> If somebody asks me what I do for a living, I say, "I'm a fruit tramp." To me, fruit tramp is not an insult. I'm proud of what I do. I pick fruit. I migrate. Once, I cut out an article that listed two hundred and fifty jobs, from the most prestigious to the least prestigious. The last job, number two hundred and fifty, was migrant worker. Bottom of the list. It actually made me feel good. I chose this lifestyle and I like it. Look at what a lot of other people do—advertising and shit like that. What does that do for the world? At least I'm helping to feed somebody. I mean, it might not be much, but I'm not destroying anything. A lot of stuff I see just seems mindless to me. Just think of the jobs people have—"I'm a public relations officer"; "I'm a consultant"—What do they really do? Mostly nothing.
>
> I do physical labor. It's honest. I'm not especially proud, but I work hard. I make an honest living. I don't know what farmwork is about to everybody else, but to me it's good hard work. You know, we're all different. Everybody's an individual. . . .
>
> I couldn't handle a year-round job with maybe three weeks' vacation a year. I like to move around, to live day to day. That's the way I've always lived. That's the only way I know. To me, farmwork is about freedom.

A farmworker named Henry Dover mused:

> Farmwork is kind of beautiful. It's peaceful. In the city, there's a whole lot of killing and shooting going on. Out here, you can breathe nice clean air. You can hear the birds. You can look up and see the sky. You're not cramped. Whenever I look up at the sky, I'll be thinking about God. That's what makes me happy, just seeing the

plants, seeing how they change color, seeing the flowers. You can see all of God's nature out there.

Today's farmworkers are almost entirely foreign-born. For the vast majority of them, farmwork isn't a lifestyle choice or a preference. It's a matter of survival. Due to overpopulation, and declining commodity prices, largely brought on by free-trade agreements and First World subsidies to farmers, they can no longer afford to live on their own land in their own countries.

The migrants streaming to South Florida these days from the highlands of southern Mexico and Guatemala speak dozens of Mayan or other indigenous languages, such as Quiché, Zapotecan, Mam, Kanjobal, Tzotzil, Nahuatl, and Mixtec. For many of them, even Spanish—never mind English—is a foreign language, and communication among groups can be difficult.

In the postpastoral fields of modern, industrialized agriculture, such quaint notions as worker solidarity are unrealistic. As a former Immokalee tomato picker named Francisca Cortes told me, every morning is like a free-for-all: when the bus pulls off the highway and into the day's tomato field, workers scramble and elbow one another out of the way in a dog-eat-dog race for the most advantageous positions in the field. A row that faces the sun more directly will have riper fruit, making for easier, faster picking than a row in the shade. A row closer to the collection bin cuts the length of the heavy slog back and forth with a full bucket. Each gradient of productivity is worth another quarter, another dollar. Under these circumstances, Francisca said with a shrug, "it's just a bunch of men and some women. You're with strangers. You don't know them. You're not there to say 'What's your name? How are you? How long have you been here?' There just isn't any time for that."

In many parts of the Southeast, like the migrant ghetto where Ariosto Roblero was murdered, agricultural workers are quartered in trailer camps miles from town; Immokalee's "pickers," as citrus and tomato

workers are often called, live in plain sight, densely concentrated between First and Ninth streets, close to the South Third Street pickup
spot. Those who don't live there are forced either to walk a great distance twice a day or to pay extra for a ride to work. As a result, rents near
the parking lot are high. The town's largest landlord, a family named
Blocker, owns several hundred old shacks and mobile homes, many
rusting and mildew-stained, which can rent for upward of two hundred
dollars a week, a square-footage rate approaching Manhattan's. (Heat
and phone service are not provided.) It isn't unusual for twelve workers
to share a trailer.

Between four-thirty and five o'clock every morning, a convoy of
crudely painted red and blue school buses arrives at a parking lot on
South Third Street, a block from Main Street, to carry workers to the
fields. In the afternoon, the buses return and the sidewalks fill with
weary men in muddy white rubber boots. In the evening, some stay
home to wash their few items of clothing or cook dinner; others run er-
rands on bicycles with the handles turned up, wearing tucked-in Western shirts, baseball caps or cowboy hats, and Reebok knockoffs. Those
with time left on their phone cards line up in parking lots and on street
corners before seemingly innumerable pay phones (a staple of migrant
towns) to call Chiapas, Oaxaca, or Huehuetenango, the mountain towns
of home.

About 40 percent of South Florida's laborers are new each season,
and they are often unsure of their rights (or the idea of rights in general).
Most of these migrants come from small towns, where everyone knows
one another. While farmwork back home pays little, they say, mistreatment of workers is rare. As one immigrant from southern Mexico explained, "Back in my village, it was so small, we really didn't have
situations where a boss or a farmer didn't pay a worker. They had to
walk the same streets as the workers. If they didn't pay, word would get
out. It ended up being, you know, not like the law here, but the law of
*cojones*"—or balls. "If you didn't pay, you were going to get your *cojones*
cut off."

It's hard to imagine immigrant farmworkers in the United States cutting their bosses' balls off. In fact, in most circumstances it's difficult to imagine them getting up the nerve to complain about anything.

There are many reasons why immigrant workers in the United States are reluctant to discuss bad, dangerous, and abusive situations with their employers, much less with *bolillos,* or whites. Fear of losing their jobs and being labeled troublemakers is only one. Another reason, of course, is that immigrant workers live in constant fear of being seized by *la Migra*—the Immigration and Naturalization Service—and deported. Unscrupulous labor contractors use this implicit threat of exposure to keep workers in line. Workers often borrow money to travel north from loan sharks back home at interest rates as high as 25 percent per month. If they are deported, the loan is foreclosed. Frequently, homes are put up as collateral, so deportation can be a financial calamity for an entire family.

All of this helps explain why South Florida has rapidly become one of the most exploitive labor environments in the country, earning the designation by a former prosecutor with the Justice Department of "ground zero for modern slavery."

Nothing drives home the reality of migrant farmwork in South Florida as well as something told to me by Michael Baron, an agent with the U.S. Border Patrol who knows the area well. "You know," he said, "these workers are so vulnerable. They're housed miles from civilization, with no telephones or cars. Whatever they're told they're gonna do, they're gonna do. They're controllable. There's no escape. If you do escape, what are you gonna do? Run seventeen miles to the nearest town? When you don't even know where it is? And, if you have a brother or a cousin in the group, are you gonna leave them behind? You gonna escape with seventeen people? You're gonna make tracks like a herd of elephants. They'll find you. And heaven help you when they do."

Adan García Orozco is a stocky man, about five feet two, with ruddy, copper-brown skin, a mustache, and the broad features and round, soft eyes of Central American indigenous people. His hair is lightly gelled and buzz cut down the sides, and when I met him, he wore what appeared to be snakeskin cowboy boots, and looked much younger than his thirty-eight years. (I have changed his name, as well as the names of his family and friends.)

García Orozco gets along in Spanish, but his first language is Mixe, a Mayan language spoken by the Mixe Indians of southern Mexico. Initially, he appears to be studiously reserved. When he loosens up, however, he's a pretty funny guy. When asked, for instance, if he had ever owned any land, he almost laughed. "I don't even own the dirt under my fingernails!" He paused, bemused. "Who in the world has land?"

García Orozco lived with his wife, Concepción, and their six children in a one-room house on the Yucatán Peninsula. The town is small, like most in the area—about ten or fifteen blocks square, home to perhaps five hundred people—and surrounded by cleared pastureland. It's fair to describe it as sleepy, the kind of place where kids bathe one another outside the house in rainwater buckets and hairy black pigs saunter down the street with billy goat escorts.

Inland from the beaches and the verdant coastal plain, the Yucatán forms a low, flat plateau with shallow soils and hardscrabble limestone outcroppings. Most of the terrain is chopped into small, rocky *fincas* or *ranchos,* which raise a little bit—but never a lot—of corn, beans, cattle, oranges, mangos, bananas, and coconuts.

Like many poor areas of the world, the Yucatán is a place where most people seem to spend their time waiting. They wait in hamlets with plaintive names like Centenario or Justicia Social, and towns near crumbling temples with names recalling the area's Mayan past, like Xbonil, Xpujil, Hecelchakan, and Dzibilchaltun. They wait in houses without windows. They wait in yards of dirt, meticulously swept, beneath trees without leaves and trees abloom with fiery orange flowers. They wait by the road, on bikes, for cars, for taxis, and of course, they wait for jobs.

García Orozco began to work when he was nine years old as a farmhand, performing such tasks as clearing brush for local ranchers or harvesting sugarcane. When work was available, it paid about five or six dollars a day. However, as he explained, "Not to criticize my country, but where I come from, there aren't any jobs. And when there are, you work two, three days sometimes. Maybe sometimes fifteen or twenty. But other times there's none, and you have to go around looking for it, wherever it is. You don't want to leave your hometown, but if there's a chance there may be work somewhere else, well, you have to leave. But you end up coming out the same anyway. Because even if you earn a little more in the city, or in whatever town you go to, you have to pay for rent, you have to pay for food. You can't get by, and once again, you end up going home with nothing."

García Orozco felt increasingly unable to provide for his growing family. "People use the term 'provide for' just to refer to a plate of beans and salsa and some tortillas," he said. But it wasn't nearly enough. "I think for a family you've got to have milk. Right?" Besides, he said, one of his kids was sick, and the medicine was costing a fortune.

García Orozco's house is a mishmash of salvaged boards slapped and lashed together, with wide, irregular gaps and a corrugated roof. The yard is a beleaguered mess of tattered banana trees, an orange tree, and a junk pile, which serves as bathroom and outhouse.

When I visited them, Adan and Concepción told me they wage a continual battle to make improvements, but bricks were expensive, and it was hard to make headway. What bothered them the most were the pools of water that surrounded the house, six inches deep during the rainy season.

Inside the house I found two beds, a tangle of hammocks, five white plastic chairs, an enormous boom box with a bright neon digital display, and six—or maybe it was eight—kids, dusty, barefoot, sprawled, politely trying not to giggle: Nestor, the oldest at fifteen, then Alejandro, Enríque, Gabriela, Cruz, and Yesenia, an adorable girl of three too shy to say hi. Two of the older boys were plopped on the floor, playing soccer on a PlayStation. The current match pitted the United States against Germany. As the boys competed, madly clicking and twitching their remote controls, teasing each other, Concepción whispered to me that one of their neighbors had actually had the gall to try to *charge* kids to use their PlayStation. Did I want any tacos?

The door to the house remained open. Sunlight streamed in. I noticed a large hen carefully set atop one of the beds. Was it usual for the chickens to share the family beds? I asked. One of the kids explained that the hen had nearly expired while laying an egg earlier that day. Hours later, her breast was still heaving violently with each breath, as if she was struggling to get enough oxygen. Every few seconds she jerked her neck around as if expecting a rear attack, her beak frozen open in what looked like a surreal grimace of terror.

The game ended, and Enríque rose and strutted, boasting with mock grandeur, "I am the champion." The boys then unplugged a cord from the back of the TV and took turns shocking each other with it, alternately laughing and howling.

One of the howlers was Alejandro, the sick one. He suffered from leukemia. As a result of the chemotherapy he was receiving, he'd lost most of his hair and so wore a kerchief over his head. He also had a ten-inch scar running up his belly. Oddly, he looked vigorous and healthy.

But Concepción told me anxiously that Ale's cancer sucked up all the family's money. Every six months or so the two of them had to trek to Mérida, three-plus hours away, for a new round of treatment. She wasn't sure it was even worth it. Of the twenty kids from all over southern Mexico who originally enrolled in the hospital's special program, only three were still alive. "When we're in Mérida," she said, shaking her head, "we're begging food and medicine. The government doesn't help." She seemed resigned, as though the cancer was more of a hassle than a tragedy.

Given the sporadic, itinerant possibilities before him, García Orozco decided to leave his home in Mexico to look for work in the United States. In February 2001 he set out with two friends whose circumstances were equally meager. One of them, eighteen-year-old Rafael Solis Hernández, lived in his mother's house with his wife and baby. The other, Mario Sánchez, like García Orozco a father to six children, lived in a house built of cardboard. At forty-three, he had difficulty recalling his birthday. Shrugging at the very idea, he said, "It's never been celebrated, so I don't even concern myself with it."

To travel north, García Orozco borrowed 2,500 pesos (about $250) from a man he worked for sometimes and Hernández borrowed money from his mother. Sánchez brought what money remained from a crop of peppers he'd managed to grow the year before.

Concepción understood why her husband had to leave, but now, as a result, she seemed to spend half her time worrying about him. Concepción, who stands about five feet tall, speaks with a verbal tic that seems to pop up in one form or another in every language I've ever heard, punctuating nearly every phrase with "I tell you" or "I tell him."

"I tell him," she told me, "I say, 'You better be careful up there,' I tell him. I say, 'We just want to see you,' I tell him. 'We need the money for the baby,' I tell him. I feel bad. He's up there all alone, without his family. I tell him, I tell him, 'What are we going to do? You have to be careful.' I tell him, 'You better watch it!'

"I tell him," she said, " 'You better be careful, because you're the only hope we have,' I tell him. 'It's already a hard life here. It's a hard life we have here. I'm all alone with the kids,' I tell him. I tell you. I tell him, 'It's awful that you're in this position.' "

García Orozco, Sánchez, and Hernández crossed the border with a large group in early March 2001, in the care of a *coyote,* or smuggler. Like half of all illegal migrants entering the United States, they found themselves in Arizona. Their money had run out. The *coyote* introduced them to a man they nicknamed El Chaparro (Shorty). El Chaparro was a *raítero,* a driver who finds workers and gives them a ride, or *raíte,* to waiting jobs. He gave them—along with a group of about thirty others—permission to sleep in an abandoned trailer home. After about a week, he came back and offered to drive them to Florida, where there would be work picking oranges. García Orozco and his friends had no idea what or where Florida was, or what picking oranges was like. The issue of wages was never raised, nor were the terms of the *raíte.* The men said yes.

The three men, along with about a dozen and a half more, were packed into El Chaparro's rickety van and a sedan, and off they went.

The trip lasted three days. El Chaparro stopped once for an hour or two to sleep, but passengers were forbidden to get out, even to relieve themselves. For that purpose, a jug was passed around. When asked whether they ate during this time, García Orozco shrugged and answered, "We didn't have money."

On March 13, more than three weeks after leaving home, the men reached their destination: Lake Placid, Florida. The van and car stopped in front of a Mexican grocery store. The passengers were ordered to stay put while El Chaparro got out and talked to two labor contractors.

One of them was Ramiro Ramos—the man known as El Diablo. The other was his brother, Juan, aka Nino.

Both brothers are short and solidly built, but they couldn't have had more different demeanors. Ramiro's goes a long way toward explaining his nickname. He has close-cropped, graying hair, an impassive manner, and bloodshot eyes. Nino, with his blowsy, windswept hair and perpetual smirk, looks like a good-times kind of guy. (As an acquaintance later aptly put it, "Juan always looks like he's coming from a party!")

The Ramoses were born in Guanajuato, Mexico. They had come to the United States as orange pickers in the early eighties. By the end of the decade, they had worked their way up the ladder to become contractors. Ramiro had married a Mexican American named Alicia Barajas, whose family ran several labor-contracting operations. According to Michael Baron of the Border Patrol, "You have to be careful with the Barajases. Their name comes up a lot in law enforcement."

Together with their cousins and in-laws, Ramiro and Juan Ramos employed thousands of migrant workers, from South Florida to North Carolina. Records from one of their companies, R & A Harvesting, indicate that between 2000 and 2002 Ramiro and Juan alone employed several hundred workers.

García Orozco recalls that when he and his friends first met the new bosses, "Señor Nino asked if we had someone to pay El Chaparro for our ride." Nino smugly shoved a phone in his face, knowing, of course, that the new arrivals had no one to call. Then Nino said, "Well, okay, we'll pay for you." The workers saw him write out a check to El Chaparro.

They had no idea how much the check was for, but the Ramoses told them that they had shelled out a thousand dollars for each of them.

There was no contract. Nino simply warned the new recruits, "You're gonna have to pay us back. And the work is very hard. If I pay for you, and you leave, we're gonna beat the fuck out of you." According to García Orozco, "He didn't say it like he was joking." From that point on, seeking another job was clearly not an option. As García Orozco explained, "I couldn't have gone elsewhere. I owed the money to them. If I refused, what was I going to do?"

El Diablo took the new arrivals to their lodgings, a former bar known as La Piñita, which had been converted into a filthy, crowded barracks where workers slept six to a room, on stained bare mattresses on the floor. While passing a neighboring room with an open door, Hernández, a soccer fan, spied a small television set in one room and asked if he could arrange to have a set for his room as well. El Diablo's answer pulled him up short: "If you keep up with this kind of attitude, I'll pump you full of lead."

García Orozco, Hernández, and Sánchez spent the next month picking oranges eight to twelve hours a day, six and sometimes seven days a week. Every Friday after work, Nino or El Diablo would pull up to the groves or in front of La Guadalupana (owned by El Diablo's wife) in a pickup truck, holding a checkbook and a large sack of money. After writing each worker a check, the brothers took back the check, charged the workers a check-cashing fee, and garnished for rent, food, work equipment, the ride from Arizona, and daily transportation to and from the fields.

After one seven-day pay period, García Orozco said, the brothers deducted forty dollars for meals, thirty for rent, and another thirty for the pick sack. He was left with sixty-seven dollars. More or less was deducted, García Orozco said, depending on the bosses' whim. A worker might net fifty dollars—or twenty. It didn't really matter. Whatever remained was usually spent on food at La Guadalupana, the company store.

The three friends lived in absolute fear. Rumors of the bosses' violence abounded. In one story making the rounds, some workers were listening to a boom box. El Diablo appeared, demanding, "What the fuck are you playing this music so loud for?" Then he threw the boom box on the floor, smashing it to pieces. When one of the workers became angry and said, "Hey, that's mine! I paid for it," Ramos pulled a gun on him.

Then there was the murder of the Guatemalan van driver. And the kneecapping incident. In this story (also documented in a police report), one of the Barajas cousins and some accomplices were allegedly driving a van when they passed a farmworker walking along the road. The cousin decided the worker was probably trying to escape, forced him into their van, broke his knees with a hammer, and threw him out of the moving vehicle.

García Orozco, Hernández, and Sánchez began to realize that they were under constant surveillance. One day, when Hernández and another worker walked down the road and tried to telephone their wives from a nearby Kash n' Karry convenience store, El Diablo pulled up behind them, asked whom they were calling, and pointedly offered them a ride home. When the Ramos brothers weren't around, workers were watched by relatives and supervisors who lived in the barracks and who carried cell phones and patrolled the surrounding area. García Orozco recalled being told by one supervisor, "If you want to leave, go ahead. But I'll call the bosses, and they'll feed you to the alligators." The supervisors pointed to a lake behind the barracks and said, "They haven't eaten for a while."

Ironically, if García Orozco and his friends had only known their rights, or known how things work in the United States, they could have left any time they'd wanted and been free in a few moments. La Piñita was only a few yards away from Highway 27, which runs through the citrus belt west of Lake Okeechobee. Perhaps three or four hundred yards away was a Ramada Inn. And just behind the barracks was a well-tended, gated retiree community. At any time, the Ramoses' employees could have run to the hotel and asked for the police. But then, if they were the kind of guys remotely likely to do such a thing, they never would have been "hired" for the job in the first place.

As García Orozco described it, "When you're there, you feel like the world is ending. You feel absolutely horrible. Friday comes, and Saturday, and you keep working, and you're really tired, and they come and say, "We're going to take out this, and this." He thought of his kids back home, and how little money was getting to them. How long would it take to repay his loans? What would his wife and family do in the meantime?

For García Orozco and his friends, life in the United States wasn't quite what they had expected. As Sánchez later recalled, "All of a sudden, you realize you're completely in their pockets."

Slavery cases typically take years to investigate and prosecute, presenting a wide array of special challenges few public officials are trained to handle. Experienced Border Patrol agents such as Baron say that one enormous obstacle he and others face is migrant workers' mistrust of officials, white people, and strangers. "Workers see us and automatically think we're here to deport them," he said. "They don't give us the time of day."

From a prosecutor's point of view, a primary difficulty with modern slavery cases is the absence of traditional restraints like chains and locked doors. What must be elicited and proven in court is much more nebulous and abstract—the notion of *coercion*. As Leon Rodríguez, a former trial lawyer with the Civil Rights Division, Criminal Section, of the Department of Justice, explained, "You have a chain of incidents that add up to a crime, usually not just a single incident. So you're investigating the entire atmosphere in which your victims live and work." It doesn't help a prosecutor for workers to merely say they were *scared* to leave a camp; to obtain a conviction, prosecutors need to prove that someone issued direct threats of harm. In such cases, the evidence very often boils down to one person's word against another's.

Other prosecutors I spoke to cited an additional hurdle: migrant workers traveling from state to state without telephones are difficult to reach, much less schedule for depositions and trials. They often can't afford to miss the workdays it takes to prepare and testify for a trial. Their lives are often so contingent (the car breaks down, the weather changes, the harvest is delayed, someone gets deported, the girl gets pregnant, the baby gets sick, the guy who was going to give them a ride to a deposition decides to move to Texas) that even when workers are willing and eager to testify, they often can't control their destinies from day to day. As Rodríguez noted, "I worked as a prosecutor in Brooklyn before I went to DOJ, so I had some experience with poor and displaced communities, but these workers are completely beyond that. They don't have addresses the same way the people you know do. They're migrants, they're undocumented. They have no presence in the system at all."

Still another attorney with the Justice Department told me that unfair as it may sound, prosecutors can only pursue those slavery operations that seem like surefire wins. "It doesn't necessarily send a good message if you lose your case," she explained. "What does that tell the community? It tells them that they can get away with it." With limited resources and myriad issues and constituencies competing for federal tax dollars, she said, federal officials simply can't afford to look foolish by losing. The technical issues of a case, the solidity of proof, and the amount of evidence become higher priorities than the simpler issue of how egregious a slavery operation may be.

Many farmworkers and advocates praised the Justice Deptartment for wholeheartedly committing to fight modern-day slavery, but lamented that FBI agents—the investigative arm of the DOJ—remained atavistically oriented toward combating more traditional forms of crime, such as bank robbery, drug dealing, and Mafia activity. The fact that federal legislation had been passed and forced labor had become a nationally prominent issue didn't necessarily translate into the personnel, expertise, and insight necessary to penetrate the shadowy world of labor exploitation.

One NGO worker explained that sometimes agents didn't seem to realize that migrant workers keep extremely long work hours, requiring agents to make themselves available during evenings and weekends. He gave an example of giving a witness's address to an FBI agent, and the agent's response:

"Does he return at five in the afternoon?"

"No, you have to wait for him till seven at night."

"Okay, we'll go there on Tuesday at five."

And so, the NGO staffer concluded, "they arrive on Tuesday at five at the person's home, ask for him, he's not there—and they leave."

Another person with experience in slavery investigations (I am not naming them for obvious reasons) pointed out that some agents could stand a bit more sensitivity to migrant culture. He said, "The first thing some agents do is come in and tower over you." He imitated a diminutive slavery victim recoiling in the shadow of a huge imaginary FBI agent. There was no way such a victim was likely to relax, open up, and testify with confidence. The best agents, he said, come in, sit down, and explain slowly and calmly, " 'I'm here to talk with you about what happened in such-and-such a camp with your boss, whose name is so-and-so. We want to investigate this, and help you, so that this kind of thing ends.' " Their initial questions, he said, focus on the reason the workers wanted to talk with them in the first place: the abuse. But other agents, he said, merely asked questions from a form or a list, often including questions about the victims' prior criminal activity. The result was that frequently, witnesses felt defensive and reacted by clamming up.

Nearly all the farmworker advocates I spoke with told me that they had met several committed, enthusiastic FBI agents who cared about trafficking and were highly talented at working with immigrants. The problem was a matter of institutional malfeasance: agents are routinely—and therefore thoughtlessly—reassigned. Every time an FBI agent developed the ability to understand a slavery investigation, it seemed, the agent was instantly transferred to another part of the country to work on an entirely different type of crime. Said one source, the agency wastes its expertise as a matter of policy. "There's no institutional memory, there's no accrual of knowledge."

For these and other reasons, enforcement authorities have become increasingly reliant upon advocacy groups already involved with migrant-worker populations. These groups have the advantage of knowing the language and customs of the farmworkers they serve. Usually, they maintain residences in migrant communities and, most important, they have the workers' trust.

One successful group is the Coalition of Immokalee Workers. The

coalition has been instrumental in five of South Florida's six recent slavery prosecutions, uncovering and investigating abusive employers, locat-
ing transient witnesses, and encouraging them to overcome their
hesitations about testifying against former captors.

In 2002 I went to visit them. At the time, CIW headquarters was a
dilapidated storefront on South Third Street, next to the pickup spot
where workers congregate each morning. Inside, the paint was peeling
off the walls and the carpet was ripped and threadbare. The principal
furnishings included a lumpy old couch, two desks, a few dozen metal
folding chairs, and a large papier-mâché replica of the Statue of Liberty,
holding a tomato bucket. The walls were adorned with press in Spanish,
English, and Haitian Creole, photographs of protest marches, cartoons
depicting labor relations between bosses and workers, and a picture of
an X'ed-over Taco Bell chihuahua with the slogan YO NO QUIERO TACO
BELL!

On a typical day, workers drift by the coalition office to say hello,
sometimes wandering inside to buy tortillas, Jarritos soft drinks, and
mole-sauce mix at the coalition's co-op grocery store. In the worker-
hostile environment of Immokalee, the place serves as a comfortable
oasis, providing a relaxed atmosphere somewhere between a college social club and a Third World political-party branch office. But even
something as simple-seeming as the co-op store serves a more strategic
purpose: by maintaining the cheapest prices in town, the coalition automatically fends off price gouging by other grocery stores.

The CIW was founded somewhat informally in the early 1990s and
has grown to some three thousand current members. Joining costs ten
dollars and, technically, entails little more than receiving a photo ID.

There are many groups dedicated to helping farmworkers, and as
many opinions about how best to do it. Some of these groups have offices
in Washington, D.C., devoted to lobbying politicians to make new and
better laws. Others try to organize farmworkers or help them find legal
representation. Many are funded by churches. Still others focus on basic
needs such as health care. The coalition's focus is on *"educación popular,"*
or, crudely translated, education for common people. The term describes a method of education and organization first theorized by Brazil-

ian educator Paulo Freire, whose *Pedagogy of the Oppressed* conceived it as a means to bring complex political problems to the attention of impoverished, usually illiterate peasants. It spread throughout Latin America and the Caribbean, where several of the coalition's members absorbed it before bringing the technique to Florida. Somewhat analagous to what U.S. labor organizers call "political education," the basic idea behind *educación popular* is to use group discussions of concrete details from workers' experience to help them analyze the larger societal, economic, and political forces that shape their lives.

The coalition holds weekly meetings, conducts weekend "leadership trainings," makes outreach trips throughout the southeastern states, stages hunger strikes, and had, when I met them in 2002, recently launched a boycott against Yum! Brands, Inc., owner of Taco Bell, in an effort to raise wages for tomato pickers working in what they called "sweatshop-like conditions." The slogan for the boycott, aimed at high schools and college campuses across the United States, was "Boot the Bell!" While each of these activities may have seemed like a disparate pursuit, the thread connecting them is the way the coalition uses them to raise workers' awareness of their own power.

One of the coalition's spokespeople is a former tomato picker from Mexico named Lucas Benitez. When I met him, he was thirty-two; his teeth were silver (the signature of southern Mexico and Central American dentistry), his hair was buzz cut flat on top, and he wore a goatee and Fu Manchu mustache. Despite his relatively young age, he seems a decade older, not because of how he looks, but because he carries a certain natural gravitas.

Benitez, who began farmwork at age six, is a co-founder of the CIW. Like the group's other co-founders, he emphasized that the organization is above antiquated notions like hierarchy. "If I need a title," he said, "I use co-director. But we don't have—we are members of the organization."

The CIW has several other such nonleaders—from Haiti, Mexico, Guatemala, and the United States. They were elected by members, and for their troubles (they work seven days a week, often late into the night), they receive around three hundred dollars a week—a figure that aimed to approximate farmworkers' earnings. The organization also requires its staff members to work in the fields during part of the year, and most members I met live in trailers and shacks not unlike those of their farmworker constituents.

Without bothering to be cynical about it, Benitez dismisses the idea that lawsuits and politicians are likely to improve the abysmal conditions facing farmworkers. "If you want true change," he told me one day at coalition headquarters, leaning back in his chair with his feet up on his desk, "it won't come from Washington, or from the lawyers." Even if lawsuits are won and laws are passed, he said, you've only won the battle. The war against overall poor treatment of farmworkers will continue. However, he told me, "if you change people's consciousness"—and by "people," he means "workers,"—"the people themselves take care of it." Change from the top down is a nice thing to dream about, he said with a shrug, leaving behind decades of liberal pieties, but really, "who cares what happens to a bunch of *pelagatos*—a bunch of nobodies?"

Benitez took me with him on a walk through Immokalee's trailer ghetto while he handed out flyers. The conversation was the same with each group: *"Buenas noches."* Quick, level eye contact. "I'd like to invite you to the meeting tonight. Here's a flyer. We're right down there, on North Third." The men looked quickly at the flyer.

"Maybe we'll see you there," they said. They thanked Benitez and sent him onward with an *"Andale, pues"* (a friendly Mexicanism meaning, roughly, "Cool, all right").

It was friendly, but Benitez never got too familiar or pressed his case. To do so would be inappropriate. For one thing, workers have little energy for conversation with strangers after a day of intense manual labor. For another, most immigrant workers are loath to fraternize with anyone who might bring headaches into their lives. They simply want to work, pay off the money they've borrowed to come here, and start sending money back home to their families.

Benitez told me that now, November, was the beginning of the season, and that most of the workers were new to town. As the coalition became better known to them, the trust level would increase and he would get a better reception. But for now, hoofing it from trailer to trailer, it seemed like rough going.

Benitez slowed down in front of a labor contractor's house. It was a typical middle-class ranch home, nothing luxurious, but several orders of magnitude above the rotting trailers surrounding it. He looked through the wrought-iron gate around the house. Smiling ironically, he said, "You'll find them every Sunday in the church. Monday they're back out, taking advantage of the workers." As if by some perverse cue, a little girl in a frilly pink party dress appeared around a corner and danced across the patio with a five-dollar bill in her mouth. We headed back to the coalition office.

Greg Asbed is another coalition founder. Born in Baltimore and raised in Washington, D.C., Asbed is a handsome, perennially stubble-cheeked Armenian American man who favors old T-shirts, worn jeans, and a gold chain. He became involved in farmworker issues after graduating from Brown University, when he worked in Haiti for a peasant organization and learned to speak Creole. Still athletic at forty-three, he spends three months each summer harvesting watermelons with other coalition members in northern Florida, Georgia, and Missouri. Despite working in temperatures that often reach 105 degrees, he describes it as a nice break from the pressures of organizing.

Over a plate of one-dollar tacos from the tumbledown taquería next door to the coalition headquarters, Asbed told me a story to illustrate how education translates into power. Back in the early 1990s, he said, when the group was just getting started, a worker staggered into the office. He had been out in the fields and had requested a drink of water. His field boss said no. When the worker asked again, the boss beat him—severely. The worker held a bloody shirt in his hand.

"We decided to confront the crew boss and see what he was going to say," Asbed told me. "We invited him here to talk about it. So he came here with his attitude and his bodyguards. And we said, 'Look at this. What are you going to do about it?' And he said, 'First of all, I didn't do it. Second, I don't care. Blah blah.' And we said, 'That's all you got to say?' And he left.

"What he thought we'd be doing was filing a complaint with the Department of Labor." Asbed looked indignantly amused by the idea. Parodying himself as a hapless do-gooder, he wrung his hands and minced, " 'Excuse, me, Mr. One Department of Labor Guy for All of Southwestern Florida, who doesn't speak Spanish and who's supposed to cover every labor situation, not just in the fields but everywhere, and who can't investigate his way out of his car!' " Asbed returned to his normal self: "That's what they expected to happen. Or that Legal Services would call him and make him pay a thousand dollars or something and it would go away and nobody knows about it and the crew leader is off the hook.

"So," Asbed continued, "we organized a march in the middle of the night with basically"—he laughed—"the whole town. We left the coalition with maybe two hundred people, but en route, as we passed by, people just poured out of the camps. It was kind of surreal because it was around Christmas and all these Christmas lights are everywhere and we're out there with this bloody shirt and there were twenty-eight patrol cars around the house and cops with camouflage on from Collier County, Naples, all around here. We weren't planning on doing anything violent. But there was a sense that the peasants had come to the king's house. And what we were yelling was 'When you beat one of us, you beat us all.' "

Asbed had been gesturing with a pork taco for emphasis. Here he paused, looking for the right words. "I don't know if you appreciate— words like *radical* and *revolutionary* don't mean anything anymore. Or they mean the wrong stuff. But here, to reverse the power system from a system where the workers are totally dependent on the crew leaders— to reverse the way it's always been set up . . ." He shifted gears. "When you stay in a town like this, where nobody's from here, nobody dies here—unless there's an accident—nobody's family is here, nobody knows each other, to have five hundred guys outside a crew leader's house saying, 'You beat one of us, you beat us all.' " For most if not all the workers involved, it was a subtle but indelible first taste of power. In Asbed's estimation, "it was like the end of the old Immokalee."

He wiped his mouth and recalled a saying he'd learned in Haiti: " 'When your comrade's beard catches fire, put your own in water.' That was people's response before the coalition. When a boss would beat somebody, everyone'd look down at the ground. No one dared to get excited for fear he'd beat somebody else. When the organization started, that stopped. Because the next time somebody got beaten, they came to the office."

One Wednesday night in November, I attended the coalition's weekly *reunión,* or meeting. The point of such meetings varied throughout the year. Early on in the season like this, I would learn, the goal was to interest workers in their own situation, to offer a sort of orientation to Immokalee and the world of farmwork. Did they know where they fit into the pecking order of American food production? Did they know what the coalition was there for?

Twenty-five or thirty workers had shown up, all of them men, seated in folding chairs. Most of them, as Benitez had indicated, were new to town and unfamiliar with the coalition. They seemed shy, curious, and possibly desperate, as if they were at their first AA meeting. Seated among the men in a circle of chairs were a number of workers who had been with the coalition in past seasons and had returned to Immokalee that year.

Benitez led the meeting, showing slides featuring photos of workers, charts of tomato and orange prices, cartoons, and crude drawings. He discussed the fact that workers need to pick two tons of tomatoes to make fifty dollars. "How much is two tons?" he asked, "A truck? An elephant? Two elephants? Twenty guys like Pedro?" He pointed to a chubby old-timer and got an easy chuckle.

The meeting followed this sort of question-and-answer format in what seemed an attempt—sometimes successful, sometimes not—to engage the workers in a dialogue. Benitez used pictures of past strikes and protests, including images from the Taco Bell boycott, to spark discussion. "This is us outside the headquarters of Taco Bell, in Irvine, California." He pointed to a picture of a shiny, glass office tower and asked, "Do you think they have any money?"

Later in the meeting, Benitez passed around a newspaper account of the coalition's role in shutting down a recent slavery operation. Some of the older members read the article out loud for the group, paragraph by paragraph, all of them slowly, some almost painfully. With each paragraph came a pause for discussion, during which Benitez asked questions like "What date did the workers escape from the camp?" and "What month was it?" His questions seemed designed to be sure that everyone understood what was being read and was following the story.

As often as not, the new attendees seemed to respond to Benitez's questions with blank looks and silence. Not only did it seem uncomfortable for them, it felt uncomfortable to me as well. On some level, it seemed potentially patronizing. It was hard for me to tell. The coalition and I had gotten off to a rough start. I'd walked into our first meeting and called them "do-gooders." I'd used the term ironically, trying to convey how other people (not me, of course) might have thought of them, but it was pretty maladroit of me to expect people I'd just met to understand my own personal code of irony. Another source of tension was that not long before I arrived to meet them, they'd spent an entire month educating a reporter from *The New York Times* about their world, their issues, the reality of life for farmworkers, and so on. Obviously, for a shoestring nonprofit organization to give away so much time was a tremendous sacrifice. But after all that effort, the story never ran. The coalition felt understandably cautious about another reporter from New York showing up and asking for another investment of their time and energy for a story that might or might not run.

It also didn't help matters that although I was supportive of their cause, I was less politically informed, more mainstream, and less liberal than I had thought I was. I had believed myself (because I'm not rich, because I'd written a lot about working people, because I think rich people and corporations should pay more taxes per dollar than poor people) to be fairly far to the left of America's current political culture. Yet when I met the coalition, I was shocked by their earnestness. In a culture as ironic as modern-day America's, and for a person as ironic as myself, it caught me off guard to meet people who were enthusiastic and aggressive about something as straightforward as fighting for social justice. Hadn't we all moved on to *Beavis and Butt-Head* and political apathy? How uncool!

On another front, the group's claim to having no hierarchy—its motto is "We are all leaders"—didn't sit too well with me. It reminded me of entry-level jobs I'd had at Internet companies in the 1990s. On several occasions, on starting day or at a job interview, I'd hear the chirpy speech about how "we really don't have a hierarchy here!" Or we didn't have a boss. Or a pecking order. Or whatever. Inevitably, at each such job, I would notice that somehow, it seemed, I was always the person sweeping up the office at the end of the day. It simply made me uncomfortable when people denied such natural phenomena as hierarchy.

Aside from these relatively petty tensions, I also felt dubious about the coalition's methodology. How could "empowering" workers from one small community in southwestern Florida each year have any measurable effect on the overall powerlessness of farmworkers in the United States? After all, there are billions of poor people around the world who could easily be imported to toil in the fields of North America. If Mexicans and Guatemalans become aware enough of their rights that they insist upon fair pay, growers will simply import workers from Honduras. If or when Hondurans begin making such demands, growers will turn to El Salvador—then Panama, and so on, leapfrogging ahead to the next country where workers haven't gotten uppity enough yet to hold out for a living wage.

Benitez's *reunión* had initially seemed to me to be a sort of feel-good road to nowhere. But as I would realize about many things with the coalition, they were right and I was wrong.

When I asked the coalition about their methods, Asbed explained, "Workers in Immokalee today have come here, for the most part, from small, rural communities, places where literacy rates tend to be far lower than they are here, where there are virtually no media, and where almost all communication is oral. Plus, in most cases, the people working in the fields here were among the poorest people in their own countries. Popular education is designed precisely to encourage people to partici-

pate in group discussions on community problems. It uses a lot of images—drawings, skits, sometimes video—to provoke discussions on
sensitive subjects. Many times these depictions are kind of crude, and
may seem trite or hackneyed for more media-savvy Americans, but in a
community like Immokalee, they provide a common, concrete reference
point for people to dissect ideas." It made sense, and I realized I was seeing things through my own eyes, not those of a farmworker.

Regarding the silent, shy audience Benitez was trying to engage,
Asbed said, "Generally, if they're there at the meeting, they're eager to
participate. But even still, it's a process that takes time. Remember, in
Immokalee we have to deal with the fact that this isn't a community in
any traditional sense. Everyone's a stranger. So not every meeting's a
perfect jewel of participation. But when it works, it can move people
like nothing else and allow farmworkers to deal with issues they'd never
even think of confronting on their own, including slavery."

I learned later how effectively the coalition's methods worked. One
day, after knowing them a few months, I asked a couple of members
what they were doing over the weekend. Oh, they said, they were meeting with some second- and third-year coalition members for some sort
of training meeting, during which the workers—peasants, for the most
part, few of whom possessed more than a sixth-grade education—were
going to be learning about stocks, the nature of publicly traded corporations, and the strategies of modern corporate public relations. Not bad,
considering that most Americans don't know much about such things.

Nevertheless, in my initial observations of the coalition, I remained
dubious. Despite their impressive track record of unearthing slavery operations, it was hard to see what kind of long-term progress could be
made toward preventing future, systemic mistreatment of farmworkers
in the United States.

From time to time, during his presentation, Benitez raised his fist in
the air and roared, *"La coalición!"* Everyone, it seemed, was to find their
voice and yell together, as one, *"Presente!"* Then, it seemed, they were to
clap their hands together, once, in thunderous unison. But when Benitez
yelled, *"La coalición!"* he was joined by only three or four lackadaisical
clappers. At the end of the meeting, as he closed, he made a final effort

to exhort some crowd spirit. Roaring with his powerful voice, he asked (in Spanish), "Who is the coalition?"

The three old-timers piped up: "WE ARE!"

Benitez raised his voice a notch higher: "Who is the coalition? Is it the walls? Is it the chairs?"

Once more, the old-timers chimed in: "No, it's US!"

"Who is the coalition?"

"WE ARE!"


Asbed met his wife, Laura Germino, in college. She is a pretty, alert woman in her early forties. Her family has been in Florida for six generations. After a stint with the Peace Corps in Burkina Faso, she became involved in farmworker issues when she took a job with Florida Rural Legal Services.

Germino would make a great Hollywood activist hero, precisely because the idea of being seen as that type of person drives her crazy. Like other members of the coalition, she works seven days a week, often tearing around the swamps in her silver 1970 Malibu—her "muscle car," as she calls it—frequently concluding her days at 10 P.M. with her husband over a dinner of cereal and milk. She dresses almost elegantly, usually in sandals and a skirt, and wears no makeup.

Germino runs both hot and cold, a wealth of information who talks a mile a minute, leaping from subject to subject, expounding generously, if distractedly, on every subject but one—herself. When I asked her about how she got into this work, and about what drove her, she looked at me warily, pointedly uninterested in being portrayed as the Erin Brockovich of the swamps. "Please," she said. "Don't make me be the story. The workers are the heroes."

Germino proceeded instead to tell me how the coalition first learned about El Diablo and the Ramos operation. "It's sort of like smoke, the way you hear about things," she recalled. "We had this one woman, actually a woman who sells cassettes out of a van. What do you call them? Where they go around—a peddler. She came into the office out of the blue one time and said, 'You guys really need to go look at what is going on up there in Lake Placid.' This is, like, in '99 or something, '97. And she left a number and a name, and we called her and the number was out of order. Then another *chofer* came by and said, 'You know, they got some deal going up in there in Lake Placid, where it's pretty out of control. They're buying and selling people, and they're not free to leave.'

"You have just fragments, little pieces of this puzzle thrown at you," she explained, concluding that it would be easier for me to understand what she was talking about if I could see for myself what some of these pieces look like. So one rainy afternoon, Germino took me for a ride in her muscle car. We left Immokalee on Highway 29 and drove north, toward Lake Placid.

Agriculture, Germino explained, is "a system of layers. There's a bunch of shells or layers between the employee, or the picker, and the big money." Between the worker and the product, she said, stands a long chain of middlemen: the contractor, the grower, a processor, a buyers' cooperative or purchasing entity of some sort, another processor, a corporation, and a retail outlet for the finished product. Each entity is protected by a legal and corporate firewall. While many of the layers are formed by public corporations, whose books, at least in theory, are open to the public, growers and labor contractors are almost always private companies. Their books are closed to scrutiny, and it's almost always impossible to know whom they buy from or sell to. A further complication, Germino explained, is that labor crews often pick for a variety of growers, sometimes working directly for them, under the growers' own names, sometimes working under the names of any number of harvesting companies the growers might own, solely or along with brothers-in-law, cousins, or wives.

After about sixty miles, we left Highway 29 and pulled onto a side road. The rain had stopped, but the clouds hung low as we entered a patchwork of meandering streets laid down decades ago for a housing development named Sunnylakes that never got built. It was a decidedly eerie place. The scorched asphalt had buckled off the derelict streets and was now being gobbled up by the swamp, along with a wake of sofas, shoes, TVs, and refrigerators lining the road's shoulder. Finally, we nosed into a sandy driveway leading to a single, isolated mobile home. Germino paused to make sure we were alone. This, she said, was one of the places used by the Ramoses to stash their workers.

"Can you imagine," she asked, "what it'd be like to come to this country, stuck back here, not speaking the language, with people telling you they're gonna kill you if you try and run away?" A pair of plastic bags floated by. Something sounding suspiciously like pistols firing could be heard in the not-so-distant background. There wasn't a person in sight. "I mean, this is like *Mad Max,* right?" Germino raised her eyebrows. "You saw that movie."

The gunshots, if that's what they were, continued. Germino smirked and revved her engine. "Let's get out of here. We don't really wanna stay too long."

We drove back along a series of dirt roads, and even after what I'd seen in Immokalee, the poverty was stunning. We passed a rural ghetto of trailer homes torn through with rust, stained with algae and mildew. Chickens scooted herky-jerkily across roads with names like Orange Street and Citrus Boulevard. The roads and the yards outside the houses were lined with yet more junk—boats crashed at odd angles, abandoned school buses with broken windows and smashed hoods, dolls with missing eyes, swing sets listing at odd angles—all of it sinking back into the swamp.

The rain started again, monotonously. Germino saw someone I didn't notice and abruptly pulled back from the rain-streaked window, pursed her lips, and muttered, "That guy's back out of jail? That sucks."

Finally, we arrived at the spot where the Guatemalan van driver, Ariosto Roblero, had been murdered back in 1997. It seemed like many other places in South Florida—low, featureless, and isolated. It was both easy and hard to imagine that a man had been yanked from a van here and shot in the head while his passengers went running into the night. Ten years of rainfall had long ago washed away the blood.

We pulled back onto Highway 29, veered into a convenience store for some coffee, and then headed back toward Immokalee. Despite the rash of slavery cases making the news, Germino said, "you have never seen any of these growers, or Tropicana, or any of these other companies, express the slightest bit of remorse or shock. What you get from them is a resounding silence. And it's because they don't care."

People new to the realm of farmworker mistreatment always get stuck on the notion that modern slavery and farmworker abuse happen because today's farmworkers often lack work papers or citizenship, she said. Such a short-term view is erroneous. Agribusiness has always been this bad, and it has always been so *by design*. Since the days of officially sanctioned, legal slavery, she explained, agriculture has consistently attempted to sidestep the labor rules that have been imposed upon other industries. In 1938, during the New Deal, when the federal minimum-wage law was enacted, farmworkers—at the behest of the agriculture lobby—were excluded from its provisions. They remained so for nearly thirty years. Even today, farmworkers, unlike most other hourly workers, are denied the right to overtime pay, receive no medical insurance or sick leave, and are denied federal protection against retaliatory actions by employers if they seek to organize. Further, in many states, they're specifically excluded from workers' compensation.

"Modern-day slavery cases don't happen in a vacuum," Germino explained. "They only occur in degraded labor environments, ones that are fundamentally, systematically exploitive. In industries where the labor force is contigent, day-haul, with subpoverty wages, no benefits, no right to overtime, no right to organize—that's where you see slavery taking root." For this reason, she continued, for every case of outright slavery making splashy headlines, it is reasonable to assume that there are thousands of additional workers toiling away in abusive, sweatshop-like conditions. Conversely, she said, in labor environments with healthy worker protections—full-time positions with decent wages, benefits, overtime pay, freedom to form unions, and so forth—slavery cases simply don't exist. When was the last time anyone heard of a slavery case in the automotive industry?

Germino compares the fight against modern forced labor to the fight against lynching during the civil rights movement. Merely abolishing lynching, she said, "would have left in place the whole rotten system of segregation that enabled such vicious violence to prevail." In order to put a stop to lynching, it was crucial to address the system of segregation that enabled and supported it. Similarly, she argued, putting an end to slavery means improving labor conditions for all workers in exploitive industries.

The issue, she said, was much larger than agriculture. It concerns all working people in the United States. "Look at all the companies that used to give people pensions, and how now they're trying to hire every-one as permanent-temporary or contingent workers," she said. "People see that and say, 'Oh, there is a terrible new trend, employers are treat-ing more and more people as day laborers and temporary workers. They're not giving benefits anymore, and they're outsourcing every-thing.' That's exactly what agriculture has always been like. And now you could say the other industries are emulating agriculture. Instead of trying to improve conditions elsewhere, they're gonna resemble agricul-ture more and more. And pretty soon people who think, 'Well, this doesn't have anything to do with me,' they might start seeing their jobs look the same way, and they might get a lot more interested.

"Look what's going on in our country," she continued. "Where the gap between the rich and poor has grown in the past twenty years—phenomenally. I mean, I don't have to say it; Supreme Court justice Brandeis—he said it." And here she paraphrased the quote I cite in my introduction: "You can have great concentration of wealth in the hands of a few or you can have democracy. You can't have both."

Germino grinned, both amused and upset by the general obtuseness of the world. "That should bother everybody, right?" She went on, as if embarassed to have to say it, "I mean, I think life, liberty, and the pursuit of happiness, all that stuff in the Constitution or the Declaration of In-dependence or whatever the hell it was—I think that's all a pretty neat idea, don't you?"

To take a quick tour of labor abuse in agriculture from the Emancipa-tion Proclamation through today is to see Germino's point. Foremost among all other industries, the agricultural sector has gone to every imaginable length to avoid paying free-market, prevailing rates for

labor, as if for some reason the production of food is necessarily different from the production of other goods.

In the Reconstruction-era South, employers recently bereft of slaves
had simply to contact the friendly local sheriff and ask him to rustle up
a few hands. Unemployed free black men in the vicinity would suddenly
find themselves arrested, fined for minimal offenses such as loitering,
and locked in prison. The employer behind the scheme would gallantly
step in to pay off the convicts' fines, thereby purchasing a bargain-rate
workforce. Convicts paid their debts to society—and their employers—
by working on the chain gang. At night, workers were locked up and
guarded by force. So much for emancipation.

The post–Civil War period witnessed the rise of tenant farming, or
sharecropping. Under the typical sharecropping arrangement, landlords
provided everything a tenant family needed for farming: a house (usually), the use of land and perhaps tools and seed, fuel, and feed for animal stock. In exchange, the landlord received anywhere from a quarter
to half of the harvest. In theory, there need be nothing sinister about
such an arrangement. In practice, however, abuse proved the rule more
often than the exception.

The overwhelming majority of tenants were illiterate, had no experience bargaining or making contracts, and were utterly dependent
upon the landowner for credit in order to survive between harvests. Employers determined the interest rates tenants paid on their debts, kept
the books, and brokered crop sales. They charged what they wanted for
food and supplies and were free to levy fees for such arbitrary services as
"supervision." Because debt, rather than naked, brute force, served as
the leading edge of coercion, this variety of slavery is usually termed
"debt peonage." But as in all forms of slavery, force remained the ulti-
mate motivator.

What is most startling about sharecropping, given its exploitive nature, is both how prevalent it proved to be and how over time it mired
more and more (rather than fewer) people in poverty. In 1880, 36 percent of farms in the South were operated by tenants; by 1920, this share
had risen to 49 percent. Some eight and a half million Americans, or
7 percent of the nation's population, were reduced to tenancy in what

was then known as the Cotton Belt, essentially the lower eastern quadrant of the United States. By 1930, the number of tenant farms had climbed still higher, to 55 percent of the region's farms. Until the combined shocks of World Wars I and II and the Great Depression prompted a mass exodus of poor southerners, millions of uneducated black and white families lived a step above barnyard animals, ignorant, hungry, and housed in derelict shacks, earning little more than their keep.

In 1942, farm interests, facing wartime manpower shortages, urged Congress to enact the Bracero Program, designed to bring Mexican farmworkers across the border. The program imported four to five million workers, who typically came to the United States for nine months before returning home. As with every other "temporary worker" program since, abuse and nonpayment of workers were rife. Workers weren't free to change employers, nor were they free to organize. Employers who paid late, paid not at all, proved abusive, or provided substandard food or living conditions faced little pressure to mend their ways. Any worker foolish enough to speak up about bad conditions was branded a troublemaker, placed on a blacklist, and denied permission to return. The program expired without being renewed in 1964, after numerous instances of abuse and outcry from labor unions and religious and community groups. Even the U.S. Department of Labor officer in charge of the program, Lee G. Williams, called Bracero nothing more than "legalized slavery."

World War II proved a boon for agricultural interests when German prisoners of war came on the labor market. In 1945 there were as many as 120,000 such workers imprisoned in the United States. Hundreds were put to work in the sugarcane fields around Lake Okeechobee and paid eighty cents a day. The work of cutting and burning sugarcane was—and is—notoriously backbreaking and dangerous, often taking place during daytime temperatures of over 100 degrees. One prisoner, a man named Karl Behrens, suffered so intensely at a sugar camp in Clewiston, Florida, that in January 1945 he ran away and hanged himself from a tree.

Prisoners of war were no substitute for a more permanent underpaid labor force, however, and it was around this time that the sugar industry also devised a series of deliberately overcomplicated remuneration plans billed as "incentive systems" or "task rates." The idea was ostensibly to reward more productive (non-POW) workers with bonus pay. The real goal was to systematically dupe employees (and government snoops), keeping them in the dark about how much workers were really earning.

One such ruse is painstakingly detailed in Alec Wilkinson's meticulous *Big Sugar,* which describes the sophisticated defrauding of thousands of Caribbean cane cutters, mostly from Jamaica and Trinidad, brought to Florida between 1944 and the late 1980s. Imported as temporary workers, the islanders lived at sugar-company camps around Lake Okeechobee. The operations were typically remote, and cutters had no access whatsoever to legal or any other kind of support. Each day, when supervisors tallied up the harvest, they sent the results to the field bosses. Using the price of sugar that day on the world market to first calculate how much profit the company was earning, field bosses then decided how much they felt like paying the workers. If workers needed to be paid less than the legal minimum wage, so be it; supervisors simply reduced the number of hours on the workers' time sheets. Cutters working twelve-hour shifts found themselves making as little as eighteen dollars a day. Those who argued were deported.

What's startling is not only that such exploitation occurred but how long it continued. In the 1970s, an executive from an oil and film conglomerate with large sugar holdings took a tour of cane workers' barracks and described living conditions to be "one degree short of Dachau." In the 1980s, a class-action lawsuit was filed on behalf of twenty thousand mostly Jamaican sugarcane harvesters employed by Florida's largest sugar companies; the suit sought to hold Big Sugar responsible for the "piece rate" shell game. After endless maneuverings and appeals, Big Sugar managed to lose, appeal, win, lose, and finally succeed in splitting the case into five cases, each to be tried and decided separately. Of the five, the sugar companies won three and settled a fourth out of court. The fifth and final case has been shuttled back and forth from state to federal court and was, in 2006, decertified as a class-action proceeding.

Twenty years after the original filing, it is awaiting decision in the Florida State small-claims court.

If not exactly justice, however, the endless legal battling against Big Sugar has changed corporate attitudes toward field hands. In the last few years, Florida's sugar companies have decided that machines shall henceforth be preferable to human labor. Caribbeans have been replaced by enormous yellow $165,000 mechanical harvesters. As an article from *The Palm Beach Post* noted, "The machine doesn't sing spirituals. But it gets the job done."

South Florida, of course, isn't the only area in the United States with a bad labor track record. Another such hot spot is the area around Johnston and Sampson counties, in North Carolina, which from the 1970s to the 1990s was home to such notorious labor contractors as Willie Warren, aka "the Black Knight"; Johnny Lee Terry, aka "Johnny Dollar"; "Goldtooth," aka "Gold Teeth" and "Goldie"; and Carrie Bonds, who ran crews with her husband and son, Willie and Willie Junior.

Typically, this group of contractors exploited bottom-of-the-barrel crews of alcoholics, late-stage drunks far too wasted to keep an eye on hours or records and too dependent on alcohol to run away and fend for themselves. They were called, appropriately, "wino crews." The wino-crew boss kept workers supplied with marked-up, company-store moonshine. In the 1980s the drug of choice became crack cocaine, but the pattern of manipulation stayed the same.

I spoke with a woman named Joyce Grant, a forty-six-year-old African American and former alcoholic and drug addict who described for me her employment with the Bonds family. Born in Ocala, Florida, Joyce had grown up in a family of migrant workers. From the age of nine until 1985, she told me, farmwork had provided a pleasant life. She got by and enjoyed being outdoors. Then she met her husband, Huey, and unfortunately, the two fell into bad ways.

Traveling with the seasons, working on camps from Florida to the

Carolinas, Joyce and Huey found themselves getting drunk, high, and locked up each night in compounds ringed with barbed wire and guarded by pit bulls and pistol-whipping guards. The guards, said Joyce, were an ever-present reality. "You so far back out there in the woods you can't walk to town. They stay right there with you when you go to the store," Joyce recalled. "The town's so small there's nowhere to run. Leaky showers, half-fed people, unlivable camps. No sheets on they bed. Got you way down a clay dirt road, mosquitoes eat you up. For lunch, they bring you a little sandwich, sauce, and baloney. It already melted in the sun. It make your blood pressure high. Treated like a dog." Once, she said, she saw Carrie Bonds wringing out a tampon into the workers' food as she prepared it. (According to local superstition, not unlike certain voodoo beliefs, if you make people consume your blood, you attain the power to control them.)

Joyce said that the Bondses charged $9.50 for a six-pack of beer. A bottle of wine that ran a dollar in a store went for six out at the camp. "If you pickin' a hundred bushels of peaches or potatoes," she said, "you making thirty-five or forty dollars in that day. But you gonna come home and you gonna get some shine and some drugs. They gonna get that money you made."

One day when Joyce was too sick from drugs and exhaustion to work in the fields, the Bondses took her in a van to Atlanta, trolling for home-less men on the streets by offering them crack. Embarrassed by her be-havior in those days of addiction (she had been sober for many years when I spoke to her), she recalled, "I was telling these men how we had swimming pools and how nice the camp was. Pool tables, this, that, and the other."

Sometime around 1992, while working at a camp in Benson, North Carolina, Joyce and Huey decided to run away and clean up their lives. It wasn't going to be easy. The guards counted everyone each night be-fore bedtime and hung around outside the barracks getting drunk with their rifles beside them as the workers slept. Joyce told me that she and Huey snuck their belongings (clothes and a television) out into the sur-rounding peach fields over the course of several nights, also making contact with a sympathetic crew leader down the road. The plan was simple. Referring to Huey, she said, "When he said 'Start running,' you start running."

The scene sounds like a B movie starring the late Warren Oates as the local sheriff. When the couple began to run, the camp dogs chased them into the night. The Bondses sent out guards in cars to prowl the dirt roads. At one point, Joyce recalled, she fell into a deep ditch; Huey tumbled in after her. They almost didn't make it.

In 1993, the Bondses were charged with conspiracy to hold workers in a state of peonage, distribution of crack cocaine, and violations of the federal Migrant and Seasonal Agricultural Worker Protection Act. They were released from prison in 2000.

Incredibly, cases like Joyce's still pop up. In 2001, an African American crew leader named Michael Allen Lee pled guilty to keeping twenty-four African American orange pickers indebted throughout the nineties by providing them with crack cocaine. In 2003, a contractor named Ronald Evans, his wife, and his son were discovered luring homeless African Americans to a remote, barbed-wired camp in northeastern Florida where potatoes and cabbage were grown. Crack, alcohol, and cigarettes were offered on credit, snaring workers in debt. After a four-year cooperative effort between the CIW and federal authorities, the Evanses were convicted in February 2007 on conspiracy, drug, and financial-reporting violations and sentenced to a combined fifty-one years in prison.

But with the influx of farmworkers from Mexico and Central America, the wino and crackhead crews will soon be a thing of the past. In their place has arisen the type of case exemplified by García Orozco and his friends—the exploitation and enslavement of foreign migrant workers. Already it's possible to see minor variations in the theme.

In September 1999, Abel Cuello, Jr., Basilio Cuello, and German Covarrubias, labor contractors from Immokalee, were arrested for the smuggling and involuntary servitude of twenty-seven migrants, who had been held against their will and forced to work in southwestern Florida's tomato fields. Covarrubias and the Cuellos told their workers that their *raite* fee from the Mexican border (which in those days was typically about seven hundred dollars) was actually seven *thousand* dollars. Workers were held in dilapidated trailers and threatened if they tried to escape.

Perhaps the most vicious case of modern migrant slavery is that of a Florida-based labor contractor named Miguel Flores. Flores was indicted in 1996 for enslaving hundreds of Mexican and Guatemalan farmworkers on a camp in South Carolina.

Flores had been hired for years by large companies selling fruit and vegetables and entrusted to handle payrolls worth hundreds of thousands of dollars, despite an arrest record in Florida and South Carolina and a well-known reputation for violence. The newspaper in Flores's hometown of La Belle, Florida, the *Caloosa Belle,* repeatedly printed letters from citizens complaining about shootouts in broad daylight at a local bar between Flores and ex-employees, guards who had worked for him. Rumors circulated widely that Flores and his crew committed numerous murders and dumped the victims into the Caloosahatchee River. Charges were never brought, but as one local cop observed, "When Flores left the area, the rash of accidental drownings stopped."

His labor camps were scenes of unrelenting barbarity, with guards firing guns into the air to get workers moving along. "It was horrible for the women," a former Flores employee told me. "One of them was sixteen, seventeen years old. She was very pretty. The drivers and the bosses got talking about how they could help her work off her debt. They raped her. When they got bored with her, the workers started in, too. If the bosses could do it, why couldn't they?"

The level of intimidation was so high that even after Flores was shut down, it was nearly impossible to persuade anyone to testify against him. It took five years for CIW investigators, later joined by Mike Baron of the Border Patrol, to piece the case together. Finally, however, in June 1997, Flores was convicted and handed fifteen years. After the sentencing, in which workers recounted their sufferings at his hands and expressed their hopes that this kind of abuse might one day be abolished, a television newsman reportedly asked Flores if he had anything else to say. Flores's answer captures rather succinctly the essence of labor relations in agriculture: "Yeah. Fuck you, motherfucker."

Seventy years ago there were nearly seven million American farmers, and about 25 percent of the American population was involved in farm production. Today, fifty thousand farms account for three-quarters of American food production. The average farmer is over fifty-five years old, and it is predicted that as today's farmers continue to retire, consolidate, merge, or quit the business, the bulk of America's food could be produced by as few as thirty thousand farms.

As Greg Schell, a farmworker advocate in South Florida, explained, "The growers who prosper in today's agriculture market are diversified, vertically integrated, and grow in a number of locations (often in several countries), insulating them against the effects of short-term market price swings. Some farmers who used to sell their own crops now additionally grow for larger growers under a contract arrangement. In most instances, the large growers began as family farms, and many of them are still run by the descendants of the founders. However, the scope of their operations is usually huge. Although privately held, these farms behave much more like corporations than the traditional family farm."

The production and distribution of South Florida's tomato crop is dominated by a handful of private firms, such as Six L's Packing Company, Gargiulo, Inc., and Pacific Tomato Growers, which often grow and buy from others tens of millions of pounds of tomatoes to sell to supermarkets and corporations who sign year-round contracts.

Ownership and distribution is even more tightly controlled in the citrus industry. Lykes Brothers is a billion-dollar conglomerate with holdings in insurance, forestry, and cattle as well as citrus. Larger still is Consolidated Citrus, which owns 55,000 acres in Florida alone and produces about seventeen million boxes of fruit each year. The vast majority of the state's crop, in the form of either fruit, juice, or concentrate, goes to three final buyers: Cargill Inc., a $75 billion commodities giant and one of the largest privately owned companies in the world, with operations in fifty-nine countries; Tropicana, which is owned by PepsiCo; and Minute Maid, owned by Coca-Cola.

This transformation of the food business from ma-and-pa-style operations to big business is frequently referred to as the "industrialization" of modern agriculture. In part, this is because of the immenseness of modern food-growing operations. Additionally, however, the term refers to fundamental changes in the nature of farming techniques, namely, the substitution of small-scale, self-sustaining, home-produced "inputs" for supplies purchased from off the farm. Where once family members served as a farm's labor force, farmworkers are now typically hired from outside the family. Horses, formerly the primary source of a farm's muscle power, have been replaced by tractors. Organic fertilizers like manure and mulch have been exchanged for petrochemical-based fertilizers. While once upon a time, farmers simply reused a portion of last year's crops for next year's seed, they now buy genetically modified seeds from Monsanto, which come with a one-year license (as writer Michael Pollan describes it in *The Botany of Desire,* Monsanto now hires Pinkerton detectives to roam the fields of rural America, making sure farmers aren't violating their licenses).

As farms have supersized, and as farming has become more technology- and chemical-based, it has become, in the public conception, a more "rational" and "efficient" business. And yet an analysis of modern agriculture shows that nothing could be further from the truth.

Between 1910 and 1983, the amount of energy consumed to fuel American agricultural production increased 810 percent. It now requires ten fossil fuel calories to produce a single food calorie. According to the U.S. Department of Agriculture, pesticide use on major field crops, fruits, and vegetables tripled from 215 million pounds in 1964 to 588 million pounds in 1997. The trend is mirrored worldwide: our planet uses five hundred times more chemicals than in 1940. This monstrous deployment of chemicals, many of which are known carcinogens, has produced a temporary illusion of bounty, but one that is, in fact, beginning to fail.

Between 1945 and 1985, the number of crops worldwide destroyed by insects rose from around 7 percent to nearly 14 percent. In 1980, a ton of fertilizer applied in the United States yielded an average of fifteen to twenty tons of corn. By 1997, this same ton of fertilizer yielded only five to ten tons. At the same time, our soils are burning out. Irrigation and massive water-diversion programs have caused farmers to throw into production arid and other marginal land, resulting in massively wasteful water usage. Since 1960, the United States has lost half its topsoil. Currently, it has been estimated, we are losing topsoil seventeen times faster than it is replaced by nature.

By every measure but the most myopic, short-term calculations, modern agriculture is a debacle. The most hopeful perspective—that our environment is being sacrificed to feed the world's hungry—is sadly delusional. During the second half of the twentieth century, so many Third World economies formerly devoted to subsistence farming retooled themselves toward high-profit export crops such as sugar, coffee, soybeans, flowers, beef, shrimp, and cotton that although worldwide production of consumable calories has risen, so has the number of hungry people around the planet—by more than 11 percent. Eight hundred million people worldwide go hungry every day. Even in the United States, the world's number-one exporter of food, thirty-three million people are officially included among the world's hungry.

The last thirty or so years have seen a massive wave of mergers and acquisitions in each of the industries that touch an American farmer's business life. Every one of these fields is now dominated by a very small and still-shrinking handful of players. Whether one looks at seeds (Monsanto, Dow, and Syngenta), fertilizer (Monsanto, Bayer, Syngenta), pesticides (Monsanto, Dow, Syngenta), commodities trading (Cargill, ConAgra, Archer Daniels Midland), food manufacturing (the Altria Group, Nestlé, Unilever), or supermarket retailing (Wal-Mart, Safeway, Albertson's, Kroger), each sector is now dominated by three or four giants who control 60 to 80 percent of the business. The same holds for the processing of corn, wheat, soybeans, chicken, cattle, and pork, in addition to railway and barge shipping concerns and even suppliers of tractors and farm machinery. It is staggering to contemplate the power and vast reach of such near monopolies. We walk through the grocery store imagining thousands of brands and companies, homey little entities that put cows, farmers, rolling hills, and sunbeams on their products' labels. The reality is that nearly all of them are owned by a very few giants. To unscientifically cut and paste the products sold around the world listed on the Kraft Foods website is to behold a document over twenty pages long. (Kraft is owned by the Altria Group, which also owns Philip Morris, the cigarette manufacturer.)

Gigantic fast-food chains such as McDonald's, Burger King, and Yum! Brands (which owns the Taco Bell, Kentucky Fried Chicken, Pizza Hut, Long John Silver's, and A&W chains) buy billions and billions of dollars' worth of food each year, primarily in the form of fresh fruits and vegetables. Such massive buyers are uninterested in going from farm to local farm, buying produce from one small farmer at a time. Instead, they want a manageably small number of suppliers who can guarantee them year-round supplies. All of this is understandable. What is less easy to understand is how radically and detrimentally this consolidation has reshaped the food business.

Classic capitalist theory assures us that the law of supply and demand always finds its own level, that buyers and sellers in a free market are able to make decisions of their own free will to ensure their maximum benefit. If it costs farmers $x$ amount to raise their crop, well, then, according to capitalist theory, they will charge $x$ plus whatever profit they can get away with, depending on the number of competitors they face and the unique positive or negative qualities of their product. In practice, however, the food business is more complicated. No matter how big growers become, their trading partners have become much bigger—to a transformative degree.

In a fascinating passage about the purchasing power of large corporations, Charles Fishman, in his book *The Wal-Mart Effect,* tells the story of the Vlasic pickle company's experience "partnering" with Wal-Mart. In the late 1990s, it seems, Wal-Mart proposed to Vlasic that Wal-Mart feature Vlasic's one-gallon jar of pickles. The gallon-sized jars had only existed as something of a novelty, but for Wal-Mart, the idea—more than the product—was enormous. The gallon jars weighed twelve pounds and looked great on display cases. What better symbol of Wal-

Mart's ability to bring consumers more for their money than anyone on earth?

"And so" Fishman continues,

Vlasic's gallon jar of pickles went into every Wal-Mart, some 2,500 stores, at $2.97, a price so low that Vlasic and Wal-Mart were making only a penny or two on a jar, if that. It was showcased on big pallets near the front of stores. It was an abundance of abundance. "It was selling 80 jars a week, on average, in every store," says [former Vlasic VP of marketing Steve] Young. Doesn't sound like much, until you do the math: That's 240,000 gallons of pickles, just in gallon jars, just at Wal-Mart, every week. Whole fields of cucumbers were heading out the door.

For Vlasic, the gallon jar of pickles became what might be called a devastating success. "Quickly, it started cannibalizing our non-Wal-Mart business," says Young. "We saw consumers who used to buy the spears and the chips in supermarkets . . . buying the Wal-Mart gallons. They'd eat a quarter of a jar and throw the thing away when they got moldy. A family can't eat them fast enough."

The gallon jar reshaped Vlasic's pickle business: It chewed up the profit margin of the business with Wal-Mart, and of pickles generally. Procurement had to scramble to find enough pickles to fill the gallons, but the volume gave Vlasic strong sales numbers, strong growth numbers, and a powerful place in the world of pickles at Wal-Mart. Which accounted for 30% of Vlasic's business. But the company's profits from pickles had shriveled 25% or more, Young says—millions of dollars.

The gallon was hoisting Vlasic and hurting it at the same time.

Young remembers begging Wal-Mart for relief. "They said, 'No way,' " says Young. "We said we'll increase the price"—even $3.49 would have helped tremendously—"and they said, 'If you do that, all the other products of yours we buy, we'll stop buying.' It was a clear threat."

Finally, Vlasic was able to get Wal-Mart to agree to let them sell a smaller, half-gallon jar—for $2.49. But it was too late. In January 2001, partially due to the hit sustained by "partnering" with Wal-Mart, Vlasic filed for bankruptcy. (It has since emerged from receivership—free and clear from their contract with Wal-Mart.)

The point is not to complain specifically about Wal-Mart so much as to illustrate an example of what has come to be called "monopsony," the power that any massive trading partner wields over any smaller one. One imagines that in a truly free market, sellers of products, not buyers, dictate the price at which the product is sold. It's a great idea. But it's not always true—especially in the food business, where growers are ever-increasingly dwarfed by their business partners.

As an article from an agricultural trade magazine, *The Packer* (www.thepacker.com), noted in 2005, "Recently, Miami-based Burger King *changed its tomato pricing method* to the extreme detriment of the tomato farmer and tomato repacker." The article noted that the whole-sale purchasing co-op that buys all of Burger King's supplies is so big that it *"sets the rules by which the game is played."* (The emphases are mine.)

The effects of such an uneven playing field can be seen in what is called the "food price spread," calculated by the U.S. Department of Agriculture. In 1952, farmers earned an average of forty-seven cents out of every dollar consumers spent in the supermarket. By 1970, their share had slipped to thirty-seven cents. By 1990, it had slid to thirty cents, and in 2001, using an average basket of food products common to grocery stores nationwide, the farmer's share of the consumer dollar had fallen to a measly twenty-one cents. Florida tomato producers receive, on aver-age, nineteen cents of every dollar purchased in the grocery store. In 2000, the last year tracked by the USDA, orange producers received six-teen cents per dollar for whole, fresh oranges.

These figures only show how much farmers receive for their crops. The other side of the equation is how much farmers pay for everything they need to grow our food. And on this end, too, farmers are facing a squeeze.

To get a glimpse of the power dynamic, we need simply compare growers' return on equity—a fancy way of saying "profit"—with that of their suppliers and buyers. According to various studies by academics and the USDA, American farmers earn about 2 to 4 percent on every dollar they invest. The more dominant food firms (ConAgra, Unilever, Tyson), by contrast, generate returns of at least 20 percent. Some companies, in particular grain processors General Mills and Quaker Oats, have at times enjoyed return on equity rates of 259.3 percent and 132.6 percent, making them hundreds of times more profitable than the farms that supply them.

How do farmers respond to being forced into an unfair bargaining position? Here is where we begin to scratch at the "peculiar" ideas about labor at the heart of American agribusiness.

In December 2003, *The Packer* ran a story about Florida tomato producers' response to an increase in the price of a common pesticide called methyl bromide. The increase was accepted without a fuss as a simple cost of doing business, and farmers reacted by simply raising the price of their tomatoes a penny a pound. *The Packer* quoted one tomato salesman as saying, "There's been virtually no opposition to it." The article went on to quote the president of a large packinghouse, who said, "I guess [buyers] knew when the Florida tomato shippers decided to do something, and it was unanimous, they didn't have much choice anyway."

Such a price increase is a normal, free-market response to a common development. One player in a supply chain raises its price, and everyone affected deals with it. But this generates an obvious question: Why is it acceptable to farmers that the price of pesticides will increase from time to time but it is unacceptable that, like everything else in life, the price of labor will do so as well?

The following is a story I heard from the Coalition of Immokalee Workers. During a thirty-day hunger strike held by some of the group's members in 1998 to protest tomato pickers' low wages, growers refused to speak with them. When a produce broker sympathetic to the farmworkers asked one of the recalcitrant growers why he refused to even meet with the coalition, the farmer grumbled, "I'll put it to you this way. The tractor doesn't tell the farmer how to farm."

At the risk of pointing out the obvious, the story illustrates the degree to which unfair pay in agriculture stems from attitudinal, not economic, causes. As another Florida farmworker advocate expressed it, "Whenever anyone tries to regulate them, farmers always complain—'Oh, but we're just poor farmers!' " As she described the problem, farming had managed to maintain an aura of self-serving exceptionalism about it that no other industry in the country could have possibly gotten away with: farms produce food, and food is necessary to our survival; therefore, it is okay to mistreat brown people. Or whomever. If it sounds stupid, it's because it is.

Tomato pickers' shares of retail sales come out to roughly 1.4 cents per pound. It would require a raise of about $3,200 a year for each farmworker in America today to earn the minimum wage. This could be accomplished by raising the cost of food by about $50 per year per American household.

According to the Economic Research Service, a branch of the USDA that compiles statistics about the food and farm economies, Americans in 2002 spent 6.5 percent of their income on food—less than any other country tracked. Canadians spent half again as much. Swedes spent nearly twice as much. Japanese spent over twice as much. Spaniards spent nearly three times as much.

Another interesting statistic is that from 1929 to 1958, Americans spent between 18 and 25 percent of their disposable income on food. From the mid-1980s to the present, the share has dropped, from about 12 percent to about 10 percent. How is it that as we've become a vastly wealthier country with a far cheaper supply of food, we've succeeded in creating a food system that can't pay farmworkers a living wage?

The food sector (food, groceries, food processing, and restaurant businesses together) is worth about a trillion dollars a year in the United States and is second only to pharmaceuticals in profitability. Considering that the American public gives some $47 billion per year in direct subsidies to agricultural producers and billions more in tax breaks, research allocations to universities, marketing initiatives, subsidized water, food aid programs to poor countries, and so on, it is blind idiocy or willful deceit to say the money just isn't there.

According to the Center for Responsive Politics, a nonpartisan, non-profit campaign watchdog group, in 1998, agribusiness—through PACs (political action committees), individual donations, and soft-money contributions—gave more than $43 million to federal candidates. In 2000, they gave close to $60 million. In 2002, the figure was over $54 million. In 2004, it was almost $53 million, and in 2006, it fell back to $44 million. These figures don't include the many millions more going to state and local campaigns, or coming from additional and obscured sources, or industries beyond the "agribusiness" designation, like fast-food chains, hotels, and construction firms, with an increasing dependency on an illegal-alien labor force.

The first and foremost response from the federal government to such generosity is the deliberate blindness to the runaway population of undocumented workers in the United States. According to the General Accounting Office, in 1999 the U.S. Immigration and Customs Enforcement agency took action against 417 companies for employing illegal aliens. By 2005, that number had dropped to three. In fact, in 1999, the Immigration and Naturalization Service listed monitoring workplaces last among its five enforcement priorities. The INS, now called U.S. Citizenship and Immigration Services, devotes about 4 percent of its personnel to enforcement in the workplace, down from 9 percent in 1999.

In a well-circulated paper from January 2005 entitled "Asset Management: The Underground Labor Force Is Rising to the Surface," analysts Robert Justich and Betty Ng, writing for the investment-banking firm Bear Stearns, found that U.S. Census statistics had become so delusional and deceptive that investors could no longer rely upon them if they wanted to make sound business decisions. "As investors," the report stated, "we need not accept the accuracy of the official census immigration statistics, which are widely recognized as incomplete."

Justich and Ng used their own criteria to estimate the number of undocumented immigrants living in the United States, namely, remittances (the amount of money sent to home countries each year by immigrants), housing permits in immigrant "gateway" communities; school enrollments, and cross-border flows. They calculated that the number of illegal immigrants in the United States may be as high as 20 million people—almost double the official 10.5 million estimated by the Census Bureau. Such a reality, the authors noted, was creating a distorted view of the American economy, altering the ways in which we factor such essential statistics as the overall productivity of the economy, national rates of inflation, and the eventual tax-burden cost for society to provide benefits to workers illegally.

Concluding that employers in the United States have become "simply hooked on cheap, illegal workers," Justich and Ng stated that American employers have responded to free-market pressures of overseas competition by finding "innovative" and even "extra-legal" ways to compete. "These employers," they found, "have, in turn, placed pressure on the government to ignore the flood of cheap labor."

Far beyond merely ignoring the massive influx of foreign, undocumented workers, however, the federal government seems in recent years to have declared outright economic war on them.

In the mid-eighties, Congress declared that agricultural workers, formerly exempt, would henceforth be required to pay federal income tax (Social Security tax is also deducted from their pay). In 1996, after intensive lobbying from the agriculture industry, Congress moved to impose restrictions on providers of legal assistance who receive federal funds, including Rural Legal Service corporations throughout the country. The new restrictions forbade the RLS from representing undocumented workers or bringing class-action suits. The restrictions removed one of the last measures of legal protection available to America's most vulnerable, poor, and abused workers.

Government agencies such as the Department of Labor's Occupational Safety and Health Administration (OSHA) and the Equal Employment Opportunity Commission (EEOC), created to protect workers, have slowly seen their budgets strangled over the last thirty years under a series of labor-unfriendly administrations. The Bush administration's proposed 2006 budget for the Department of Labor recommended eliminating the National Farmworker Jobs Program, which allocated $81 million for migrant and seasonal farmworker programs. The results of this kind of deprioritization of labor regulation is palpable: In the 1950s, the Wage and Hour Division of the federal Department of Labor had one inspector for every 46,000 workers. By the 1990s, there was one inspector for every 150,000 workers.

As recently as 2007, the primary public interface of the Department of Labor's Wage and Hour Division in Fort Myers, Florida—serving an area with perhaps a hundred thousand Spanish-speaking migrant workers—consisted of an answering machine. The outgoing message enumerates in bland, English bureaucratese the few types of complaints the office does handle (and the many more that it doesn't). The recording further explains that the office has no full-time staff and that it's open only once a week, on Wednesdays, for half a day. There is no option to hear the recording in Spanish.

Laxness with regard to abusive growers (or any other malfeasant employer) has become mind-boggling. In one instance, in 1998, the Department of Labor cited a large North Carolina tobacco and sweet potato farm for stiffing a group of Jamaican temporary guest workers out of an aggregate $100,000 in wages. The grower was ordered to pay up and fined—$650. After the 1999 slavery conviction of the Cuello brothers, in Florida, the Department of Labor was tasked with collecting back wages for the enslaved workers. The department was also supposed to levy a fine against both the contractors and the growers who employed them. No such actions were taken.

Even the Supreme Court has gotten into the game of denying farmworkers' rights. In a complicated case from 2002 called *Hoffman Plastic Compounds* v. *National Labor Relations Board,* the Court essentially ruled that while foreign workers in America are as entitled as Americans to engage in union activity, as protected by the National Labor Relations Act, employers who illegally fire foreign workers for participating in such activity will face no penalty whatsoever. The ruling not only flies in the face of the law's intent (to protect the activity of would-be labor organizers), it makes illegal workers far more attractive to hire—in the eyes of antiunion, discriminatory employers.

But the most hypocritical instance of federal intervention to protect abusive employers surely has to be the manipulation of the 2000 anti-trafficking bill.

In 2000, the Department of Justice, alarmed by the increase in human trafficking, worked with allies in Congress to pass the Victims of Trafficking and Violence Protection Act. The essential proposal was to create a federal felony charge for holding people in involuntary servitude, updating the Thirteenth Amendment's prohibition of slavery to take into account the combination of debt peonage and psychological coercion that characterize modern slavery.

The original version of the bill was introduced into Congress by Representative Chris Smith (R-NJ) and focused primarily on sex slavery. Several cases of forced prostitution had recently made headlines, and as one congressional aide involved in the bill's evolution told me later, "It was a big winner that everyone could get behind; people on the Christian right were really repulsed by the issue and wanted to nail it, and the feminist left were also very against it."

As House Democrats studied the bill, however, they became concerned that it ignored other victims of slavery, like farmworkers and garment workers trapped in sweatshops. They reasoned that if modern slavery is to be a crime, it should be a crime wherever and however it occurs. In response, the Democrats, through Sam Gejdenson (D-CT), introduced a competing bill, which included provisions relating to what they called "labor trafficking."

Early drafts of the bill provided a prison sentence for any person who makes a profit "knowing, or having reason to know," that a worker will be subject to involuntary servitude. What this meant, my sources (who, I should mention, both worked for Democrats) explained, was that "if you had a case where you had field workers who were basically being enslaved, and you were in charge of that field, and you knew that these guys were in slavelike conditions, and you benefited from it, then you could go to jail for twenty years."

To the great surprise of all involved, even after extremely intense negotiations in multiple committees, the bill managed to pass muster with both parties, and in November 1999 a compromise was reached. As one of my aides described it, the legislation that resulted was a rare example of "true bipartisanship."

Suddenly, however, as Congress moved toward the Christmas adjournment, the bill hit a roadblock—namely, Senator Orrin Hatch (R-UT), head of the Judiciary Committee. In the words of one aide, "Hatch felt that agricultural enterprises would be too vulnerable. He didn't want the higher-ups to get punished for turning a blind eye." The senator and his staff sat on the bill, refusing to pass it on. Until and unless the "pro-labor" provisions were removed, the bill was not going to come to a vote.

Hatch's staff disputed this characterization of the bill's evolution, countering, "Hatch wanted the bill to pass. He was just concerned about the federal government prosecuting people for crimes because 'they had reason to know' as opposed to whether they actually knew or not. The standard was so broad that you could hold a salesperson selling a shirt in Kmart criminally liable because he is 'profiting' from the sale of goods that were produced overseas because he had a 'reason to know' that some of the overseas factories have such poor working conditions that the workers were 'basically' enslaved."

The bill passed—with the provisions regarding "knowing, or having reason to know" left in place for sex slavery but removed for labor slavery. As a result, the penalties for involuntary servitude apply virtually only to labor contractors—the lowest rung of employers in the long chain that brings produce from the field to the table.

"My personal view," concluded my source on the Hill, "is that the Hatch staff were going to be damned if under their watch, they were gonna open up new avenues of attack on corporate America."

End users of Florida's agricultural commodities, such as Tropicana, the largest buyer of Florida oranges, employ supervisors who roam the fields and test for such things as quality and sugar content. They keep abreast of soil-moisture content and prices in world commodities markets. For all intents and purposes, they control the harvest, dictating what fields are picked when, and to which local processing plants the harvests go.

Not surprisingly, however, when confronted by the fact that several of South Florida's recent slavery cases involve workers picking oranges, a Tropicana spokeswoman with whom I talked denied anything like responsibility. In a sympathetic, perky voice, she informed me that "Tropicana no longer owns any actual groves in the state of Florida. We purchase from companies that own groves." She clarified this position, adding, "We're really not in the business of policing the groves. We're a business and we have to rely on what's in our purview."

When asked whether Tropicana had a position regarding the treatment of the laborers who supplied its product, she replied, "We do our very best to make sure our growers operate at the highest ethical standards." When asked what that actually means, she explained, "We have a written policy in the growers' contract. When they sign that, they say that they're committed to following the labor laws that all companies in America do." When asked what Tropicana would do if it was discovered that one of its suppliers was engaging in unsavory labor practices, she answered, "Well, if it came to our attention, we would take action. We would terminate the contract." When asked if they had ever, in fact, terminated a contract, however, the answer was no. When informed of the ongoing case against the Ramos brothers, who worked for two of Florida's largest orange growers, Lykes Brothers and Consolidated Citrus, Tropicana responded, "Well, we don't actually buy from Lykes Brothers."

According to Jonathan Blum, vice president for public relations of Yum! Brands, the parent of Taco Bell, which in 2003 bought some eleven million pounds of Florida tomatoes, the company does not divulge the names of its suppliers. When I asked Blum about the boycott against the restaurant launched by the Coalition of Immokalee Workers, he said that his company wasn't responsible for helping farmworkers negotiate with local growers for better pay and conditions. "It's a labor dispute between a company that's unrelated to Taco Bell and its workers," Blum told me. "We don't believe it's our place to get involved in another company's labor dispute involving its employees." As for the

relationship between slavery in South Florida and his company's chalu-
pas, Blum said, "My gosh, I'm sorry, it's heinous, but I don't think it has
anything to do with us."

On the night of May 27, 2000, the following two calls were received by
the Highlands County, Florida, Sheriff's Office. Highlands County
is one county north of Lee County, home to Immokalee. Both counties
have a population that is for two-thirds of the year at least half Hispanic.

The first call is answered by a dispatcher with a heavy southern
twang. "911 police emergency."

A male Hispanic speaks with a panicked, high-pitched voice. "Uh,
eh-speak eh-Spanee?"

The dispatcher answers curtly, "No. You speak English?"

The caller pauses. "Okay. *Mire* [look]. Um—"

The dispatcher cuts him off. "You need police, ambulance, fire, or
what?"

The caller panics. "El Mercadito! Lake Placid!"

The dispatcher's concern, unfortunately, registers like impatience.
"*Where?*" she barks.

The caller's panic surges commensurately. "Eh-store Mercadito!
Lake Placid!"

The dispatcher begins to understand him: "At the *store?*" she asks.

The caller answers, "Jes!"

Dispatcher: "What street?"

The caller says, "Twenty-seven."

The dispatcher sighs. "Okay, what's the problem?" She's met by silence, then panic. There are shouts in the background. Something is
happening. "What's the problem?" she shouts. "Is there someone there
that speaks English?"

The phone is hung up. The dispatcher says, into the night: "Hello?"

The phone rings again. The same dispatcher answers, "911, what's
yermergency?"

A different male, with a slightly better command of English, speaks.
"Yeah, I need a cop over here 'coz there's been fight with gun!"

The dispatcher asks, "Where at, sir?"

The man answers, "El Mercadito store!"

The dispatcher literally shouts at him: "I'm not understandin' what you're sayin'! Slow down!"

Bedlam breaks out in the background. The man begins to panic, like the first caller. "El Mercadito! Is the store!" he screams.

The dispatcher is confounded. "Marguer—spell it!" she commands.

A third man now grabs the phone and shouts, "Hello? Hello?"

The dispatcher shouts back. "Yes! Where you at? I am not understandin' where you're at! Are you in Sebring? Avon Park?"

The man sounds more urgent when he screams, "Plis! Is emergency! *Here!* Come quickly! Hello? Emergency! Emergency! Everybody have gun!"

The phone clicks.

Dial tone.


Deputies were able to trace the call to a phone booth outside the El Mercadito grocery store on Highway 27. When the sheriff's officers arrived, they found four vans with smashed windows, forty-odd petrified Guatemalan and Mexican migrant workers, and a man named José Martínez lying on the ground with a bloody lip and a split forehead.

Martínez, the owner of an Immokalee *servicio de transporte* company, had stopped at El Mercadito to make a pickup. There was nothing unusual about it; the citrus season was ending, and pickers were heading north to the Carolinas and beyond. At approximately 11:30 P.M., however, while Martínez's caravan was preparing to leave, two pickup trucks arrived. Six or seven armed men jumped out and began to attack the drivers. While one group of attackers held the passengers at gunpoint and smashed the vans' windows, others demanded to know who the boss was. When they found Martínez, several attackers surrounded him while at least one of them pistol-whipped him with a Llama .38, splitting his forehead open and shouting, "You're the motherfucker who's been taking my people! I'll kill you, you motherfucking son of a bitch!" When Martínez tried to call 911 on his cell phone, his assailants kicked the phone from his hand and continued beating him until he collapsed in the dust, unconscious, his face and shirt covered with blood. During the mêlée, the passengers and one of the van drivers managed to get away, making two calls, one to the police, the other to the Coalition of Immokalee Workers.

Laura Germino and Lucas Benitez arrived around midnight. At least three of the attackers had managed to escape, but police had arrested Juan and Ramiro Ramos, along with a cousin, José Luis Ramos. A gun was found in their truck. Germino recalled that if the reason behind the attack hadn't already been clear, it became so when she saw one of the cops at the crime scene shaking his head, saying, "It's the same guys who did this three years ago. Only last time they killed the guy."

The coalition soon obtained a copy of the unreleased police report describing the 1997 murder of Ariosto Roblero. The similarities between that attack and the current one were too numerous to be coincidental. The circumstances strongly indicated conditions of involuntary servitude. As Germino explained, "Cutting off people's escape routes is the same as locking them behind a fence or holding guns to their heads. There's no difference."

Local prosecutors failed to see the larger picture, however. Ramos, his brother, and their cousin were charged with assault, a misdemeanor. Their lawyers reached a plea agreement with the state attorney whereby the suspects each received a year of probation and a bill for Martínez's van windows and broken cell phone.

Coalition members started making inquiries. Once Ramiro Ramos's nickname began circulating through the membership, reports began to filter back rather quickly: "Oh, El Diablo, yeah, he killed a guy a few years ago right up there!" In little time, it became clear that Ramos was indeed the head of a large and awful operation.

To find out more about the Ramoses, a nineteen-year-old coalition member named Romeo Ramírez volunteered to go undercover and work for them. Ramírez, a Guatemalan, approached the brothers, asked for a job, and went to live in La Piñita, the barracks where García Orozco, Sánchez, and Hernández were held against their will.

Illustrating by example why FBI agents (until and unless the Bureau

starts hiring Guatemalan agents) may never be suitable for such undercover work, Ramírez explained how he approached the job. "You have
to come in as being very humble, innocent about life, and be with these
people, be one of them," he said. "You do it the *indigena* style. I pre-
tended to know nothing."

Inside the camp, Ramírez said, living quarters were "the ugliest I
ever saw in my life. I have lived in bad conditions, all types of conditions,
but this was the worst. In one room where a couple would barely fit,
there were four people. The beds seemed to have been retrieved from
the garbage. There were cockroaches all over the place; the floor was
black. The worst was the stove. Horrible. And the bath, forget it." Acting as if he were merely asking for advice from his fellow workers,
Ramírez made his inquiries: Were people getting paid? Were they free
to go when they wanted? The answers to both questions were no.

Armed now with an eyewitness confirmation that the Ramoses were
holding workers by force, the coalition approached the authorities.
Would the FBI help liberate the workers? According to the coalition,
the FBI declined. One reason given was a lack of material evidence;
without witnesses, victims of the Ramoses, who were available to be interviewed, the FBI couldn't get involved. Another excuse was that it
would be too dangerous. The CIW was on its own.

As the Easter holidays approached, the coalition decided to make a
surprise visit to the Ramoses' workers. They surmised that the Ramoses
would be in church on Palm Sunday. If so, the coalition reasoned, their
cell phones would be turned off, and the goons guarding the barracks
would be unable to warn their bosses. So on Palm Sunday, 2001, several
coalition members visited the workers at La Piñita and began handing
out generic booklets from the Mexican consulate, which, Germino
explained, said, more or less, "Welcome to the U.S. and here's some
guidelines." Slipped underneath these pamphlets, however, were some
coalition handouts, advising the workers of their rights and urging them
to call if they had any problems.

"It was an incredible moment," she recounted. The coalition had
known about the workers' situation for so long but had never been able
to approach them directly. Ironically, because that day there was a reli-

gious event, the workers were more accessible than usual. After months of investigation, Germino said, "we were able to actually speak to people without interruption. We had at least twenty minutes there." Once they could talk, Germino said, the first thing out of their mouths was "We're not allowed to leave." Finally, a bus came with more workers and guards, and the first group of workers said the coalition members better leave. The Ramoses showed up a few moments later, asking questions about what had happened.

The following Saturday, Hernández sneaked out of the barracks to the Kash n' Karry and called the coalition. As Benitez recalled, he said, "We want to get out of here. We're really, really, really afraid. We want to try and leave."

An escape plan was set for later that evening. Around midday, however, Juan Ramos (Nino) showed up at La Piñita in a rage. A worker had escaped the night before. Nino swore and shouted at the remaining workers, then asked for their IDs. When one of them asked why he wanted them, he answered, "Because that way I can find you faster and kill you."

For the three friends, it was too late to change their plan. García Orozco recalled his feelings about entrusting his fate to strangers. "We were shivering," he said. "We were shaking. Because we thought maybe they are his people, too, and they might kill us." However, he said, the group decided "we couldn't endure it any longer. So we thought, Oh, well. If we're going to die anyway, better to die trying to escape." As a final precaution, García Orozco tucked a pair of scissors into his boots. The three men went into the yard outside the barracks, trying to act as if they were simply passing the time.

Around sunset, a white Mercury Grand Marquis with tinted windows pulled off Highway 27, a short distance from La Piñita. Lucas Benitez emerged and raised the hood, as if checking an overheated radiator. From the balcony of the Ramada Inn, across the highway, Asbed and Germino signaled that the coast was clear.

García Orozco, Sánchez, and Hernández sat on a railroad tie at the camp's edge, near the highway, debating what they were about to do. Then, leaving all their belongings behind, including their Mexican documents, they walked slowly toward the roadside. As they neared the Grand Marquis, they broke into a sprint and jumped into the backseat as Benitez slammed the hood closed, got behind the wheel, and gunned the engine. The terrified passengers kept their heads down until they were twenty miles down the road.

Two days after the escape, FBI agents arrived and interviewed the freed workers. Realizing the size of the Ramos operation, they organized a raid on the Ramos camp involving dozens of officers from the FBI, Border Patrol, Department of Labor, and the INS. Unfortunately, they made the mistake of parking their vehicles in plain view one town over from where the Ramoses live, and—more ineptly—using buses marked DETENTION AND DEPORTATION. It wasn't an especially swift move, considering that the Ramoses' extended family included cousins and in-laws living throughout the area, each quite capable of using a cell phone. When agents arrived at La Piñita, they found food, stoves still warm, and sleeping bags, but not a single worker. (Lucas Benitez later told me he could see fires out in the orange groves, obviously campfires of workers spirited out to the fields to avoid detection. The enforcement agents evidently didn't notice them.) The Ramoses were arrested. Now, however, instead of having dozens, or hundreds, of witnesses to choose from, the Department of Justice would have only the three workers sprung by the coalition.

The trial of Ramiro Ramos, Juan Ramos, and José Luis Ramos began on June 4, 2002, in the U.S. District Court for the Southern District of Florida, in Fort Pierce. The defendants were charged in a four-count federal indictment with conspiracy to hold people in involuntary servitude, interference with interstate commerce, use of a firearm during the commission of a violent act, and harboring illegal aliens for the purpose of financial gain.

Fort Pierce is a doleful-looking city about 125 miles up the coast from Miami. The town proper includes a lackadaisically restored six-block square "historic district" flanked by a mini-slum, sprinkled with Haitian-style hand-painted signs for establishments such as Granny's

Kitchen, Da Hair Boutique, Mae J Da' Musik Den, and the Being Serious Unisex Salon—by Teresa. Less quaint are the signs advising NO LOITERING, NO DRUG DEALING and NO STANDING OR DRUG SELLING. What seems to connect the different parts of town is a bizarre preponderance of characters whizzing around in electric wheelchairs. Some seemed aged and disabled, others too obese to walk; a good number seem merely to prefer them to other modes of conveyance.

Rumors circulate before the case gets started: K. Michael Moore, the presiding judge, who lives in Miami, hated Fort Pierce; he wanted to rush the trial in order to start his summer vacation; Moore is extremely conservative but fair; he almost automatically hands out maximum sentences; John Ashcroft, then attorney general of the United States, had requested weekly updates about the case; a feather—assumed to be a kind of mafiosi-style warning—was reportedly left at the local FBI office. None of these rumors was verifiable.

What was ascertainable, however, was the contrast between the defense and prosecution. On the right side of the courtroom, the Civil Rights Division of the United States Department of Justice was represented by three prosecutors, Daniel Velez, a goateed, amicable-looking former assistant district attorney from Brooklyn; Adrianna Vieco, an acerbic, no-nonsense former district attorney from Queens; and Andrew Huang, a quick and eager assistant, new to the Justice Department. All three attorneys were focused, tidy, and self-assured, a modern, multiracial, updated version of G-men I'd seen all my life in movies and books.

A blond twenty-eight-year-old paralegal named Amy with very tanned, strong tennis arms assisted them. Amy had a satchel with a Department of Justice patch on it featuring a slogan in Latin that looked like something from a superhero cartoon. When the attorneys needed an old case for a legal citation, it was Amy's job to sift through the dozens of immaculately organized plastic bins, each bearing hundreds of well-arranged, smartly labeled folders.

The lead strategist for the defense, representing El Diablo, was Joaquin Pérez, a handsome Miami Cuban in his fifties with thoughtful eyes, a full head of lightly gelled black hair, and a flair for stylish suits. Pérez had a history of representing high-level Colombian drug dealers fighting extradition to the United States. He also happened to represent Carlos Castaño, the notorious head of the Colombian paramilitaries, who are reported to kill around two thousand people each year.

His colleague, representing Juan Ramos, was another Miami Cuban named Nelson Rodríguez-Varela. A third attorney, Alfredo Horta, a Mexican from Orlando, represented the Ramoses' cousin José Luis. He had never tried a federal case before. In contrast to their opponents' meticulously organized library, the defense lugged in a few bruised cardboard boxes, haphazardly crammed with folders and loose papers.

After the first day of court, I returned to the Radisson Hotel, just north of town. I was about to go for a run on the beach when in the elevator I bumped into Rodríguez-Varela. I'd introduced myself to both sides during the lunch recess, and the government lawyers had politely told me they were forbidden to discuss the case during the trial. Rodríguez-Varela, on the other hand, grinned and invited me to dinner, adding, "Hey! You should go running with Joaquin! He's about to go!" Moments later, I found myself running down the beach with Pérez.

He was eager to discuss the case. He wasn't going to earn nearly the amount of money he would make from his drug clients, he said, but from a legal and even an anthropological point of view, he found the case engaging nevertheless. "I mean, slavery—it's exciting, right? It's sort of sensational! It raises a lot of issues." He compared the Ramoses to his usual clients. "When it's like, 'Okay, you got caught sitting on fifty kilos of coke,' or if they've shot someone and the corpse is there, and they're going, 'Oh, it was self-defense!' it's very hard to feel sorry for them. But here, it's not so clear-cut."

Chugging along in the sand, he practiced his arguments for the jury. The trial, he said, was clearly for show. Why else would the government bother with only three witnesses out of seven hundred workers employed by the Ramoses? It was a bullshit case, stemming from the CIW's need to make headlines about slavery and the feds' need to seem proactive.

Pérez laughed wryly at the idealistic pretensions of the Coalition of Immokalee Workers. "I used to be very liberal. I worked for Florida Legal Services in Liberty City," he said, referring to the African American slum in Miami famous in the eighties for rampant carjacking. "I was like those people in the coalition, you know, 'Let's change the world!' " He paused and smiled a little ruefully. "But you can't. You don't change anything." In the end, he said, you had to look at the facts. The case was really quite simple, he said. "They got the wrong guy."

For the first few days, the defense tried to paint the plaintiffs as disgruntled employees, crybabies, in fact, who found orange picking too difficult and ran off to avoid paying legitimate debts. The alleged slaves didn't always shine in the courtroom. Their shyness and fear sometimes seemed to read as indifference or vagueness.

Rodríguez-Varela volleyed effectively with Hernández, the youngest of the witnesses, when he grilled him about his expectations of life in the United States. "Was it a possibility in your mind," he inquired, "that things here were free?" Had the witness felt he simply deserved to come to America and be given free food, work equipment, and housing, even though he had no experience whatsoever picking oranges? Why should a boss be willing to give him all these things? Rodríguez-Varela then asked Hernández if he had ever paid his thousand-dollar debt for the ride from Arizona. The witness admitted that he had not. By the time Hernández left the stand, it seemed plausible that he'd possibly pandered to an overeager prosecution, overstating his case for a green card.

The defense also managed to bar several pieces of evidence as hearsay—things the Ramoses had not actually said but rather utterances their workers had heard from others. It eventually became clear that the Ramoses had never, in fact, actually harmed any of the witnesses. It also became quite evident that had the workers wanted to "escape" at any time—as they eventually would do—all they had to do was walk out the door to the highway nearby. No guns had been drawn, no bars had been placed over the windows. Was this really slavery?

Each night, after trial and a run on the beach, I met up with the Cubans. After hours, both lawyers fancied casual clothes, flowered guayabera shirts, and sweatpants. We often had a drink at the hotel bar, then went to a local restaurant called Nora's Ribs. Rodríguez-Varela, a tall, boisterous, light-skinned, frat-boy sort of a guy with an amiable, chubby face, liked to tell jokes and stories. "Hey, John," he asked me one night. "Have you ever fucked a black girl? It's really not so bad!" When his wife called on the cell phone every night around the time of his second gin and tonic, he would break into a naughty, buoyant grin and answer, "Hey, little *mami*!" Pérez, who does not smoke or drink, would smile and try to seem present, but his mind was clearly taken up with the case. On several occasions he told me he hadn't slept the night before.

The prosecution's most important witness was García Orozco. He took the stand looking nauseous with fear, his eyes heavy-lidded, as though he hadn't slept the night before, either. Speaking through a translator, he described his shack back in Mexico but refused even after repeated questioning to name his hometown. During his entire testimony, he did not once look at the Ramoses. His jaw muscle stuck out like a walnut.

The prosecution's next most important witness was the van driver, José Martínez. Martínez looked a bit like the late actor Ernest Borgnine—sweet, lovable, hardworking. A regular guy's regular guy who'd been working since the age of seven, Martínez testified that he had nine kids, had lived in Immokalee for twenty-four years, worked seven days a week, and ran a general store called Zapatería El Oasis, selling shoes, CDs, cassettes, belts, clothing, and tickets for his van service.

When it came time to describe the attack, Martínez identified the three defendants, singling out Ramiro Ramos as the one who'd said, "You're the fucking son of a bitch who's taking our people." He recounted the assault on him, crying a bit, then minimized the pistol blow to his face. "No, it wasn't painful," he said. "It just felt like fingers touching me." He showed the scar from his hairline to the bridge of his nose, and another one on his lip.

The Ramoses made bad impressions throughout the trial. Ramiro had an unseemly tendency to crack his knuckles loudly, then sit back with his fingers laced behind his neck, glowering impassively. Juan simply looked unkempt, as if he was on a bender. Ramiro had a tendency to seethe, smirk, and roll his eyes at testimony he found dubious. When Martínez started to cry, Ramiro made a big show of suppressing a laugh and turning to the ceiling, as if unable to stand such blatant foolery.

The defense ultimately attempted to prove that the citrus industry, not the Ramos family, should be on trial. Pérez called Jack Mendiburo to the stand. Mendiburo, a tall, stalwart man, was the safety, labor, and environmental compliance manager for Consolidated Citrus. Consolidated, the largest citrus grower in the state, owns 55,000 acres of citrus groves and produces 30 percent of the state's crop. The Ramoses had worked for the company for years. Mendiburo testified that in May 2000, after accounts of the attack upon José Martínez were published, the company became concerned about the Ramoses' "issues with labor." To discover whether the accounts had any merit, Mendiburo went out to the fields, pulled about a dozen of Ramiro's workers aside, and asked them if they were being treated okay. Although one of the workers, Reuben Rivera, answered that he wasn't being paid, that he was only getting deeper into debt, Mendiburo concluded that there was no cause for concern. The Ramoses remained in company employ.

Pérez asked Mendiburo to describe how pickers were paid. Mendiburo described an elaborate system in which paychecks were made out to the workers themselves but only after passing through an account held by the Ramoses. The Ramoses, however, were legally and technically unable to access the account. Nevertheless, Mendiburo emphasized that his company was not the employer of the pickers. When Pérez asked to what extent the company felt responsible for the workers, Mendiburo answered that Consolidated was reluctant even to use terms like "co-employer" when referring to its relationship with orange pickers. Explaining further, he said, "It would bring to our company certain dynamics that we do not want."

Next, Rodríguez-Varela called Rich Hetherton to the stand. Hetherton was the director of Human Resources at Lykes Brothers, one of Florida's largest citrus growers after Consolidated. Lykes Brothers had also worked with the Ramos brothers for years. Rodríguez-Varela asked him if his company owned the groves. Hetherton affirmed that this was correct. Rodríguez-Varela next asked Hetherton if the pickers who harvested the oranges for his company were his employees. Hetherton denied that this was so.

A: We don't employ those people.

Q: Technically you don't, but they are in your groves all day picking fruit?

A: Yes.

Q: They are on your property picking fruit from your tree?

A: That's correct.

Q: They are loading oranges into containers that are shipped to companies that process fruit based on your contractor?

A: That's correct.

Q: So it is your fruit, it is your worker, too, isn't he?

A: No, he is not my worker.

Q: Because there's a piece of paper that says he is provided by a contractor? That's it, right?

A: Our relationship is with the contractor to provide workers.

Hetherton then described for Rodríguez-Varela a check-writing process identical to Consolidated's, and Rodríguez-Varela asked him if it wasn't strange for someone to write a check to someone who does work that benefits them but then refuse to call that person an employee. Hetherton said he really didn't know.

During both witnesses' testimony, Judge Moore leaned forward. It was the first time during the entire trial that he seemed engaged and interested. Indeed, the testimony of the growers' employees seemed momentous.

I remembered the moment, a few days earlier, when Ramiro, now looking very small and scared, passed by me outside the court when no one was looking and shyly asked me in a surprisingly small, squeaky voice, "What do you think they will do? Do you think they will find me guilty?" It was hard to look at him and his brother after the growers' testimony and feel the same outrage I'd felt earlier. El Diablo and his brother looked like shrimps, two guys about five feet three inches tall, dressed in cheap, gray flannel pants, white polyester shirts, and inexpensive black fake-dress tennis shoes.

In a sidebar, the defense approached the bench and asked Judge Moore to dismiss the charges on the ground that the prosecution of the Ramoses was selective and arbitrary. As Pérez asked, "Do you not think for one moment, you know, that the growers don't know what's going on? . . . Everyone knows that somebody has to buffer them."

The judge considered the request but answered, "That's the way the whole system works. I'm not defending it. You come up with proof of that, and maybe you can talk to the U.S. attorney's office about it and expose the whole system for what it's about." The motion was denied.

By the end of the trial, the government's case had become impregnable. When it came out that of 680 Alien Registration Numbers used by the Ramoses for payroll and Social Security documentation, exactly 10 were correct, you could almost hear the defendants hitting the mat on the charge of harboring aliens. After José Martínez's testimony about being attacked by the Ramoses while trying to conduct his business, it seemed pretty inarguable that use of a deadly weapon and interference with interstate commerce had been proven. When García Orozco, Sánchez, and Hernández took the stand, they were credible enough. Never mind the rumors of violent conduct the judge didn't allow; the direct verbal threats established the climate of fear necessary to prove forced servitude.

The Ramoses were found guilty on fifteen of sixteen counts and sentenced to twelve years; their cousin José Luis was sentenced to ten. They were also ordered to surrender $3 million in company and personal property. No one had expected anything so absolute. After the sentences were pronounced, Judge Moore, without excusing the Ramoses' actions, gently admonished the prosecutors not to devote the lion's share of their resources to the "occasional case that we see from time to time that this case represents" but, rather, to recognize that "others at a higher level of the fruit-picking industry seem complicit in one way or another with how these activities occur."

Juan and Ramiro Ramos were given five minutes to cry and remove their belts, watches, wedding bands, and cash. They handed them over and kissed their wives and children good-bye before being cuffed and led out of the courtroom. Rodríguez-Varela shook his head and dried a tear. He told me, "You never get used to that. I don't care how many times you see it." Pérez had already flown back to Miami to start the next case. Yet another defense associate, Lorenzo Palomares, moved in to handle the seizure of the Ramoses' bank accounts and properties. Rodríguez-Varela couldn't stand it. He asked me for a ride back to the hotel.

As we left the courthouse parking lot, we passed El Diablo's wife, Alicia. She held her husband's belt in front of her, looking a little like Lady Macbeth, stunned, numb, sleepwalking. The sight of her launched Rodríguez-Varela into a full-out tantrum. He punched the dash of my car while fulminating against the citrus industry and the government. "What a bunch of bullshit! The whole thing—these guys, Juan, Ramiro—they wouldn't have had a problem except for that stupid incident on Highway 27!"

In March 2003, the Coalition of Immokalee Workers was honored with the prestigious Robert F. Kennedy Human Rights Award. In February 2005, it received a letter from FBI director Robert Mueller thanking it for its assistance with the agency's antislavery efforts. The coalition has been invited to participate in training seminars for FBI agents and local law enforcement agents around the country. But perhaps most important, it has begun to convince major corporations that by and large—at least, when they're aware of it—the American public prefers not to buy goods produced with slave labor, or anything like it.

In March 2005, Yum! Brands agreed to the coalition's demands in return for an end to the four-year boycott of Taco Bell restaurants. The boycott, ignored at first by company officials, had gained widespread support from church organizations, former president Jimmy Carter, and the Student-Farmworker Alliance—a group that spearheaded the campus-based movement. Eventually the protests resulted in the banishment of Taco Bell restaurants and products from twenty-two schools.

Yum! Brands not only agreed to commit to paying an extra penny per pound directly to the workers who pick their tomatoes—a move that will nearly double the pickers' wages—it also consented to work with the coalition to develop and enforce a tough new code of conduct for its Florida tomato suppliers. Negotiations are under way, but it is hoped that before the end of 2007, Yum! Brands will announce that the rest of its restaurant chains—KFC, A&W Restaurants, Long John Silver's, and Pizza Hut—will participate in the top-to-bottom "pay-back" policy to help bolster farmworkers' rights and wages.

Soon after the boycott's end, the coalition and its partners took aim at McDonald's, asking the chain to follow Taco Bell's lead. McDonald's responded by partnering with the Florida Fruit and Vegetable Association, or FFVA—a powerful growers' lobby—and hiring a public relations firm to counter negative public sentiment. McDonald's then commissioned a study that found that farmworkers in Florida are, in fact, very well paid and receive as much as eighteen dollars an hour!

Unfortunately for McDonald's public relations efforts, one of their suppliers, Ag-Mart Farms, Florida's largest grower of grape tomatoes, hired Abel Cuello, the labor contractor convicted of slavery in 1999. As media reports surfaced that he was back in business, allegations arose that he continued to exploit his workers. According to farmworker advocate Greg Schell in an e-mail from 2006, "Sadly, it appears that Cuello was not rehabilitated in federal prison. Last week, our outreach worker spoke with a group of workers from southern Mexico who had just arrived in Immokalee. Each of them owed a substantial debt to Cuello for the cost of being smuggled in from Mexico. As he had done prior to his peonage conviction, Cuello had placed the workers in an overcrowded trailer that he controlled, and withheld most of the workers' paychecks to recoup the smuggling debt."

In 2006, grower Frank Johns, the 2004 chairman of the FFVA, McDonald's labor-compliance partner, made news when one of his labor contractors, Ron Evans, after investigation by the Coalition of Immokalee Workers, was convicted on conspiracy and drug charges for luring homeless black men into his employ with crack cocaine, alcohol, and cigarettes. Johns, whose Tater Farms had hired Evans, said the issue had been typically overblown by the media. "I'd like to think our operation is a little above average, and I think Ron Evans is an above-average crew leader," Johns said.

When, only months later, in April 2007, McDonald's announced that CEO Jim Skinner would receive $13.4 million in mostly profit-linked compensation, public outrage boiled over. Days before the coalition and its student-group and religion-based partners gathered for a huge march on McDonald's corporate headquarters in Oak Brook, Illinois, the company cracked and agreed to participate in a program nearly identical to Taco Bell's.

What is most significant about the farmworkers' victories is the way in which they leapfrog over the notion that state or federal governmental efforts are any longer up to the task of looking after farmworkers on American soil. As Eric Schlosser, author of *Fast Food Nation* and a long-time coalition supporter, would write in a *New York Times* editorial about the victorious boycott, "The failure of government to protect the weakest and most impoverished workers in the United States has left the job to corporations and consumers."

In the end, the coalition's activist tactics turned out to be far more effective than I had imagined they could be. By skillfully educating and motivating a fairly small group of peasants with sixth-grade educations, they had managed to make national news and force change throughout the system. Who if not them? As Benitez had said, "Who cares what happens to a bunch of *pelagatos*?"

The agreement with Yum! Brands will affect only about one thousand workers, and the agreement with McDonald's adds another thousand to fifteen hundred. Two thousand five hundred workers out of a million and a half or so migrant farmworkers in the United States is clearly a long way from victory. There are some who question whether the efforts of groups such as the coalition are anything more than symbolic.

The most hopeful way, perhaps, to view the coalition's gains is not by measuring their material impact, but in asking what they mean for the future of America's worst-paid, least-protected workers. When in the 1960s African Americans successfully boycotted the segregationist policies of the Montgomery, Alabama, public bus system, the victory didn't trigger an instant transformation of black Americans' material circumstances. The significance of the victory, of course, was the birth of the civil rights movement and the sea change in public attitudes it heralded: Black citizens had triumphed over a white-owned company, thereby marking the beginning of the end of generations of systematic abuse and exploitation. With luck, the coalition's protests and the beginning of an ultimately positive corporate response might be the dawning of widespread acceptance—that general conditions in the fields of Florida are untenable, and that labor relations in American agriculture are an embarrassment to modern notions of human rights.

Since leaving the Ramoses' employ, García Orozco, Hernández, and Sánchez have worked in Georgia, South Carolina, Missouri, Indiana, and Kentucky. Today they share a tidy one-bedroom apartment in a working-class neighborhood in Florida lined with palm trees and live oaks. Inside the doorway are several pairs of cowboy boots, polished and standing in a row. A lime-green stuffed dog sits on top of the TV, between the rabbit ears. In the corner are a set of keyboards and a guitar. On the stove are pots and pans filled with Mexican, Chinese, and Italian food—the result of a foray into international cuisine.

The three men relax in the living room. García Orozco wears a long-sleeved striped shirt, white jeans, and cowhide boots. Sánchez is wearing tennis shoes, and Hernández strums a guitar. The three have found jobs in a furniture warehouse. (Since the trial, in exchange for cooperating with the prosecution, they have received papers allowing them to work in the United States.) García Orozco says that he likes his job. He has learned to drive a forklift, which he enjoys, and his bosses never tell him to run or hurry up. "I work like a normal person, and they treat me like a normal person." He works from two in the afternoon until eleven or midnight and is earning enough to call home frequently and send money to his family to buy food and medicine for his sick son.

Hanging from a mirror is a commemorative ID pass that García Orozco wore at a recent march with the Coalition of Immokalee Workers. He's been to several protests, including a road trip to Taco Bell headquarters in Irvine, California. He likes them. "I get to talk to people who've been through what we went through," he said of the coalition marchers. "You know, thank God. Because if they hadn't done anything, we wouldn't be free right now, and we wouldn't be here." All three men hope to become more involved with the coalition, but whether that's possible depends on money and work opportunities. Most likely, they'll follow the summer watermelon harvest through Florida, Georgia, and Missouri, then return to Florida.

One contribution Hernández has already made to the coalition is a *corrido,* a type of Mexican folksong that usually tells tales of heroism and courage. In a note to the coalition, he wrote, "This ballad is about what happened to us. I hope you all like it. I'll be there soon to sing you all the song."

> *I'm going to tell,* señores, *the story of a great friend.*
> *He was called Rafael Solis Hernández and came from Campeche.*
> *He came to the United States to seek his fortune.*
>
> *One day, the twentieth of February, he consoled his wife,*
> *"Don't cry, I love you, you are the owner of my soul.*
> *I'm leaving, but I'll be back soon, and you won't be lacking in money."*
>
> *A famous* coyote *recommended by many*
> *Crossed all of them over the mountains, through the pasturelands,*
> *And once in Arizona, distributed them all over.*
>
> *In Lake Placid in Florida, his boss awaited him.*
> *He promised to give them work, but he never paid them.*
> *He treated them like slaves, and took everything from their checks.*

*They are famous gunmen, the kind who kill and bury,*
*With numerous crimes that they're now paying for*
*Awaiting their punishment in the county jail.*

*Ramiro Ramos is the name of the cruelest one I've ever known.*
*I hope that one day in prison, they sing him my ballad*
*Just to remind him that in his court I was a witness.*

García Orozco, Sánchez, and Hernández are to this day reluctant to talk about the Ramoses, fearing that it might be taken as a provocation. Hernández said, "You know, I'm a pretty cocky guy. I like to joke around a lot. But I'm scared. I'm still having nightmares about guys coming after me with machetes and stuff. I'm gonna be looking over my shoulder for the rest of my life."

García Orozco looked up from the TV, concurring. "That's called 'trauma.'" He continued. "When you're in the kind of situation we were in, you feel like the world has ended. And once you're back here on the outside—it's hard to explain. Everything's different now. It was like coming out of the darkness into the light. Just imagine if you were reborn. That's what it's like."

# Tom

When I published an article telling the story of García Orozco and his friends, its subtitle was: "Does Slavery Exist in America?"

It might seem strange to ask. After all, a court of law had found the Ramoses guilty of holding people in involuntary servitude. But even after thinking about the subject for two years, I felt slightly hesitant about using the word *slavery*. Wouldn't it be just as appropriate to say that García Orozco and his friends had simply been intimidated, threatened, and unpaid for a few weeks' work?

The answer to my question, I would eventually realize, is no.

The means by which tribes, ruling elites, religions, kingdoms, and legislatures justified, arranged, codified, and promulgated slavery have varied with almost infinite complexity. Likewise, the quality of life and degree of oppression for those enslaved have varied immensely. Some slaves worked full-time, constantly on call, every moment of their lives, every calorie's worth of productive effort given over to their masters. Others worked part-time, a few months per year, for their master, the rest of the year for themselves. Slaves working the mines and farms of ancient Rome led lives of donkey-level drudgery, limping, wounded, and suppurating in heavy chains till early death. In other cultures, notably African, slaves were treated much like members of the family that owned them. Sometimes, such slaves even married into their new families.

In many societies, slaves were allowed to own businesses, property, and even other slaves. In others, terms of bondage were limited to three, five, seven years. In some settings, slaves were occasionally granted far more power than average private citizens, given command of armies and governmental departments to run like their own private fiefdoms. Eunuch mandarins in China, for example, were enormously powerful, highly educated, and unleashed by preeminent warlords to rule over and humiliate enemy chieftains.

Despite these many variations, what all forms of slavery share, including that of García Orozco and his friends, is the temporary or permanent condition of having one's rights and one's person utterly controlled by another. What does "utterly" mean? As Frederick Douglass, who knew from experience, wrote in the *Narrative of the Life of Frederick Douglass, an American Slave,* "A mere look, word or motion,—a mistake, accident, or want of power,—all are matters for which a slave may be whipped at any time." To be a slave meant one's body was not one's own; it was for another—to use, to beat, to rape.

As Harvard sociologist Orlando Patterson found, most slave owners in most societies that had slaves treated them better rather than worse. After all, slaves were property. It was better to keep them alive and happy and useful (for labor, for sex, for abusing at some later time, for whatever) than to have them be sick, miserable, and dangerous. But still, the fact remained that a slave was a slave, a lower-class entity with no legal rights and no social status or claim whatsoever. If a slave dropped an earthenware pot when the master was having a bad day, what was to stop the master from lashing out?

When I first began to write this book, I realized that achieving even a general understanding of the intricacies and dynamics of thousands of years of slavery would require an immense sifting through the thousands of books and opinions about the subject. There would have been no way to do so with any thoroughness or objectivity, so I decided to hire a research assistant. I posted a notice at the Columbia School of Journalism and, in the end, hired three recent graduates, each on a part-time basis. It was my first experience in almost twenty years with managing employees. (The last employee I'd had was in the 1980s, when I had a house painting company. His name was Tom. He wasn't a great painter. One morning he showed up to work and confessed to me that he'd spent the previous evening drunkenly making out with my girlfriend. I fired him.)

My researchers and I got along fabulously, I like to think. I realized that there were better jobs than working for me for fifteen dollars an hour, one and a half days a week, and partly to compensate them, partly out of genuine interest in their ideas, I offered any assistance they might want with stories, pitches, and career strategizing. For this, I expected a certain amount of loyalty. By and large, I got it, and to this day we remain friends.

But there was a moment when our mutual happiness took a little dip. During the course of an otherwise overwhelmingly positive work relationship, two of my researchers and I found ourselves in the middle of what I later realized must be one of the occasional, ordinary, and inevitable disappointments that pop up between employers and employees.

I was traveling a lot, fourteen time zones away, to the island of Saipan, reporting on what would be the third part of this book. And suddenly, I couldn't get my employees to do what I wanted them to do. It felt to me like they were reneging on a promise. A month came and went. I e-mailed them a few times, asking how things were going, but received only vague answers. Six weeks passed. I cleared my throat—as well as one can do over the Internet and by answering machine. Nothing. By the time six weeks became eight weeks, I was furious.

Eventually, I reached That Point—the point where an employment situation becomes emotional. I undoubtedly would have lashed out at them in some way—even an unlawful way—if I could have. At the very least, I would have fired them for sure, and perhaps, if asked by some future employer about them, I would have given them poor references.

What was amusing and enlightening for me was to see that there I was, the supposedly nice guy writing a book about slavery, social justice, and so on—yet I was as capable as any employer of becoming murderously pissed off.

In a different time and place, what might I have done to punish my employees? If I were a nobleman or a high priest, assigned by God to occupy my station in life, and they were mere lackeys, serfs, disposable wretches protected by nothing but the vagaries of my whim, would I have resisted the urge to chop off a finger as a little reminder that things go better for people who don't break promises to me? If they had come from a class of people—Christians, Muslims, Belgians, barbarians, war captives, debtors, red-haired people, people with big ears—deigned beneath me by fate, circumstance, or local law—would I have had the slightest hesitation about punishing them?

What kept me from killing my employees in cold blood was more than me being a nice guy. It was the consequences I would have faced in modern America if I hadn't acted like one. Even if I'd just chopped off one finger, the little ingrates could have gone and squealed to the police. They'd have run off and complained to their families. Even if I went on the lam, word would get around the publishing world that I was sick, dangerous, scary, and mean—and criminal. I would discover that I couldn't get work anymore. I'd be ruined in my community. And then I'd be arrested.

If it sounds like a far-fetched scenario to invent, it's not. This kind of treatment of workers by employers was the norm for most people, most jobs, most workers, throughout history. What's far-fetched, when viewed against the backdrop of time, is the fact that modern employers are at least nominally required to play by the same rules as their employees.

Before the advent of modern industrial capitalism, laborers in their physical person—not labor itself—were the perceived commodity. Before, during, and even after slavery, in Europe and in the United States, early industrial labor relations between nonslave workers and their employers were appalling. As Ted Nace wrote in *Gangs of America,* a history of modern corporate evolution, workers in England's industrial revolution toiled for eighty hours a week. What spare time remained was often spent under duress in church, learning the virtues of productivity under the instruction of teachers and clergy hired by workers' employers to keep employees in line. If workers didn't want to spend their "free time" being told what to do and where to be, they would be dealt with in the prisons, workhouses, and orphanages with which most large employers had relationships. Troublemakers were taken care of. In the American colonies, the idea of "free labor" was pathetically unfree by modern standards in most countries of the world. It wasn't even until 1843 that American courts stopped permitting employers to beat their employees.

Somehow, between the bad old days and now, American workers completed the transition from peons to persons, free to sell their hours to the highest bidders—or not. The employer buys only a worker's time and labor, and everything else in life remains the property of the worker. What happened?

What happened was a reappraisal of human rights, freedom, and workplace rights that continues to this day. Laws were passed allowing workers to change jobs when they wanted to, to join unions, to be compensated at standard rates, to be paid extra for time over forty hours a week. Still more laws were passed, codifying and limiting the right of employers to interfere with workers' off-the-job lives, seeking always to level—at least, to *try* to level—the playing field between workers and their employers. Laws forbade employers to discriminate against workers for reasons of family, culture, religion, dress, sexual preferences, political orientation—any reason an employer could use to try to treat one person differently from another.

The result of all these laws, naturally resented by employers as unwarranted intrusions upon *their* freedom, was the creation of freedom for workers. Freedom to spend time with their families, to read, learn, attend school or church, to enjoy the fruits of labor—to have a life outside of work—a sense of self, a self, period.

These laws have come a long way to create the psychosocial infrastructure of what we call "modern, free" society. As much as freedom of speech and freedom of assembly, it is workplace rules that provide the essence of modern life. But to imagine that simply because slavery has been banned, made illegal and uncommon, the underlying, organic tug-of-war between employers and workers has gone away or will ever go away, is naïve.

Recently, in *The New York Review of Books,* an article called "Inside the Leviathan" by Simon Head described the formula used by Wal-Mart's senior management to force higher levels of productivity from their workforce:

> When deciding how many workers to employ, Wal-Mart management relies on a formula guaranteeing that the growth of the labor budget will lag behind the growth in store sales, so that every year there will be more work for each employee to do. In her paper "The Quality of Work at Wal-Mart," presented at the conference in Santa Barbara, Ellen Rosen of the Women's Studies Research Center at Brandeis described in detail how this squeeze on labor works. Each year Wal-Mart provides its store managers with a "preferred budget" for employment, which would allow managers to staff their stores at adequate levels. But the actual budget imposed on the store managers always falls short of the preferred budget, so that most Wal-Mart stores are permanently understaffed. The gap between the preferred and actual budgets gives store managers an idea of how much extra work they must try to extract from their workforce.

The intuitive *legal* solution would be for managers to ask workers to work extra hours. But such a solution would require paying overtime. And in fact, Rosen found, managers who let their workers work more than forty hours per week are guilty of a company "offense" and can be terminated. As a result, managers are forced to connive with their workers so they can put in extra hours off the clock.

Such practices fall considerably short of slavery or even physical abuse. Yet it's fascinating to observe: here is a wildly profitable company that has already killed off much of its competition but that nevertheless continually seeks to further its gains, even if it means that some of its practices will violate the bounds of legality. If it were not for the law stating that workers logging more than forty hours a week are entitled to higher overtime pay, the company would surely become more brazen in its tactics.

I used to think of such greed and senseless aggression as evil. I now see it to be the nature of power. It would be no more productive to get mad at water for being wet than it is to be shocked that power seeks to enhance and justify itself.

In a country like the United States, where the rule of law is reliable, if imperfect, most kinds of power—religious, economic, and political— are held in check. If someone does something against the law, there is a counterforce to punish him or her and to corral the behavior back toward what we, as a society, have deemed preferable. But what about in the world of globalization, where suddenly we have people, employers, and businesses with First World money and power meeting up with workers from other countries?

Americans have spent three centuries fighting, arguing, debating, and legislating for a relatively peaceable playing field within their own country. But suddenly, in the era of globalization, employers have found vast workforces in other countries with few labor rights and lower wage expectations. It's an alluring temptation: profit. Like a magic drug, the lure of inequality proves irresistible. Call it profit, opportunity, or whatever you want: as consumers, as employers, we in the First World want access to the fruits of these weaker people. And if we can't go to their countries to do business with them? We'll bring them to ours.

# TULSA

J ohn Nash Pickle, Jr., stands about six feet tall and dresses like a man on his way to Dollywood. His hair is a catchy silver, playfully flipped to the side like an old-school country singer's. He wears cowboy boots, an inexpensive, checked sport jacket, square, seventies-style wire-rim glasses, and lamb-chop sideburns. He speaks with a strong Southern accent, quickly, making steely but not unfriendly eye contact, broken only to turn his head and cup his ear. At sixty-five, after a lifetime of machine-shop din, he has become hard of hearing.

I'd met him at his trial, but it was hardly a convenient place to talk. When we spoke a few months later, he remembered me instantly. "You the guy writing a book or something, wasn't ya?" Without much more prompting than that, he launched ahead. "I'll tell you the story of me. I was born in Mississippi, 1937, and we was raised on a farm. Forty acres we farmed. And I have to say these words right to you, we had Afro-Americans on the place did the farming. We was cotton and corn. Had hogs and cows. Had an outhouse. Had a big chicken house with lights on it. My dad had this Ford—little two-row tractor."

It was, he said, "the hardest life you can imagine. I hear these people talk about being poor, ain't got anything—well, when the cow didn't have babies, we didn't have milk for three months. Had two pair shoes, two pair pants, many Christmases I never had any Christmas. One time I got two apples and two oranges. So people whine to me that they was raised poor, piss on 'em.

"See," he explained, "I'm one of them Americans, one of them assholes, that works eighty to a hundred hours a week. And I've done that since I was about ten years old. I've had five two-week vacations in forty years. I come from nothin', got to where I am by myself. I never had no mentors, no partners, no nothin'. I don't socialize with anybody. I don't even socialize with kinfolk, hardly. You know, if you want a piece of the world, you go get it. That's the only way I know."

And that, he concluded, "kinda gives ya who I am, where I came from."

He knows I'm writing a book about slavery. So I jump right in and ask him to clarify what he said about how "Afro-Americans on the place did the farming."

"We'd call 'em sharecroppers now," he explained. "If we made five bales of cotton, they got the money from two and we got the money from three, and we furnished the mules and the land and the fertilizer and they got so much corn and so many cows." He said he couldn't really remember all the details; he was just a kid at the time.

When I asked how everyone got along, whether there were any racial tensions or anything like that, he nearly roared. "We all worked together, man! I slept with 'em, ate with 'em. Hell, I didn't learn about integration until I left home! I *was* integrated! I didn't know niggers and whites—they was just black and I was just white and we was all just sumbitches that worked the same. That's the way I was raised."

But was his family's house, say, for example, *bigger* than the sharecroppers'? I asked. "Definitely!" he boomed. "White people's house is different than the black people's house. 'Cause they was the landowners. That'd be just like, 'Is the company owner's house different than the people that work for him in the company?' " It didn't matter, he said. Whatever prissy distinction could be made between his family's life and the sharecroppers', existence was miserable for everyone involved.

Pickle and his family worked every day from six o'clock in the morning till dark—like slaves. In fact, he said, "we worked harder than the colored people lived on the place. We had food—of some kind—at each meal. And clothes on your back. But it was farm life, farm life as it was at that time. Shit in the outhouse, use the Sears, Roebuck catalogue to wipe your ass." Toilet paper, he said, "that's some shit I seen after I got married and left home."

He paused briefly, eyes twinkling, perhaps with regret, over the meagerness of his upbringing but also with a twinge of pride at having escaped it. "I told myself, 'When I get outta high school, I'm a-goin' down the road and do something else.'"

In 1972, John Pickle and his wife, Tina, started a small steel-cutting company out of their garage. With $5,000 in savings and a $20,000 loan from the Small Business Administration, they launched the John Pickle Company. By the 1990s, JPC had come to specialize in the manufacture of enormous two-hundred-ton pressure tanks, used by oil refineries and power plants. The firm had prospered. Sales reached $15 million a year, and at its peak, the company counted 120 employees.

Pickle had watched the domestic oil business decline for a long time (certainly since the 1920s, when Tulsa was the self-designated "Oil Capital of the World"). What he hadn't counted on, however, was the abject free-fall of American manufacturing, beginning in the 1980s, brought on by foreign competition.

It was pathetic. Not only were foreigners moving in and stealing American market share, American firms were being perpetually hamstrung by their own government. Foreign firms, Pickle said, "don't have the U.S. government fuckin' with 'em like they do over here! Their government don't have all these rules, and regulations, and EPA, and OSHA on your ass! Their wages are a lot cheaper. Any country—Korea, China—any foreign countries, they don't get taxed hardly as much or any a'tall!"

Pickle's day of reckoning came in 1998, when a Korean firm outbid JPC on a pressure-vessel job fifteen miles from Tulsa. When he realized that he could no longer compete, even in his own backyard, Pickle said, he sat down with JPC vice president and chief operating officer Joe

Reeble to have what he called "a head-knocking session." The two men agreed that if something didn't change, the company would be history in ten years—or less.

Pickle and Reeble decided that JPC's best hope was to reestablish it-self in the Middle East. Not only was the oil business still booming in that part of the world, but governments there offered a vastly more favorable tax and regulatory environment. JPC could continue to manufacture in Tulsa, but as demand in the United States faded, they reasoned, the firm's technical expertise would be transferred abroad. Pickle could take a 6 or 7 percent commission on sales (as opposed to the half a percent or so he was currently making), and the JPC name would survive.

It didn't take long for the company to break into the Middle East. In October 1998, the Kuwait Oil Company discovered cracks in nine pres-sure vessels in its Burgan Field natural-gas operations. Fearing an explo-sion, it yanked the facility from production—at a loss of $2 million a day. An immediate call was put out for replacement tanks. It was an ideal op-portunity for an otherwise unknown player like JPC. While better-known firms from around the world submitted bids requiring nine to eighteen months to manufacture replacements, JPC daringly promised to deliver the goods in *three*. The Kuwaitis took a risk, and on Christmas Day 1998 signed a deal with JPC for $5.5 million. It was, company liter-ature enthused, "an unforgettable Christmas present." In ninety days, the Tulsa factory had cranked out all nine steel-clad, whale-sized tanks, packed them up, and flown them to the Middle East—on time.

The quick delivery established JPC as a trusted vendor, and almost immediately offers came pouring in from foreign firms wanting to team up with the company. For John Pickle, his company's success at global-izing was a clear-cut case of "the American dream coming true."

The company signed an agreement with the Kharafis of Kuwait (listed by *Forbes* magazine as the twenty-ninth-richest family in the world) to form a joint venture, and a new, international arm of JPC was born: JPME—John Pickle Middle East.

Pickle's American welders were uniformly uninterested in relocat-ing to the Middle East. As Pickle later told me, "I kind of threw it out to a couple of them: no way. Their fishing boat's here and the deer is here.

Americans is not going to go over there. They're not going to leave their family, their kids." Moreover, he added, "everybody in the world wants to come to America. Why would America go to another country in the world?"

Kuwaitis couldn't be hired, Pickle explained with a laugh, because "Kuwaitis don't work." (The Kuwaiti economy, like that of other oil-rich Gulf kingdoms, relies upon massive numbers of "guest workers" from Egypt, Syria, Jordan, the Philippines, India, Bangladesh, Pakistan, Sri Lanka, Thailand, China, and Korea to do the heavy lifting. In Pickle's words, Kuwaitis tended to stick to "higher management.")

The obvious solution was to import a staff of foreign guest workers. But from where? Pickle had heard good things about Indian welders. As one of his employees later testified, around the time of the Kuwait venture start-up, she had overheard him extolling their virtues to another employee, saying, "You bring them in, pay them two or three dollars an hour, give them a little food, give them a place to stay. That's cheap labor. And they're the hardest-working sons of bitches you'll find—harder than any white man you can find around here."

Pickle and Reeble hired an Indian-born American named Ray Murzello to select and hire a workforce. Murzello, born in Mumbai (formerly Bombay), had more than forty years' experience in the Middle East, setting up manufacturing plants and joint ventures. He seemed like the ideal guy for the job. Murzello suggested that JPC contract with a Mumbai labor-recruiting company named Al-Samit. The company had been in business for thirty years, supplying skilled workers to Russia and many of the Persian Gulf States. They'd recently supplied labor for the Halliburton subsidiary Brown & Root to perform work at the U.S. prison camp in Guantánamo Bay, Cuba.

The directive was given to Al-Samit to find the very best welders in India—men with the most time at the best firms and with the highest level of skills.

Murzello would further explain to me later, in an e-mail:

In the first selection process, we evaluated over three hundred candidates' CV's and selected a hundred and fifty for testing! Of these only 22 or so made the grade by passing all tests put to them. These workers, although experienced and proficient in their individual skills, were then sent to JPC's Tulsa plant for further training to imbibe the JPC "culture"! This we felt, would bring them up to speed and put them on a par with American work standards, which we were hoping to duplicate at the JPME plant in Kuwait.

As Pickle later amplified, he wanted the Indians to learn to work in what he called "the American way." Asked to define what that meant, he answered, "Five times faster than they ever saw in their life." Elaborating further, he said, "Americans are American. I don't care how big, how short, how long, how wide, men, women, or whatever: they have one way of doing it. And as soon as you go somewhere else, they have another way of doing it. I wanted the American way. That's what this— this was to teach the American way."

Pickle, by his own description, is not the detail-oriented type. He thinks of himself as more of a "hands-on" guy, a manager more comfortable on the shop floor than in the head office. Accordingly, he left the details of the recruitment plan to Murzello and Reeble. In turn, Murzello and Reeble made a series of decisions about the training program that would, it's fair to say, prove fateful for all involved.

They opted to procure for the Indians something known as a B-1/B-2 visa. The permit is most commonly granted for business training—a sort of business tourist visa. It is designed for foreigners who wish, on their own or at the behest of their employers, to observe American business operations or processes. The terms of the B-1/B-2 visa specifically prohibit visitors to the United States from being actually employed by a company, paid for, or engaged in actual, productive work. But what Murzello and Reeble had in mind was for the Indians to get "hands-on" training. They would be working alongside John Pickle's American employees, learning "the American way." It wasn't quite what the visa seemed intended for. And yet, Murzello and Reeble applied for the B-1/B-2.

They also perhaps took a little shortcut when they decided that rather than employ the Indian men themselves, they would designate

Al-Samit as the employer. It would save everyone a ton of trouble. As long as the Indians remained employees of Al-Samit, the recruiting agency, JPC wouldn't have to go through the hassles and formalities of meeting U.S. labor laws, filling out the endless paperwork, paying Social Security, insurance, workmen's comp, et cetera. After all, the workers weren't really going to be *working* in Tulsa, they were only going to be *training* there. Besides, the company reckoned, it seemed kind of silly to pay the Indians the U.S. minimum wage of $5.15 an hour, then turn around and force them to spend most of it on housing, food, and transportation. As company literature, written in John Pickle's voice, explained, "Sure, I could have had the recruiting company pay them minimum wage, then let the guys pay for their housing, food and transportation, but they were only here visiting for a short time, no credit, no Social Security number, no reason not to treat them as the guests of America they were."

Later, in court, after testifying about the details described above, Robert Canino of the United States Equal Employment Opportunity Commission would have occasion to pursue the following line of questioning with John Pickle:

Q: Okay. When you were thinking about—you and Ray and Joe were thinking about putting this together, did you consult any other companies to find out how might be some good ways to do it?

A: No.

Q: Do you know if Joe or Ray did?

A: No.

Q: Mr. Pickle, is it fair to say that you don't know all the details that went into the negotiation of each of the terms in this . . . agreement?

A: I don't—no, that's—that's a right statement.

Q: Are you still president of John Pickle Company?

A: Yes, I am.

Q: And how long have you been president of JPC?

A: Thirty years.

Q: And in that time, have you ever taken any courses at a college or seminars on employment discrimination?

A: No.

Q: How about human resource management courses?

A: No.

Q: Have you ever attended any courses or seminars on harassment?

A: No.

Q: How about the Fair Labor Standards Act?

A: Nothing.

Q: Okay. How about any laws relating to pay generally?

A: Nothing.

Q: Immigration issues?

A: None.

Q: Now, tell me why, if you've been president for 30 years and you haven't taken those kinds of courses or training, why is that, Mr. Pickle?

A: I worked with some pretty sharp people and kind of put myself after them. You know, just learned.

In early 2001, JPC brought over its first six trainees. This first bunch, according to company literature, stayed in Tulsa for three months, and their experience was deemed a success. A second group of twenty more was brought from India to Tulsa later that spring. This group stayed four to five months—an even bigger success. As company literature later enthused, the first group of workers "had an almost insatiable appetite for learning." For the first time in their lives, these Third World workers "were given the freedom to make suggestions . . . taught to think for themselves and make decisions on their own." Even more satisfying, they had bonded with the Tulsa workforce in a way that was downright touching.

At the Awards and Appreciation Dinner for a batch of the second group of workers leaving for Kuwait, company literature stated, "the recruits spent hours taking pictures, making speeches, and exchanging personal gifts, laughing and reminiscing. We gave them framed Certificates of Accomplishment, other awards, had some wine, made many toasts, and really spent a wonderful evening."

The remaining Indian trainees left two months later. "This time," the literature gushed,

> grown men, shop leaders raised in the steel business, tough as nails, had tears in their eyes saying their "goodbyes" to these men. These guys who had the guts to leave their families and all they ever knew, to come 10,000 miles to learn from us. *From our guys!*
>
> I will never forget the feeling of those days: my company with such talented employees freely teaching all they knew to guys they would never meet again, to provide our new venture in a place they would never know, a world-class staff. God, I was proud of these men.

The Indian welders trained in Tulsa proved to be an able staff. The company was up and running, the Kuwaitis were happy, and, most gratifying for Pickle, he was helping poor Indians get ahead in the world.

As he told me later, the wages earned by the "Indian boys" were more than enough to feed their immediate families. Said Pickle, quoting one "boy," " 'Hell, we don't feed the family, Pickle. What money we're making, we feed the whole damn block.' "

Two other "boys" broke down right in front of him one day, bawling with gratitude. According to Pickle, one of them said, sobbing, "You know, I never had nothin' but one handful a rice at noon and one at night. That's all I've ate in my life."

The program was a success on every level. According to company literature, the training program devised by John Pickle Company was "by some accounts, the most visionary and forward thinking in the history of cross-cultural international business." It seemed like a cinch, JPC figured; why not bring over a third group?

One Sunday in November 2001, Mark Massey sat with his wife, Dawna, in their customary pew in the fifth row of Hale Pentecostal Church. Their daughters, Heather, Christin, and Charity, were up in front, singing with Sister Regina and the rest of the choir. At the pulpit,

Pastor Smith preached, as he often did, about the committed life, about pressing forward and making stronger commitments to the Lord.

Hale Church is a nearly windowless cinder-block building with a teal-colored double door framed beneath a twenty-five-foot triangular entryway—the sort of exuberant touch common to inexpensively built churches from the 1960s. The church, home to a small but devoted congregation of forty-odd parishioners, stood on a grass and gravel lot in Tulsa, Oklahoma, offering a minor touch of cheer in an otherwise gloomy working-class neighborhood of one-story houses, highway overpasses, and struggling businesses.

The church also happens to be located across the street from what was then the John Pickle Company. The JPC facility was similar to many industrial concerns—enormous, outscale, and somewhat intimidating. The main factory building spread out over seven hundred thousand square feet; the surrounding sixty-acre lot was littered with old train cars, disused cranes, and rusting, gargantuan pipes fifteen feet in diameter. A railroad spur ran beside the property line, and the factory yard was enclosed by chain-link fence, topped in places with concertina wire.

Massey described services at Hale as typical charismatic Pentecostal preaching, similar, he said, to "what you used to hear on Jimmy Swaggart and some of those. It's very old-fashioned. The women wear dresses and have long hair. You come in. You have your old hymnal songbooks. You sing 'Amazing Grace.' You sing 'I'll Fly Away.' It's real conservative."

There are many different styles within the charismatic movement. Some charismatic churches, Massey said, might display just "a little more clapping or peppier singing than a Baptist service." Other services "manifest" speaking in tongues, but worshippers are taught to follow a script of sorts, chanting and dancing together in a prescribed fashion. Hale Pentecostal is part of what's known as the "old-time holiness movement." As Massey explained, "There's nothing really planned." Congregants are free to do whatever they want—"whatever's in their heart," he said. "Some people might lift their hands in the air and say things in English like 'Praise the Lord,' 'Thank you, Jesus,' and 'I love you,

Lord.' " Others might be moved to speak in Chinese, Arabic, or even what Massey called "heavenly languages." In such cases, he said, "if you were standing next to them, you wouldn't understand what they're saying."

In other words, Sunday-morning services at Hale can get quite fervent. "If you come in thinking, 'Oh, what's for lunch? I wanna be outta here by twelve' "—here Massey laughed—"you're not gonna get the experience. 'Cause sometimes we might stay here till dinnertime, till midnight, till one o'clock in the morning."

A lot of "weird stuff" happens at Hale, Massey said. "We've had sermons where demonic people have come and had demons cast out of them. It is like electricity hits everybody in that place sometimes. One time a man got so moved he leapt up and ran across the pews. His eyes were closed and his head was lifted toward heaven, and he just ran across the pews."

Another time, Massey recalled, a skeptical aunt of his came to a service at Hale. "She thought it was the devil, or at least crazy," he said. "But finally, she came in and said, 'Lord, if this is real, let me feel it.' And for the next two to three hours she was baptized by the Holy Ghost. And she spoke in many tongues. Many tongues. That don't happen to too many people, but it happens to some people. And she sang beautifully. Afterward, she couldn't speak in English for a while. She had to write down on a piece of paper, 'Will I ever be able to speak English again?' "

Whatever "weird stuff" Massey had witnessed at Hale, nothing could have prepared him for the journey he embarked upon this particular Sunday. Services had started, and congregants began to join in, clapping their hands to the music. A few were already speaking in tongues. And then it happened, the event that would change the course of Massey's life: two men with brown skin entered the church.

It wasn't their color, Massey said later, but the way they carried themselves that caught his attention. As he observed the men taking seats in the last row, he felt that they were troubled. "They seemed scared," he recalled. "They were acting like they were somewhere they weren't supposed to be."

Massey remained distracted during the ceremony, wondering what might be wrong with the men, and after services ended, he tried to engage them.

Massey is in his mid-forties, slightly heavyset, descended from French-Irish stock. He stands about five feet eight in Wal-Mart loafers, with green-blue eyes, thinning auburn hair, and a default expression of fretfulness. He and Dawna married when he was nineteen and she was, he said, "fixin' to turn eighteen." He has worked for most of his life as a building manager, repairing and restoring low-rent properties, doing much of the painting, drywall, carpentry, heating, plumbing, and electrical work himself. He doesn't seem especially suave, gregarious, or even at ease with himself. He does, however, come across as sincere and nonjudgmental—in a word, trustworthy.

But try as he might to reach out, the Indian men remained tight-lipped. "We had a little bit of small talk," he told me later, "but you know, I really didn't have a big picture of what these people were doing here." Both men had a fair command of English, but their accent was almost indecipherable to Massey, and in any case, he said, they remained "real reserved." All he could gather was that they were welders, they had come from India, and they were working at the John Pickle Company.

As the men started to ease their way out of the church, Massey followed them outside, toward the JPC gate, trying, even a little overeagerly, he worried, to let them know they were welcome to return anytime. He had no idea if they'd understood that. Watching them crossing the bleak factory yard, he felt sure he would never see them again. As he later told me, he felt like he'd blown it. "I probably overdo myself sometimes."

To his surprise, however, the Indians returned the next Sunday. This time, they were a bit less shy, and he was able to speak with them a little more. He invited them to a church dinner the following week. The men attended.

One night, during such a church dinner, one of the men let it slip that he was making only two dollars an hour at the John Pickle Company. "I didn't really make much comment about it," Massey remembered. But after the men left, he mentioned it to some of his fellow congregants, saying, "Now, if I understood them right, they said they were making two dollars an hour." The group discussed it, and it was decided that Massey must not have heard right.

After all, as he knew, when employers bring foreign workers to the United States, it is presumably to do highly skilled work Americans can't do. Furthermore, Massey assumed, "for someone to go all the way to India to get these guys, and bring them here to work and do work Americans can't do, they must be making big bucks. You know?"

What Massey slowly learned, detail by detail, over the next three or so weeks was how wrong he could be. Each time he met with them, the Indian men told him more and more troubling details about their employment situation across the street: JPC had confiscated their passports, crammed fifty-three workers into a squalid barracks on factory premises, and was feeding them disgusting, unsanitary food, verbally abusing them, constraining their movements, and forcing them to work six days a week. The company had even hired an armed guard to keep them from escaping over Thanksgiving weekend. Whenever anyone tried to speak up—about the food, the hours, the pay, or the living conditions— they were called names and threatened with deportation.

Some of the men had become so distraught they were considering suicide. There was nothing they could do. They were trapped.


When I met Uday Dattatray Ludbe, in September 2003, he wore a long-sleeved button-down shirt tucked into tidy blue jeans. Ludbe could almost seem like a sort of preppy engineer, but from up close, his bald crown, bushy temples, and tiny wire-rim glasses give him something of a mad-scientist look.

Ludbe was born in India's Maharashtra State. He's forty-six years old, stands about five feet one, and weighs perhaps 125 pounds. In a country where per capita income is $720 per year (compared with $33,050 in the United States), his family, he said, is "not rich" but "not poor, either." Although the caste system has been banished and no one is supposed to care about such things anymore, he's well aware that he's a member of the Khsatriya caste, which is just below the Brahmin caste, the highest.

His father had been a teacher, and education was a priority for the Ludbes. In order for the children to attend better schools, the family moved from a provincial area to Mumbai. Ludbe attended technical college and majored in engineering. Three years into his degree, however, his father became ill, lost his sight, and was forced to stop teaching. Ludbe has two brothers and a sister. To support his brothers' education, he quit school and took the quickest, best-paying job he could get—as a welder.

When asked if it wouldn't have made more sense for him to stay one last year to finish his degree, Ludbe explained that as the oldest brother, he had the responsibility of looking after his younger brother, to "let him get educated good" and enable him to study without working. When I asked him if he wouldn't have made more money for the family if he had simply finished his degree first, *then* paid for his brother's school, he nearly became upset. "To just go and look selfishly to think about my life—it was not accepted by the community and the community don't like. We cannot see people doing like this around. See, this is intimacy. This is *intimacy*."

By his own reckoning, Ludbe was something of a playboy in his teens and twenties. "Sometimes I was chasing for the beautiful girls," he admitted with a grin. As he matured, he said, he realized that outer beauty was fleeting and unimportant, especially compared with qualities like wealth, family reputation, and character. But even as he became emotionally ready to settle down, he told me, he felt steadfastly reluctant to do so on a welder's wages. As a result, interludes between flings became longer, and he spent a lot of time alone. As he wryly described his predicament, "You know: no money, no honey."

Ludbe's family had tried and failed several times to arrange a marriage for him, but he managed to find fault with every prospective bride. Finally, his maternal uncle cornered him; he had found the perfect girl. And he had taken the liberty of telling her—and her family—that Uday would be delighted to marry her. There would be no backing down this time.

As Ludbe told it, he wasn't angry. He was lucky. His marriage has been a happy one, and he feels that his uncle did the right thing. But his financial concerns remained unabated. And now, of course, there were two Ludbes to worry about money.

One hot day in August 2001, a friend of his mentioned something about an advertisement he'd seen for an overseas recruiting agency seeking welders for an American company. Normally, the agency was swamped, with applicants lining up around the block, waiting days to be seen. But since Ludbe was a highly qualified welder, the friend suggested, perhaps if he hurried, he would be given preference for one of these coveted jobs. As Ludbe well knew, the money earned abroad by overseas workers was transformative when relayed back to India— enough to buy homes and high-quality educations, and to raise an entire family in high style.

Ludbe and his wife discussed the unappealing notion of a possibly years-long separation. Weighing the unimaginable loneliness of being apart against the all-too-palpable strains of staying together in poverty, they came to feel that if they were ever going to have a chance at happiness, Ludbe would have to risk going abroad. As he revisited the decision-making process with me later, he remembered with a sort of "Whattayagonna do?" shrug a saying he'd once heard in India: "God gives you one hundred years. The first twenty-five are for you. And after that, you're married!"

Ludbe gathered all of his training and work certificates and went to Al-Samit, and the clerk there was impressed by his credentials. All of Ludbe's jobs had been in welding, fitting, piping, and vessel fabrication, and he was certified for ASME (American Society of Mechanical Engineers)–coded jobs and pressure vessels. His résumé showed that whenever a company had laid him off, usually because of work slowdowns, it tried to hire him back later—an indication that he was a reliable, productive employee.

Ludbe was told to come back the next day with his passport to take a written test. When he returned to Al-Samit, the clerk passed him on to another man, Mr. Hamid Tole, a manager. Tole told Ludbe that if he could pass his written test and, later, a physical welding test, the job was his—with one hitch: he would need to pay a fee of 100,000 rupees, or about $2,200.

Ludbe wasn't surprised that there was a fee; such things were common in India. What put him off was the size of it. A skilled welder with a very good job and full-time employment was lucky to earn $2,200 in an entire year. Moreover, Ludbe knew enough about how things worked in India to be wary of handing his money to strangers. If he'd been dense enough to have asked for a receipt or any paper proof of the transaction, he said, the clerk would have laughed in his face and told him, " 'Okay! Come back in ten days!' " This was the problem with India, Ludbe said. "If you want to go by these agencies, you don't ask for the certain things that are legal. They'd just make you go on the runaround."

On the other hand, Ludbe reasoned, maybe the fee would be worth it. Both Tole and the clerk had told him that the job in America would be long-term and that the salary was approximately $880 a month— with a $100 raise after six months. Ludbe grinned as he recounted this, relishing the irony of something Tole had told him. Emphasizing how fortunate Ludbe would be to land such a job, he said, "It would be a very good life in America."

Ludbe was just one of fifty-three men being chosen to come to the John Pickle plant in Tulsa. The others were now streaming toward Al-Samit from all parts of the country—Gujarat in the west, Kerala and Andhra Pradesh in the south, Bihar in the northeast. Some of them were Hindus, others Catholics and Muslims. They had names like Roy Justus Panackalpurackal, Pauly Perumbully, Krishnankutty Kunjipillai, Jitendrabhai Prabhudas Patel, Peter Jeron, and Marshall Suares. Not only did they represent the wild diversity of India, but they were the crème de la crème of Indian manufacturing. Some had won national competitions for their skills. Many of them had long experience with large international industrial firms. Most were leaving good jobs. Several of the men had worked in the Middle East before, and others had worked at Louisiana's Avondale Shipyards in the late nineties. Quite a few were leaving what is called a "permanent job," an Indian workplace designation akin to tenure at an American university, a status guaranteeing industrial workers employment until the age of fifty-eight. Still other welders were leaving their own successful businesses.

And yet, as well fixed as they might be in India, each of them had, like Ludbe, reckoned it was worth it to leave the comforts of home—and to pay $2,200—for the opportunity to work in the United States.

It's hard for anyone in the United States to imagine the risks undertaken by an Indian to borrow such a vast amount of money. For an American to owe a year's worth of a middle-class salary (comparable to what the welders made in India) might mean an indebtedness of $50,000 or $75,000 dollars. It's a lot of money, to be sure, but people in the States do it all the time to finance new homes, second homes, and higher education. Certainly, it is no picnic to pay back any kind of loan. (I speak from experience, having spent eleven years and counting paying back a student loan that at one time had ballooned to $110,000.) But in the United States, where repayment can be difficult, stressful, and even depressing, it is still a financial transaction guided by laws. Unless your loan came from Vinnie the Loan Shark, no one is going to kill you if you don't pay it back. One can usually haggle for more time over the phone or down at the bank. And of course, as two million debtors did in 2005, one can declare bankruptcy, thereby suffering the stigma of ten years' bad credit.

For a multitude of reasons, the case is entirely different in India. While some of the workers in Ludbe's group had borrowed their fee money from banks, most had obtained it from informal lenders. (Ludbe was lucky; he managed to borrow three-quarters of the money from his mother-in-law and the rest from a sister-in-law.) The interest rate for such informal loans across India are usuriously high—usually around 14 to 18 percent monthly. This translates to 120 percent annually. Since informal lenders can set whatever rate they wish, however, rates frequently reach twice that.

Most Indians live with their extended families on ancestral plots of land. Their homes and these plots are usually all they have with which to secure loans. To lose the collateral on a loan, therefore, means putting your entire family on the streets. The loss goes beyond mere money; a family's reputation and social status are at stake. To be without a home is, of course, to be homeless. But it is also a banishment to the status of dirt, from which no return to respectability or comfort can be expected. For even a shabby-genteel, lower-middle-class family to fall to this level of poverty is a humiliation beyond the imagination of most First World citizens.

It has been fashionable recently for pundits like Thomas Friedman to cite India as a shining example of the many benefits of globalization. Indeed, it is uplifting to read the accounts of high-tech hot spots like Bangalore or Hyderabad, with their Starbucks, shops, software programmers, and Internet start-ups. But most of India has been ignored by the magic wand of free trade, and the fact remains that the vast majority of the population is still deadly poor. As the writer Alexander Cockburn explains rather evocatively: "Remember, India has a billion people in it. Maybe 2 percent of them get to fly in a plane or go online. Around 10 percent are well-off, another 10 percent doing OK. By the most optimistic count we're left with more than half a billion of the poorest people on the planet."

In other words, while "average incomes" in India have been rising at 3 to 4 percent a year and have doubled since the mid-1980s, one in three Indians still lives on less than a dollar a day. As Cockburn notes, while "market reforms" of the 1990s were stimulating some industry sectors, tens of millions of rural Indians were forced to flee from villages to city slums. By 2003, children across the nation, who once averaged nine hundred calories of food intake per day, were now receiving six hundred calories per day. Two million of them die each year. To be thrown into such a seemingly bottomless well of misery is indeed a different degree of duress than enduring, say, ten years with no Discover card.

John Pickle arrived in Mumbai during the first week of October 2001 to meet his prospective hires—including Ludbe—at the offices of Al-Samit, the recruiter. As Pickle later described it, it was "just a good-old-buddy interview." He asked about Ludbe's experience, his age, family, height, and weight. At the end of the interview, Pickle later testified, he shook Ludbe's hand. He also did this with the other workers, in such a way as to make sure the men's hands had been toughened by hard work.

Afterward, Pickle met the workers in a group. According to affidavits signed by Ludbe and fifty other welders, Pickle told the men that they'd been hired to work in his factory in Tulsa, and that the jobs would be for at least two years. He said that as his employees, they would receive free food and accommodations, free medical facilities and insurance. Driver's licenses, he promised, would be given to those who had had them in India. And finally, he said, if the workers' skills were up to par, they could hope for a permanent visa, allowing them, eventually, to bring their families to the United States. Nothing was ever said about going to Kuwait.

A few days later, on October 9, Ludbe returned with his baggage to the Al-Samit office. It was time to go. He was nervous. Not only was he leaving home, but he was forking over the last five hundred dollars of his recruiting fee. If anything went wrong from here on in, he would be bankrupting his in-laws. His life and theirs would be ruined.

By early evening, the men had all gathered at Al-Samit. The plane was to leave at two in the morning. As the night wore on, according to the affidavits of Ludbe and the others, they received their visas, their passports, and their return air tickets. What seemed strange, however, was that they hadn't received their contracts yet. It was getting late. Wasn't that kind of . . . odd?

The men were then given a piece of paper upon which they were supposed to write a statement attesting that Al-Samit had never asked for nor taken any money from them. It seemed shady, of course, and by now the men were worried. Where were the contracts? Finally, quite late in the evening, the men received a piece of paper labeled "Offer Letter." To the chagrin of Ludbe and the others, the letter detailed a set of terms they'd never seen before. The $880 a month they'd been promised had become $550 a month plus overtime. The two years' employment they'd been promised had become a "Period of Training." When Ludbe asked Mr. Tole what "open period" meant, and what was meant by "training," he was assured it was only a formality. In the wake of the

September 11 attacks on New York and Washington—only a month before—immigration enforcement was jittery. The provisions were
merely designed to grease the visa process. Ludbe shouldn't worry, Tole
said. He should just hurry up and sign.

Every worker present later recounted his shock at what was described as a classic bait-and-switch. They'd paid their fees. Some had
traveled from many hundreds of miles away, two days' ride by train.
They were camping out in Mumbai, crashed on friends' couches and, in
some cases, sleeping on the streets because they couldn't spare money for
lodgings. They'd said good-bye to their families. Sure, they could have
refused to sign. But it would have meant certain and immediate loss of
their life's savings. "What else was there to do?" said one of the men. "I
signed it."

As Ludbe told me later, he believed Tole and Pickle. He thought it
was dishonorable for the men to complain out loud. He was ashamed of
them for grumbling, and, he said, he didn't want Pickle thinking, " 'Oh,
it's just the Indians doing all this bullshit.' " As Ludbe reasoned, why
would a man of John Pickle's caliber need to pull a scam? "He's a big in-
dustrialist. He's a big American guy. He wouldn't do that."

The Indians arrived in Tulsa on October 10. A bus picked them up
at the airport and took them to the John Pickle plant. Several of the men
later remarked in their affidavits that the quality of the bus was much
better than they had encountered in previous work experiences abroad.
They took this to be a hopeful indication that accommodations at JPC
might be equally plush.

But when the bus pulled in to the JPC lot, the men received several
surprises. The first was meeting Tina Pickle, a heavily made-up blonde
with striking blue eyes, a little reminiscent of Tammy Faye Bakker. Mrs.
Pickle greeted the Indians, then asked them to surrender their passports,
I-94 immigration forms, and their return tickets. When the men asked
why this was necessary, they were told by a JPC supervisor named John
Holcomb that, like the "training" clause in their contract, it was just a
formality—nothing to worry about.

If the men were unsettled by having to surrender their documents, they were shocked when they saw their lodgings—a crude arrangement of bunk beds in an unfinished room on company property, inside the factory walls.

One of the welders who had worked abroad before remembered, "When I saw the door to the dormitory I lost all confidence. The door was enormous and heavy, made out of steel. It reminded me of the door to a jail."

Another Indian with fifteen years' experience in the Middle East recalled that the barracks "had the appearance of a municipal hospital in India. There was only one light switch for the entire building, which meant we could have lights on to write, read, or do other things or turn off lights for sleeping." The door, he said, was so heavy that whenever anyone closed it, it clanged so loudly it woke everyone lucky enough to have been sleeping.

A welder with previous work experience in numerous countries around the world, including the United States, said that the moment he saw the barracks, he knew something was deeply wrong:

> The rooms were filled with beds so close together that it was difficult to walk between them. The top bunk of the bunk beds was within two and a half feet of the ceiling. The dorm was only a very small house. The entire space, including a garage, which we utilized as a common room, was approximately 1,500 square feet. There was no carpet on the floors. The only place for all of our belongings was in our luggage underneath our bunks. We had no private place for our belongings. The dorm provided no privacy. It had four showers, two urinals, and two toilets. We had one place to wash our hands between thirty men. After three weeks, three more washbasins were provided, but this was still insufficient for 30 men. The dorm was also equipped with only one washing machine and one dryer.
>
> Initially, there were no tables to sit at to eat. After one week, a small table for about eight people was provided. Most of us had to stand or sit on the floor in the garage while we ate.

As this worker, Krishnankutty Kunjipillai, surveyed the depressingly shoddy dwelling he would now call home, he could reach only one conclusion: "I immediately told my friends that we had been cheated."

The Indians began to work on October 15. As Ludbe remembered, while the men were actually on the job, welding, "the work was good and the supervisors and co-workers were very good to us." The problem, he said, was virtually every other aspect of employment with the John Pickle Company.

A few days after their arrival, Pickle put the Indians to work nailing and plastering Sheetrock, sanding, and painting what was to be their new, improved accommodations. Later, he had them cleaning bathrooms, kitchens, and even visiting his home to help with lawn work. The men, chosen for their welding skills, deeply resented being deployed as common day laborers and felt these tasks to be degrading. Pickle and Reeble insisted that the duties were part of the Indians' "training."

According to the men, the new barracks was barely any improvement upon the old. (Eventually, the place would come to be known as "the Cram-a-Lot Inn.") Partial walls, four feet high, were the only concession to privacy between beds. Bunks near the showers got habitually splashed with water; those near the toilet stank. Two bunks were placed a paper-thin wall away from an X-ray machine, used frequently and around the clock to check welds. When the hot water ran out, as it often did, the men had to walk several hundred yards to the old barracks just to wash their hands. Meals were still served in the old dormitory as well, keeping the men running back and forth during their half hour lunch break. Perhaps most insulting of all, the men complained, was that there weren't even enough plates for everyone during meals, so latecomers had to wait for others to finish before they could eat.

The most vehement protests concerned the food. Although Pickle had hired two professional chefs from India to serve the men, the workers complained unceasingly. Some said the food was boring, that the same thing was served every day: rice, curry, vegetables, and sometimes turkey. Quite a number complained that the quality of the ingredients was low, that the food tasted bad and was causing "gas problems." Others described the food as "inedible," "nasty garbage." Moreover, the men said, Pickle rationed like a Scrooge, limiting servings of apples, for example, to one quarter per man.

Perhaps most alarming, if less of an issue at the outset, was the feeling among Ludbe and the others that they weren't quite free to come and go as they pleased. John Holcomb, the supervisor, had told the welders upon their arrival that it would be advisable not to leave the premises. He warned the workers, Ludbe and others said, that "there were black men in the area who smoked crack and took drugs and were dangerous." Pickle had assigned an employee named Sharon Sartin to take the Indians around town to shop for necessities but warned the men against leaving on their own for any purpose. "He told us," Ludbe said, "that Americans were very angry about September 11, and that it was a difficult time and that we should not be out in public."


In the second week of November, JPC managers called a meeting with all fifty-three Indians to ask if they were satisfied with conditions. One of the men, Baburajan Pillai, summoned his courage to speak up and told Ray Murzello that he had worked extensively in the Middle East and that in his opinion, the food and housing at JPC were the worst he had ever seen. Murzello became indignant and told Pillai and the others that they should feel lucky for the food they were getting. After all, he said, they had been "dying of hunger" in India. Pillai countered that he'd been doing just fine in India, and that until working for John Pickle, he'd never seen any company—in any country—so stingy that it rationed apples to a quarter a man. Murzello responded angrily that if Pillai didn't like it, he could go back to India. Pickle, also angry, asked if anyone else had complaints about the food. "Anyone who does," he said, echoing Murzello, "we can just send you back to India."

Despite the warnings about staying put, some of the more adventurous Indians had been leaving the factory lot to shop at nearby stores and even to visit friends. Those who ventured out had usually found the gates open. Over the Thanksgiving holiday weekend, however, workers would later testify, the gates were locked. Additionally, that weekend, a notice was posted in the dorm stating that no one was to leave without permission from John Holcomb or Dale Chasteen, another JPC supervisor. The notice also stated that any violation would result in immediate return to India.

The threat of deportation soon became a pattern. One weekend, an unidentified worker took a company vehicle for a joyride around the lot. After he punctured a tire, a meeting was convened with several supervisors and the Indians. The supervisors demanded to know who had driven the vehicle. No one spoke up, and Chasteen became angry. With Ray Murzello's wife translating, Chasteen called the workers "sons of bitches." Next, John Pickle called the men "fucking bastards," and threatened to deport the wrongdoer and anyone else found to have known about the incident. (According to the men's affidavits, what was most discomfiting about the incident was the fact that Pickle had shamed himself and all of them by using abusive language in the presence of a woman.)

A few days later, Holcomb stormed into the dormitory in a huff and ordered Pillai and another worker, Rajasekharan Cheruvoth, to pack their bags. When the men asked why, he told them: Rajasekharan had been fingered as the unauthorized driver of the company vehicle. Pillai was being made an example for complaining about the food. Both were being sent back to India. The men panicked. Rajasekharan immediately ran from the dormitory. Pillai was not so fortunate. Holcomb escorted him to the airport.

The next day, however, word reached the remaining workers that Pillai had run away at the airport. He'd never even boarded his plane. Furious now, Pickle fumed to the Indians that anyone caught running away from JPC would eventually be caught and thrown in jail. Did they understand?

What seemed clear, both to the Indians at the time and, I imagine, to anyone reading this now, is that the John Pickle Company's "visionary" and "forward-looking" training program was an amateurish sham from the start—and was quickly falling apart. After the incident with Pillai and Rajasekharan, additional workers began to run away from the dormitory. (The use of the term "run away" is clearly a misnomer, I should point out, and one I use only ironically. There is no job in the United States where it should apply. People quit jobs. Sometimes they abrogate their duties. But "run away" is a term normally applied to dogs, troubled teens, and prison inmates.) Pickle's response was to hire an armed security guard and place him in front of the barracks.

The men's unhappiness with conditions at JPC grew. In December, Ludbe's eyeglasses were damaged by sparks from a torch. Remembering Pickle's promise in India to cover medical expenses, he asked for help, but Pickle dismissively told him to call India for his prescription. When another welder, Marshall Suares, dropped a thirty-five-pound steel spool on his toe, Pickle and his wife, Tina, gave him over-the-counter medicines and refused to take him to a hospital for an X-ray. (Two years later, Suares was still receiving treatment for the injury.) When the chefs, who had been given the bunk beds nearest the X-ray machine, complained about being so close to a known cause of cancer, Pickle suggested they take some Anacin, closing the matter by snapping, "Shut the fuck up. You talk too much."

Workers continued to "run away" from JPC, disappearing to parts unknown. Management began to worry that they would overstay their visas and, in Murzello's words, "sour" relations with the U.S. embassies and the INS. In response, Murzello sent an e-mail to Al-Samit, requesting that the president, Mr. Gulam Pesh Imam, "put pressure on the families" of the workers in India. "Knowing Gulam as well as I do," Murzello said in a memo to JPC management, "if this fails . . . Gulam has further recourse and can file a case quickly against these individuals with the Mumbai police." In the memo, Murzello lamented with good humor that it was too bad "we cannot send them (the men, that is) airfreight or FedEx, which would assure a quick, guaranteed delivery!" He also joked that the annoying reprobates should be sent in handcuffs.

Soon after this, during a meeting in Joe Reeble's office, the Indians were gathered to listen in on a conference call from Mr. Pesh Imam. As they leaned in to listen, Pesh Imam threatened that if the men didn't stay put and cooperate, someone would "break one of their goddamn legs."

"Not a bad idea," Reeble said with a laugh. He later testified that it had been a joke. Really, he insisted. Even some of the Indians had laughed.

One day, during the civil trial of the John Pickle Company, I met Mark Massey for dinner. He recommended we try the Rib Crib. I learned later it was a franchise in a chain of restaurants, but I'd never heard of it before. The décor of the Tulsa outlet was unlike any restaurant theme I'd ever seen. The walls were festooned with old hot-water pitchers, deer heads with antlers, deer antlers without heads, Christmas-tree lights, snowshoes, carved wooden birds from Guatemala, old statues of American Indians, gear purportedly belonging to old, dead American Indians, and Coca-Cola posters from the 1930s. The aesthetic seemed to pay homage not to a particular spirit or time period, or even a hyperreal, reimagined but specific vision of the universe, like, say, Planet Hollywood, but rather to the general idea of "the rustic." As the host seated us at our ur-wooden resort chairs trimmed with fake plastic tree bark, the weirdness of it all dawned on me. I had flown to Tulsa on a modern airplane guided by state-of-the-art computers to have dinner at a place with faux "ye old lodge" furnishings, undoubtedly manufactured in China, to talk about slavery with a man who sees lightning bolts at church and sometimes sings praise to Jesus in Arabic.

Massey appeared as always, neither comfortable nor relaxed, a little prim but never officious, and he was present, I gather, because he wished to serve justice. With me, during our several meetings, he was consistently friendly, but somehow not in the way most people would call warm. If anything, he seemed exhausted and uptight. At no time, however, did he seem like an attention hog or an unreliable narrator of events.

Massey told me that the two men who had initially come to Hale Pentecostal began to bring their friends. One Sunday there were three Indians, then there were five, and eventually seven. Massey still couldn't understand most of what the men were saying because of their accents. It was frustrating, and out of concern for what seemed to be their plight, he enlisted a friend of his to translate. The friend, a man named Louis whom Massey knew from a local hospital, was Indian but had lived in Tulsa for a long time and had a more acculturated accent.

Massey brought Louis to meet the workers a few hundred yards from the factory, at a defunct burger-joint parking lot. With Louis translating, Massey finally learned what was going on. "They began to tell me that they were being held there, you know, and that they didn't have their passports. Uh, and just telling me a little bit about the situations that were going on there. That things wasn't so good."

At the time, Massey was working on a condemned property he'd bought with a partner for $2,500. He had put in new windows, and the rehab was almost done, but it was still unoccupied. It was only about a half mile from the JPC plant. He showed the men where the house was, left the key under the mat, and told them that if any of them ever had a problem, they could go stay in the house.

It didn't take long for them to accept. "I guess they were already threatening people," Massey said. "They had some pretty rough meetings where they were, you know, making life pretty rough." A few days later, a group of men left the Cram-a-Lot Inn to stay at Massey's.

Massey took them to meet with an immigration lawyer to find out what they could or should do. The lawyer told them that Pickle had no right to hold the Indians'—or anyone else's—passports. When Massey asked the lawyer how the men might obtain visas that would allow them to work legally, the lawyer jokingly suggested that they could marry American women. Or hey, the lawyer said as an afterthought, they could also try to obtain student visas.

Massey discussed the idea with a pastor from a church with a Bible school. Why not enroll the Indians? It sounded like a terrific idea. Except that in order to obtain the student visas, of course, the men would need their passports.

In January 2002, Mark Massey visited JPC. He met with Joe Reeble and explained the situation. It was a relaxed encounter, as Massey describes it, with Reeble "kicked back in his chair, behind his big desk." The pair spoke for two hours, Reeble explaining "about the work thing and what he was doing." Massey said that Reeble took pains to get him to understand that "this is a new age, a new time to compete with the world, and to be competitive in the world market, people had to make changes. Had to do things different." Reeble refused to hand over the men's passports.

During their long conversation, Massey said, John Pickle had been rushing in and out of the office, scarcely noticing Massey. Eventually, Pickle returned to the office. When he finally had time to recognize Massey, Massey recalled, "his blood pressure—I mean I thought he was going to have a heart attack. He was just about to come unglued. There I'm sitting. I'm sure they done know who I am because I had been . . ."

He didn't finish the thought. But indeed, Pickle "done knew who he was," because for weeks JPC had been tapping the men's phones and monitoring their e-mails. Pickle had known even before Massey's visit that morning that a group of workers was planning to "run away" to Bible school.

Not to be outsmarted, Pickle had called the Tulsa County Sheriff's Office and reported a "disturbance" at the plant. Three deputy sheriffs' cars, under the command of one Captain Billy Bass, had promptly arrived, and while Massey was indoors, chatting politely with Reeble, the deputies had escorted the workers to a local bank to close their checking accounts. Then they dropped the men at the Tulsa airport, where, supervised by a former Green Beret aquaintance of Pickle's, they were to board a flight to Mumbai via Atlanta. At the airport they were handed envelopes containing their passports and back wages. One worker said that when he opened his envelope, he found only seven dollars.

When Massey found out what had happened, he and the other Indians panicked. He called government immigration officials in Atlanta, and at his frantic behest, they reviewed the Indians' documents. The Indians, some of whom had already boarded and taken their seats, were informed that their I-94's and visas were good for another three months. Literally moments before the plane departed, the men learned that contrary to what Pickle had been telling them, they were free to go anywhere they wanted.

For Massey and the Indians, it had been a nightmare. Massey said he felt particularly stupid because there he'd been, blabbering away with Reeble while the men were being forced to the airport. He also felt conflicted, because in a way he was at fault for intervening and provoking Pickle's response. He remembered speaking with one of the nearly deported guys when he'd come up to the fence near Hale Church. The man was Hindu. Massey had talked to him for a long time about Christianity and the Christian concept of God. "I was telling him about the Lord. And, you know, 'The Lord is wonderful' and he would help us in the situation. And I thought, you know, here I told him how good God is, and how, you know, about prayer and everything." Massey laughed with embarrassment. "Then he was shipped off! I thought: 'Man, man!' "

Massey said he had been especially concerned about Pickle's high-handed abuse of power. He gave me a letter that he had filed with the Tulsa County sheriff:

On January 28, 2002, around 10:15 in the morning 7 men from India were escorted by Tulsa Sheriffs to a bank, where the men were forced to close bank accounts and later to the Tulsa airport, wher [sic] the men were forced to get on an airplane bound for Atlanta. The men tried to communicate with the officers but were told to remain silent. My concern is that these men did not get a fair opportunity to defend themselves or get legal assistance. I wonder if the Sheriff's office could do the same to me. It appears to me that there has been an abuse of power. I was told by a dispatcher that the officers were originally called out for a disturbance. I can't imagine how a call for a disturbance can result in a police escort in support of a private individual's attempt to forcibly remove people from the United State [sic].

By now, word of the messy goings-on at JPC had leaked out into the community and attracted the interest of local newspaper reporters.

In a *Tulsa World* article dated February 1, 2002, Reeble was asked to comment about allegations beginning to surface. He explained that the men were simply trainees, that they were staying in Tulsa for only six months, and that in any case, they weren't employees of JPC, they were employees of Al-Samit, the Indian recruiting company. When reporter Michael Overall, who'd spoken with some of the Indians, brought up the fees they had paid, Reeble responded sympathetically. Speaking of India, he noted, "It's a corrupt society over there. I don't condone it. But I can't stop it. It's unfortunate, but I think some of these guys might have been taken advantage of."

When the Indians read the article, they were shocked. Pickle, they said, had told them they were going to be working for two years—at least. Not six months. And what was this business about "minimum wage"? People working in the United States were supposed to make at least $5.15 per hour? The Indian men had been making only $2.89 to $3.17 per hour at the John Pickle Company. The two cooks had been making even less—about a dollar an hour.

The end was near. Pickle, apparently making a homegrown, final attempt at damage control, hired three lawyers and held a videotaped meeting with his managers and four of the Indians. One of the lawyers stood directly in front of the door. Another asked the men if they had any complaints. The workers cited the entire litany of bad conditions: the terrible food, the cramped housing, the lack of privacy, the humiliating treatment, the verbal abuse, the broken promises, the restraint of movement. Perversely, after the men had finished their exhaustive recitation, the lawyer rejoined, "Yeah, yeah, okay. But besides that do you have any complaints?" The point of the video seemed to be to get the men to say on tape that they had never been locked up. But no matter how many times the Pickle lawyer asked them if the door to their dormitory had ever been locked, the men seemed unable to answer. From the tape, it's hard to say whether the language was confusing, the question itself was confusing, or the Indians simply didn't know how to answer. Certainly, they had been made to feel unfree to come and go. The fact was that the door to the dormitory had, in fact, been locked on at least one occasion. But it's not clear who knew it, who had locked it, and whether it had been locked on other occasions. Finally, after the management team and its lawyer had run through the question as many times as anyone could bear, the lawyer moved on. "Now," he asked, "if you had a choice to come back here again, knowing what you know now, would you still do it?"

The Indians looked confused. They understood the words, it seemed, but the question itself didn't make any sense to them. The camera lingered on a movie-star-handsome, self-assured guy with a *bindi* on his forehead named U. C. Patel. Patel considered the query for what seemed like an interminable pause, as if trying to frame it any way that might help. He looked to the other Indians for guidance, then back to the lawyer before finally repeating, rather quizzically, "Choice?"

When the John Pickle Company's "training program" came crashing down, it made a big noise. On February 2, 2002, Tulsa's three news channels led their broadcasts with the story of the Indians' dramatic mass exodus from JPC. Footage showed the Indians grimly hustling their belongings out of the factory barracks to a group of waiting vans and drivers, led by Mark Massey, and arriving at Massey's own home, which soon looked like a chaotic refugee camp.

The Associated Press picked up the story, which quickly went national. *The Washington Post* wrote a feature about it, and Tom Brokaw on the *Nightly News* gravely described the plight of the Indians—"new arrivals whose American dream has become a nightmare."

The word *slavery* figured prominently in most of the coverage, although nobody seemed to know exactly how to use it:

"Workers from India say conditions were almost like slavery."

"Local man accused of holding fifty-four welders from India in 'virtual slavery.' "

". . . subjected to slave-like conditions."

One attorney, speaking for the Indians, asserted, "This is a slave-labor case because these men were forced to eat and sleep and work in the same place."

Another local attorney was quoted: "I don't know what else you would call it. It's like slavery."

"What they have done is really not that much different than slavery," said Roosevelt Milton, president of the Oklahoma City Chapter of the National Association for the Advancement of Colored People.

To me, the most surprising thing about the coverage was the confidence with which Pickle countered the charges against him. In his every TV or newspaper quote, he seemed to carry himself with utter sincerity—almost charmingly exasperated, irritated, and irascible. There was nothing in his demeanor to suggest that he had done anything remotely wrong.

In one bit of TV footage, he protested, "I feel like I bent over backwards to help these people, and I'm getting shot in the back." In other moments he insisted, "No worker has ever been mistreated here." Certain gates, he said, were sometimes locked to protect company property, but never, he swore, had workers been locked up. "They have never been locked in those barracks," Pickle said. "Absolutely not." As to the legality and legitimacy of his dealings with the Indians, he said, "Never a doubt in my mind from the get-go," he said. "If I had, I never would have done it. I'm a straight shooter the whole way."

What was also curious, I thought, was the amount of public sentiment—not a majority but a substantial amount—that ran with Pickle and against the Indians.

One letter, written by a Tulsa resident to the local paper, read:

On July 17, NBC ran a story about the John Pickle Company. It was terribly slanted towards the Indian workers and their supposed plight. NBC failed to tell the whole story.

If these men were so abused how did they get to a church to whine? How many of us are given living quarters—of any kind while learning a trade? They were given a terrific opportunity to learn the welding trade. How many of us get those breaks?

The Indians need to go home! Let's start a fund to send them home. I'd be the first to contribute—of course with the stipulation that they'd never come back. I'm sick to death of the "bleeding hearts."

Another comment, read over the Channel 2 news program, stated: "It sounds to me like the arrangements for these guys were probably all made out in the open, before they came over here from India, so I'm sure they knew what they were getting into."

Pickle's American employees came out strongly in favor of their employer. Tulsa's Channel 6 featured a Pickle welder named Bob Thomson wearing a camo-colored baseball hat, convincingly swearing that John and Tina Pickle were "kind-hearted employers. . . . There's not a guy who's been here [at JPC] very long where he doesn't know their wife, he doesn't know their kids are going to college," Thomson attested. "And over the years, I've seen John pull thousands of dollars from his pocket and give to these people that was in need that maybe didn't make it between paychecks and didn't require it back."

Supervisor John Holcomb was quoted in an article for the *Tulsa World* saying that if JPC employees had witnessed the kind of abuse alleged by the Indians, they would have taken action to stop it. "We are Americans, Christians and family people," Holcomb said, "and would have left if we thought that was happening. My girlfriend even made them plum cakes because they wanted some and we couldn't find them anywhere. Why would we do all of this if we weren't treating them right? We did not treat them badly. It's all lies." The Indians, Holcomb charged, were simply desperate to stay in the United States, willing to do anything, legal or not, to get a toehold in this country. "We never thought it would come to this," he swore. "What they said did not happen."

As one article followed another in the *Tulsa World,* each referring to the Indians as "virtual slaves," investigations of JPC were launched by the Occupational Safety and Health Administration (OSHA), the Food and Drug Administration (FDA), the FBI, the Immigration and Naturalization Service (now a division of Homeland Security), the Department of Labor (DOL), the Department of Justice (DOJ), the Environment Protection Agency (EPA), and the Equal Employment Opportunity Commission (EEOC), in addition to Oklahoma state health and fire officials.

Over the coming months, JPC, feeling itself "buried" by the negative press, began to issue a series of press releases and statements. One of them read:

Based solely on the news accounts, government agencies started tearing through us. The Department of Labor Wage and Hour Division sent two investigators to find out about the Indians [*sic*] wages, then 7 months later filed suit against us for underpayment of minimum wage. The Equal Employment Opportunity Commission (EEOC) filed suit based on allegations of "slavery" and discrimination. The Fire Marshall and State Health Officials wanted to see the kitchen and the men's quarters. They all wanted to see where we had "locked up the Indians". The Occupational Safety and Health Administration (OSHA) brought in 4 investigators and spent days combing our plant on two separate occasions. Some days, we had three government agencies here at the same time.

In the end, JPC asked, what had the government found? Not much. OSHA, the company said, cited the company for thirty-one health and safety violations. JPC successfully challenged twenty-two of them. The EPA, the FDA, the FBI, the INS, the DOL, the DOJ, and state health and fire officials had all called off their investigations. Only the EEOC's investigation and a lawsuit filed by a local lawyer remained active.

JPC insisted that the Indians had lied to the media, describing the workers as legally savvy connivers who had learned that if only they claimed "slavery" (as opposed to other, lesser forms of labor abuse), a gullible press and public would believe them and allow them to stay in the United States. Under the Victims of Trafficking and Violence Protection Act of 2000, mentioned earlier, a special form of visa had been created for immigrants agreeing to testify in slavery cases. Anyone with Internet access could look this up.

Many of the company's claims seemed far-fetched, but one of them at least piqued my interest. JPC had always maintained that the workers' contracts had been signed well before they had met with Pickle—not, as the Indians claimed, at the last moment, under duress, on the night of their departure. If this was true any claims about a bait-and-switch on issues of salary or living conditions were almost certainly bogus.

Why, I wondered, would Pickle or any other businessperson wait until the night of departure to sign contracts? He would have had to purchase plane tickets for all fifty-four workers, at about $2,000 apiece. Why would anyone spend over $100,000 on airfare for workers who hadn't yet signed contracts? Wouldn't he have to have the name of every passenger to even buy their tickets?

From the very beginning, it was clear that the John Pickle Company had been guilty of labor violations and some sort of visa fraud. On the simplest level, it was guilty of evading minimum-wage laws. And of course, the company had taken the men's passports. Certainly, it sounded like Pickle and his management team had attempted to intimidate the men into staying put. But to what extent was what had unfolded in JPC's "training program" a case of slavery—versus run-of-the-mill labor abuse? And did it matter?

As opposed to the Mexican workers in Florida, who seemed very uneducated and guileless, the Indians I'd seen and met with to discuss the Pickle case seemed calm and cool—sophisticated enough, perhaps, to be able to successfully manipulate me. After all, I don't pretend that my gut feelings are infallible. And when it comes to lies, lawsuits, people, and money, I've never been able to forget the words of a personal-injury attorney named Jamie Wolfe, whom I interviewed years ago, speaking about his clients:

> I have never, and I mean this, never met an honest man. I have had rabbis lie. I have had priests lie. I have had witnesses of every color and denomination and persuasion lie. Clients come to me and tell me that they were caused to have an accident and they were injured in a certain way. But the truth is that it usually didn't happen *exactly* the way they say it happened. The client may be fundamentally and inherently a good and honest person, but when it comes to their case, their theory is, Well, it's a goddamn insurance company, and they've got more money than God, and it isn't right, and it isn't fair. And so it's okay if, on the margins, on the fringes, they improve or enhance their story a little bit.

Pickle might be guilty of all manner of things, but still, as an "objective journalist" (there is no such thing, but everyone tries), I had to scrutinize everything that the Indians had claimed.

After all, consider the following: a foreigner who testifies in a slavery case receives a green card. As is well known, green cards are usually a viable stepping-stone to U.S. citizenship. If a thirty-five-year-old welder employed full-time in India makes around $2,500 per year and retires at around the age of fifty-eight, he stands to make about $45,000 altogether. Give that same worker a green card. Let him retire at age sixty-five. He will have earned well over a million dollars more than he would have earned in India. He will receive additional thousands of dollars from Social Security, Medicare, and Medicaid. His family will in likelihood be enabled to immigrate to the United States, and presumably, at least some of them will find gainful employment and contribute hundreds of thousands of dollars or more to the family income.

Why would any sane poor person not be tempted to lie, even just a little bit, and especially against an employer who had treated him as Pickle had? I know that if exaggerating a little bit meant raising my entire family out of poverty, having babies unthreatened by diarrhea and bad water supplies, having clothes, good, healthy food, electricity, a chance to be educated, to own a home, I'd consider myself an idiot not to try it.

On August 30, 2002, the John Pickle Company closed its doors. In a postmortem, Pickle wrote:

> This is not about the faceless "John Pickle Company" you have read about. It is not about a "rusty old plant" just west of downtown. . . .
>
> It's about the demise of an American business. . . . About how a legal system and its pundits could file a lawsuit without a single piece of evidence of slavery, or deceit, or mistreatment, or malnourishment, or discrimination . . . to make a media splash, and put seventy-five Tulsans out of work. . . .

And of course, there's Mr. Massey, the savior and local hero; who never missed an opportunity to play the media, to publicly parade his newfound converts and capture headlines from reporters too naïve to know they were being "played."

On every single charge, the Indians were lying, Pickle said. Regarding the food, he claimed, he had taken the cooks twice a week to a local Indian-food distributor and told them to buy anything they wanted—within reason. The Indians back at the plant, however, were insufferably picky. If the cook bought fish, they wanted lamb. If the food was hot, they wanted it medium hot. Every one of them wanted a gourmet meal, Pickle said with a snort. "Hell, I could've bought 'em lobster, too. I did not do that."

What burned him the most, obviously, was the charge of slavery. What had happened at his plant, he said, wasn't slavery. "Real slavery," he said, "would be where you bring the guys in, you lock 'em up, you don't let 'em go anywhere, you feed 'em a certain amount of food. The man works so much, but you don't compensate 'em *anything*."

He shook his head bitterly. "They had me on national TV one night, somebody did," he said, almost spitting. " 'Virtual slaves.' They say it over and over and over. 'They was locked up.' Unbelievable. You've heard that a thousand times, on every news report here right in the United States. How many times you seen they been locked up and couldn't get out and all that shit? Just unbelievable. Unbelievable. I'm telling you: this thing is phony, man. It ain't what you see a'tall."

The Indians had been free to come and go whenever they wanted from the moment they'd arrived in Tulsa, Pickle said. "John Holcomb took the men to the Catholic church four times. Sharon Sartin was being paid twenty-five hours a week to take the men around."

Yes, he said, he had put up a sign telling the Indians to let supervisors know when and where they were going if they left, but this was only because he worried about the men, whose English skills were sometimes poor. If he had had anything to hide, he protested, why would he have called the INS and the FBI every time he was worried about missing workers? How would he have gotten the men visas and arranged the whole thing with the permission of the U.S. consulate in India?

Once, he said, he had believed in the media. He had thought that if he read something in the paper or saw it on the news, it was true. Now, he said, he had learned how easily the media could be deceived. All the workers had had to do was cry "Slavery!"

As the lawsuit against JPC chugged through the courts, generating continued press coverage of the story, public outrage over the Indians' "plight" seemed to flag. With the crisis past and the Pickle plant closed, whatever had happened seemed like less and less of a big deal. Within six months of the men's dramatic breakout, the once-sympathetic *Tulsa World* had demoted the men from "virtual slaves" to "alleged virtual slaves" and even gently derided them for being publicity hounds.

Indeed, the workers seemed to be doing quite all right for themselves. Most had managed to get visas enabling them to stay in America and work legally. If that is in fact what they'd wanted, then it appeared that by alleging they'd been "enslaved," they'd gotten it.

I had met and interviewed the lead counsel for the men, a Tulsa attorney named Kent Felty. Felty was actually one of several lawyers who had helped the Indians file a lawsuit against Pickle. Some of the lawyers had dropped out of the case; others lent a hand when they could. In an unusual but logical turn, to avoid two trials concerning the same facts and claims, the defendants' case was "consolidated" with the EEOC's; together, their suit alleged that JPC was guilty of civil rights violations, discrimination on the basis of national origin, intent to avoid minimum wage, fraud, false imprisonment, and intentional infliction of emotional distress.

Felty had been good enough to give me a folder's worth of EEOC depositions he happened to have on his laptop. I became excited when I stumbled across the testimony of Jacon Harbour. Harbour was, at the time, a guy in his twenties, and his job at JPC was to administer the computer network. As he put it, he was the "resident geek." He was also by far the most notably Indian-friendly American employee at JPC. When the Indians first arrived, Jacon started practicing a few words of Hindi he'd picked up from the Internet, mostly to say "Hello" and "Thank you." This soon led to socializing and forays into Tulsa nightlife.

The nature and quality of this nightlife would become the subject of much concern over the course of the JPC trial. According to Felty, Harbour "claims to be a legitimate vampire, over one thousand years old." At any rate, as the deposition read, it appeared that on two occasions, Harbour took some of the Indian men to a hangout of his, a club called the Other Side, where, evidently, "shows" of some sort took place.

In the deposition, Harbour was asked about the shows. He described them as "fire fetish acts" or "hot-wax stripteases." As Felty understood it, the parties Harbour had taken his new friends to were cultish affairs, where "people dress in Goth stuff, they paint themselves with latex and come in semi-naked with chains, dragging each other around." Felty didn't pretend to understand the whole thing but nevertheless couldn't help finding some humor in the situation. "I don't think this is a common practice in India," he drawled laconically. "I think it freaked the guys out a bit."

Whether Harbour was or wasn't Count Dracula was beside the point, but what I felt about him while reading his transcript was that he was perhaps the ideal witness to whatever it was that had gone on at JPC; after all, he seemed to be neither a company man, nor a racist, nor a redneck. Nor, despite his acquaintance with the Indian men, did he appear to be so friendly as to be in league with them. I was especially intrigued by his answers to Felty's questions regarding the Indians' alleged confinement at JPC.

Q: What do you—is there—what do you think of the claim of false imprisonment?

A: Laughable.

Q: Why is that?

A: Because if they were in prison, then me and my friends all throughout town wouldn't have been able to party with them.

When I spoke with the Indian men about the parties, they made no attempt to deny that they had socialized with Harbour. When I asked

Uday Ludbe about the parties, he seemed a little worried I might lump him in with the Goth crowd. Quickly, he explained, "I'm a man who likes to do some experiments always. You want to know only what is there actually. We just went out of John Pickle Company to find such a bars like this." In other words, he was bored and the Indians merely wanted to see what life was like in the United States.

I assured him that I just wanted to know what the parties had been like. "This was the first party for us," he explained. "So we were . . . really got scared. We were confused as what to do because all the girls. The drinking. They were looking at our face and we are watching their faces and girls come in with minimum clothes. Yeah. That was a taboo. You know, because traditionally we don't go with our bodies like that.

"And actually," he said, "we didn't like that party because—you know, the rhythm, the music, the songs—it's drink and dance. Drink and dance! If you drink more, you're going to dance. If you don't drink, you're not gonna dance. We had not that much money. I drank one beer when I was there."

Another Indian worker, younger and cooler than Ludbe, was more nonchalant about the evening's proceedings. "He's not really a vampire," he said of Harbour. "This is their fashion. They don't do nothing, really. It's just an imitation. They're just dancing with a big sound and enjoying that. I don't know. They have their own style and dancing steps. Different rhythm." He laughed heartily.

After thinking more about it, I didn't really care what kind of party the men had gone to. I just wanted to know more precisely about their freedom of mobility. I wanted to know how intimidated they had really felt. Later I had the opportunity to track Harbour down to ask him more questions. (Before or during the trial, he'd moved from Tulsa to Denver to accept a position "freelance fire performing.")

First, I wanted to ascertain if he was the relatively neutral source I'd hoped he was. How had he personally felt about John Pickle? I asked him by e-mail. He wrote back, "I liked Mr. Pickle . . . somewhat . . . he didn't understand my culture or mindset, and I didn't understand his. He was a hands-on man, I was a long hair freak sitting in a room with a bunch of computers doing nothing."

Elaborating about the men's freedom of movement, he wrote, "They came and went as they pleased, they went to strip clubs, I even took them to a few fetish balls and gothic clubs. They went roller-skating with me and my family and friends."

Of the Cram-a-Lot Inn, the barracks provided for the Indian workers, he wrote: "It was just as good as any dorm I had for camp or even college. I had came in and setup 2 computers that were nice, not top of the line, but still very good, they had DSL in their rooms and even setup voice chat for them to talk to their families."

I asked him what his impressions were about the most contentious— if seemingly unimportant—subject of all—the food. "Let me bounce this off you," he replied. The chef, he said, "was great." The food was "fantastic." He went on:

> I tried to eat there morning, noon, and night. It was every bit as good as anything we would go pay $20–$30 a plate for at a restaurant here. Now, you have to realize, there are around 28 states or districts I think they call them, in India. Each one of those is like a new country, different language, culture; even religions differ greatly as do the language. So this guy tried making food that could be appreciated by everyone. Of course, some loved the food, other could care less, and some hated it. Ever try to get a hick from Texas to eat sushi? So, yeah, some went to the media and said that the food was horrible, I think the one that said that was vegetarian also . . . so there you go there.

In Harbour's telling, the Indian workers at JPC had been fine—until they met Mark Massey. Of Massey, he wrote: "He struck me as an ass. He had this total 'Christian' attitude that his way was the only way that there could be. He started telling them that the area they were staying in was horrible and started going directly to the news with it."

After interviewing Jacon Harbour, I had come around full circle. It felt like a particularly dumb circle; I had spent months investigating a slavery case that suddenly didn't seem much like slavery. No matter whom I talked to, I got a different answer. Many of the perspectives were interesting. But they were too conflicting to sort out with any clarity.

Usually, I try not to get my information from people who are paid to dispense it. Or at least, I try not to rely upon the information they give. It's too hard. Public relations people, spokespeople, lawyers, politicians—if they're any good at what they do, they're better than my ability to pick it apart. I don't like assuming people are lying. I feel rude when I do. I generally want to believe what people say. What I find fascinating about my job, however, is that whether or not people lie to me, all I have to do is represent their view on the page. It's like hunting. If I wait long enough, the truth always comes. Lies have a weird way of dissolving, and truth has a lovely habit of making more and more sense over time.

In his own telling, Kent Felty had been feeling somewhat at sea before the fifty-three Indian plaintiffs walked into his life. When Massey brought the men to see him in January 2001, Felty was sitting in his office, "staring at my calendar, trying to figure out how I was gonna keep everything together." He was forty-one years old at the time; his practice specialized in bottom-of-the-barrel legal carrion—car wrecks, divorces, and misdemeanor criminal work. Dryly describing the kind of cases he'd been taking, he pitched his voice unctuously to inquire of an imaginary witness, " 'And how sore *was* your back, sir?' " He laughed and stage-cringed. "It was a miserable life, truthfully. I was not successful. I was never successful. I had managed to basically scrap it out and keep my doors open for ten years, just by grace."

Felty is perhaps the most laid-back lawyer I've ever met. Neither short nor tall, dumpy nor skinny, he has sandy brown, lightly graying hair and a darker mustache and goatee, and he seldom wears a suit outside of court. He speaks plainly and ironically, and while he's happy to talk about the JPC case, his attention wanders most naturally toward the football exploits of his only son, Matt, who at the time played linebacker for the University of Oklahoma.

Felty said that when he met the Indian men, "they seemed scared. Nice guys. Very, very little English. That was the overwhelming deal, is they were really scared. They looked like they'd been sleeping at a bus station. They looked like they'd been through hell, like they'd been beat up." Felty's first impulse, he said, was more humanitarian than legal-minded, and he simply "went into comfort mode, just trying to tell them that it was gonna be okay."

However sympathetic he felt, he soon started wondering, "How am I gonna get paid?" Most of the work he'd been doing was already pro bono, he joked—but unintentionally. "A lot of my clients were indigent, and I never had the heart to collect. And so I was preoccupied with money. Put that in your book. 'Lawyer preoccupied with money.' That'll be very unusual." He laughed.

However, he elaborated, "once I got rolling on it, the spiritual aspect of it kicked in. And I got a little bit less self-centered." The feeling was transformative. After a lifetime of doing work that lacked dignity and seldom paid, he described fighting for the Indians' rights as feeling "like being married to the right person."

Felty's version of the story is that Pickle brought the first group of Indians to Tulsa for training. They worked out fine, and he shipped them off to Kuwait. Then he brought the second group of Indians to Tulsa. They worked out fine as well (as far as anyone seems to know, according to Felty, Pickle, and the EEOC, those men are still employed by JPME in Kuwait). As to what happened with the third group, his plaintiffs, Felty said, "I think it was a fluid situation. I think he got these guys over here, and they were working cheaper than Americans. I know it would've crossed *my* mind: 'How long can I keep 'em? Maybe I can have an Indian workforce here that'll cut my costs.' " Felty said that he had always assumed Pickle would have eventually sent the men to Kuwait. However, he mused, putting himself back in Pickle's frame of mind, "as long as they could stick around in Tulsa for a while and fill orders more cheaply than Americans, why not keep 'em awhile?"

Felty then told me an interesting story. Shortly before the case came to trial, he heard that Ray Murzello, JPC's liaison to Al-Samit, who often traveled the world on business, was at home in Tulsa. Felty called him and asked if he could come by and have a casual talk. Murzello said it would be fine—but only if he came alone.

In Felty's telling, the night couldn't have been more surprising. He drove to Murzello's. "I walked into his house. And I'm his enemy, remember. And he's there with his wife. His house is beautiful, his wife is very attractive. And they offer me some very expensive Scotch. His wife is very religious; his kids are beautiful. Wonderful family, very accomplished kids." Instantly, Felty realized he was in over his head. Murzello was seventy, sophisticated, articulate, deadly charming, and, in Felty's words, "way smarter than me." Felty compared him to a confident old lion.

After a couple of Scotches, Felty said, the two men began rolling up their sleeves. Felty tried to "flip" Murzello, meaning he tried to get Murzello to agree to testify against John Pickle. Murzello knew the FBI was still investigating the case to see if it merited criminal prosecution. Felty told Murzello that if he came clean, Felty would broker a deal, if possible. After all, it's the first to cooperate who gets the reduced sentences in conspiracy cases. All Murzello had to tell him to get it started was "who thought the whole scheme up."

During their long conversation, said Felty, Murzello "was very, very careful to deny that the [Indian] men had been lied to. It was very obvious that he was not going to implicate himself in a fraud. He was more casual about admitting that minimum wage had not been paid, food and accommodations were substandard, et cetera. He admitted that the trainee status was bullshit, and that he thought Pickle was dumb for not treating the men well in terms of food and accommodations." What struck Felty, he told me later, was that Murzello didn't seem the least bit morally troubled by what had happened. "Basically, he seemed only to regret the loss of money and the business opportunity. I know he told me specifically, more than once, that he could have made millions with these men."

The more Murzello talked, the more obvious it was to Felty that neither Pickle nor Reeble could have authored the plan. They weren't smart enough or experienced enough. After all, it was Murzello who had the international business experience, the necessary contacts and sophistication, to process the whole thing through American consular officials overseas. Of course! He was the one who had educated Pickle or Reeble on what to do.

Now it became Murzello's turn to try to flip Felty. Having declined to name names (because he *was* the name, Felty was certain), Murzello began to feel Felty out for a number. He wanted, Felty told me, to know "what I personally needed out of the deal—how much it would cost to settle the lawsuit."

At a certain point during the discussion, Felty said, Murzello became markedly bored. "He looked at me like this was irrelevant," Felty said, like "all this race and moral stuff was kind of childish." It was at this point in the conversation that Murzello asked Felty if he had ever been to India. "He told me if I had, I would understand things a lot better." Felty interpreted this to mean that "these men were Indian and Indian people are poor and used to working cheap and not having enough to eat. Two bucks an hour is two bucks. It's twice as good as they were making before." So what was the problem with the John Pickle Company training program again?

Felty chuckled at his naïveté. There was nothing he could say. Murzello seemed like a nice guy. Felty had enjoyed his company. At the end of the night, he told me with a laugh, "I gave him and his wife a hug! I was laughing at myself as I was doing it." Felty paused and shrugged. "Shoot, if I was amoral, I'd hire Ray in a second!"

I had been hesitant to ask Felty about Jacon Harbour. Finally, I mentioned that my e-mails with Harbour had left me wondering about the veracity of some of the Indians' claims. Felty dug through some pages of testimony from the Indians, found a passage, and handed it to me. In the testimony, it came out that Harbour, as resident tech geek, had been the person who had spied on the Indians' computer usage, watching where they were going and what they were writing. As it turned out, he embraced his role, and had even played games with the Indians, sending them instant messages saying things like "I am watching you. I know exactly what you're doing." So much for Harbour being a neutral witness. As for Harbour's animus against Mark Massey, Felty pointed out that whether he was a Goth or an actual vampire, it seemed a good guess that Harbour didn't like Christians a whole lot.

Getting around to whether the case was a matter of forced servitude or merely labor abuse, Felty answered, "On a sliding scale? I personally don't know." Comparing Pickle to slaveholders of the 1800s, he said he thought Pickle was obviously a racist, but it didn't mean he was necessarily or intentionally cruel. "Slave owners back in the day," he said, "I don't think they hated the people that worked for them. I think that in their own distorted way, they cared for them. The fundamental problem is that they were controlling other people's lives."

Pickle, Felty imagined, "had been to India, was shocked at the conditions, and felt like he was appointed to raise these men up and teach them how to be Americans. No matter what he did, it couldn't be worse than what they came from. 'So what's the harm if I exert a little control? These men need guidance, anyway.' "

Whether you preferred to call it slavery or something else, however, American laws had been broken, Felty said. The problem with guys like Pickle is that they choose to live in America, but they exploit the realpolitik of a globalized world to their selfish advantage here in the United States. Imagining the point of view of such an employer, he said, "If you can, then why not do it? If they're willing to work for a dollar a day, then so be it. I mean, they're poor people. Who cares? Why think about it?"

The trial of John Pickle and his company (both were listed as defendants) was broken into two parts. The first, which took place in September 2003, centered on whether or not the fifty-two Indian plaintiffs could legally be considered trainees. Implicit to the determination was the subsequent validity of the charges of deceit, discrimination, minimum-wage violations, false imprisonment, and infliction of emotional distress.

The U.S. Department of Labor lists six conditions that must be met in order for workers' activity to be considered part of a bona fide training program:

1. the training must be similar to that which would be given in a vocational school;
2. the training must be for the benefit of the trainee;
3. the training must not displace regular employees;
4. trainees must work under close supervision;

5. an employer may derive no immediate advantage from a trainee's activities; and

6. trainees must understand that they are not entitled to wages during the time they're in training.

JPC was represented by the husband-and-wife team Philip J. and Linda McGowan of Carpenter, Mason & McGowan, a local firm with a general trial practice. The McGowans' strategy seemed to revolve around the idea that the Indians were such god-awful welders that Pickle could not have been trying to profit from them. Due to the trial, the negative publicity about the Indians, and the fact that they had left his employ, he had lost money by hiring them. Therefore, they *had* to be trainees.

The defense called a Pickle loyalist named Brent Goodfellow to articulate what, in his experience, made or didn't make a good welder. Goodfellow, a likeable-seeming guy, tried to explain it. "If you look inside yourself," he said, "and if you don't—I mean—if you ain't a welder when you look inside and that's what you see, then, you know—some people—not everyone's a welder."

From this somewhat cracked foundation, the defense launched into hours of technical terminology and expert testimony about different kinds of welds and welding classifications, a strategy that might have been useful for numbing a jury into submission but that confused no one present. In fact, the defense from the get-go seemed so amateurish as to be kind of a joke.

The first pretense to be demolished was that Al-Samit, the Indian recruiting firm, was the actual employer of the fifty-three Indians. As was easily demonstrated, the Indian firm had made no decisions whatsoever about what type of work the men were to perform, nor on what products, nor on what shifts, nor within which product divisions of JPC. All of these decisions were made at JPC. The fact that JPC had been sending the men's payroll money to India, for Al-Samit to then send back to Tulsa, convinced no one that Al-Samit was anything more than an agent in a ruse perpetrated by JPC.

It did not help JPC's case when testimony showed that management had created the paperwork documenting the "trainee program" only after the media had started writing bad things about the company. Director of Manufacturing Dale Chasteen admitted that Vice President Reeble had instructed him in December (the Indians had arrived in October) to create evaluation forms proving that such a program existed. These "records," however, were so clumsily forged that some of them were dated prior to the Indian men's actual arrival. Others assessed performance of workers supposedly employed by Pickle who had, in fact, left Tulsa months before.

JPC's claims were further undercut when the plaintiffs showed that since leaving Pickle's employ, most of the Indians alleged to be such incompetent welders had, almost to a one, found jobs in shipyards, power plants, and chemical companies paying between fifteen and twenty-five dollars an hour, some including cushy per diems and living allowances. Not a one of them appeared to have required any additional training or education regarding "the American way."

The plaintiffs also demonstrated that the Indian "trainees" had worked during their time at Pickle on products that generated millions of dollars for JPC, and that the company had laid off thirty American workers during the Indians' tenure.

Finally, the plaintiffs showed that the Indians' claims about the food were absolutely merited. It would be revealed that Pickle ordered the men to throw away rotting food prior to an FDA inspection of the barracks kitchen, and in court, a sales representative for a local food distributor would testify that despite bringing in more than fifty-three workers, Pickle had told him to outfit food for only twenty-five to thirty men.

In short, the Indians hadn't fibbed or exaggerated about a thing. It appeared that everything Felty had surmised had been right on the money. Pickle had noticed that having top-grade Indians work for three dollars an hour was a great way to save money. If the workers had not become aware of their rights, gotten mad enough to run away and make trouble, there's little reason to suspect Pickle would have had any problem employing them—or replacement "trainees"—for as long as he could have.

But was it slavery?

Toward the end of the trial, the plaintiffs' lawyers called as an expert witness one of the nation's leading authorities on contemporary slavery, Dr. Kevin Bales, president of the Washington, D.C.–based human-rights group Free the Slaves. Bales had agreed to testify for free because he thought the Pickle case was so important. In his opinion, what had happened at JPC was indeed a form of slavery. The Victims of Trafficking and Violence Protection Act of 2000 enumerates several forms of trafficking, including, he said, "the recruitment, harboring, transportation, provision, or obtaining of a person for labor or services, through the use of force, fraud, or coercion for the purpose of subjection to involuntary servitude, peonage, debt bondage, or slavery." What was so tricky to understand? The men had been forced to work in a situation they had not freely consented to and had been made to feel unfree to leave. This was against the law. It did not matter what life is like in India. It mattered what we understand in the United States to be normal ethics and workplace conditions.

What had happened at JPC, Bales felt, was a matter of subtle coercion. He cited several types of coercion that seem to repeat themselves in cases of modern slavery, namely, threats of force or future harm. The type Pickle had employed, Bales said, was "use or abuse of the legal process." Every time Pickle or his officers issued threats like " 'If you misbehave, or if you don't do what we say, we're going to get the police after you,' or 'We're going to send you back,' or 'We're going to have you deported,' " Bales testified—"those are all coercion."

The sum total of JPC's actions—the constant threats of deportation, the confiscation of the men's passports, immigration permits, and plane tickets, the tapping of their phone and monitoring of their e-mail—was, in Bales's estimation, a crude, ham-handed attempt at "classic coercive control." On the stand, as he ran through the list of JPC's actions, he even laughed a little. In his ten or so years of experience with slavery cases, he'd never seen anyone leave a paper trail as long or as oblivious as JPC's. Pickle, he told me later by e-mail, using an English expression, "seemed like a man who was too clever by half."

Somewhat echoing Kent Felty, Bales imagined that Pickle had probably just wanted to "pull a fast one on immigration and get some cheap welders." Unfortunately for Pickle, however, "I really think he had no idea what he was playing at. This was just a little scam on the INS, like plenty of others all around, that are never investigated, and if they are, rarely punished. Think of the millions of 'illegal' aliens working for U.S. employers who know full well what they are doing."

For Robert Canino, Felty's co-counsel with the EEOC, wherever the case fell on what Felty had called "the sliding scale" of slavery, the legal nexus of the case was about the relationship between race, discrimination, and freedom. In the eyes of many, he agreed, the whole affair might seem like meddlesome bureaucratic twaddle, political correctness at its worst. He was certainly aware of how and why many people viewed the federal government as far too intrusive, an agent of oppression rather than a guarantor of freedom. But what people didn't usually understand, he said, was the relationship between racism and freedom. Not only is it an injustice when people are discriminated against and treated unfairly, but in the very act or moment in which they are constrained, they become a disruptive, radical force. In a free market and an otherwise free world, they suddenly became agents of unfreedom. It wasn't just a matter of saying one ethnic group or another smells bad or behaves in a funny way. Instead, it's that if any one group of people is allowed to exploit any other group of people, the exploiters soon expect they have the right to exploit *all* groups of people. Everyone suffers. The idea, Canino explained, is antithetical to the concept of democracy and the free market.

If employers go unpunished for discriminating against foreigners, there remains no incentive to motivate them to continue hiring Americans. Why would anyone pay minimum wage if it were legal for them to pay half that? In Canino's opinion, people will probably be racist until the end of time. That wasn't his problem. His job was simply to come up with mechanisms to financially "disincentivize" racism in the workplace. I had never thought of it this way. Suddenly, meddlesome bureaucrats like the guys who work for places like the EEOC began to seem like freedom fighters.

In Canino's opinion, JPC and its lawyers weren't putting up such a

lame defense because they were inept. They had probably just decided
not to waste money on the trial. Pickle, Canino guessed, would try to
make himself "judgment-proof" by selling the company and hiding
whatever assets the government might try to seize. Canino called it the
"empty bag" strategy. It was typical.

However, Canino said, the defense had left him in an advantageous
position. It allowed the EEOC not only to win its case but to do so in a
way that could be used as a model for future, similar cases of immigrant
abuse. Previous to the Pickle case, victims of slavery had one remedy: to
mount a criminal slavery case, like the case against El Diablo. But as I'd
learned from the prosecutors discussing the Florida case, criminal cases
are incredibly complicated and expensive. Few slavery cases end up
being solid enough to be prosecuted. Civil means of redress were far
cheaper and easier because the legal standards for such cases were far
simpler. Lawyers such as Felty could be hired on a contingency basis and
offered a chance to profit by nailing guys like Pickle, opening up the way
for a truly free-market battleground between workers and employers.
Again, Canino used the term "financial disincentive." If it became easier
for workers to fight against discrimination, it became more expensive
for employers to discriminate.

After phase one of the trial, Canino, like the McGowans, prepared a
brief for the judge called a Proposed Finding of Fact. The document offers both plaintiff and defendant an opportunity to link their evidence to
case law throughout history to support their argument. Canino told me
later he'd had a hard time preparing his brief. The long, dry, technical
legal arguments about training and coercion had left everyone forgetful
about the cruelty at the heart of the case. It was impossible for Americans to understand the terror, the absolute panic, that his clients had felt
in Pickle's employ. To keep fresh the memory of what his clients had experienced, Canino collected a sampling of phrases and statements from
their testimony.

> That's a day I cannot forget in my life. In this country, when all the
> people celebrate and enjoy during a holiday season, I was being
> locked inside a company and it felt like a prison without no freedom.

scared to go out; didn't know what to expect . . .

exactly like a prison experience . . .

like a criminal . . .

I was afraid . . .

something bad is going to happen . . .

they got angry . . .

very disturbed and distressed . . .

emotionally very upset . . .

too much tension and stress . . .

terrified . . .

Why are they treating me like this and putting so much pressure and fear in me?

no freedom to talk . . .

nobody shook my hand . . .

humiliated . . .

they were getting into my private things . . .

we are unable to tell anyone . . .

Is this my fate?

what has happened to us that, we have to live at the mercy of others . . .

While I was changing my clothes . . . they were just standing there watching me . . .

I never had people watching me taking a shower . . .

lost my dignity coming here . . .

I didn't think that this is how people are treated in America.

On May 25, 2006, Judge Claire Eegan of the Federal Court for the Northern District of Oklahoma ruled on the JPC case. She ruled for the plaintiffs, agreeing with them on every legal claim asserted. The defendants had made misrepresentations to the Indians as to their pay, food, insurance, and duration of the job. The "training program" was clearly fraudulent, a naked attempt by JPC "to expand their labor force in a manner that violated U.S. law and took unfair advantage of the workers they recruited." The court also found that the "trainee program" had resulted in the permanent displacement of thirty American workers. The

John Pickle Company was also guilty of visa fraud, violating the Fair Labor Standards Act, and false imprisonment. In total, for missed wages and punitive damages, JPC was assessed $1.3 million.

Later that year, for his work on the case, the American Bar Association would award Robert Canino a prize for being the Federal Labor and Employment Attorney of the Year.

During the time I watched the Tulsa case unfold, stories about chicanery and abuse of immigrant laborers seemed to spawn with numbing frequency. There would be the scandal at Tyson, one of the nation's largest meat processors, caught encouraging illegal aliens from Mexico to procure false work papers and join their production lines in Tennessee. Twelve Mexican migrants would be found locked and baked to death in a boxcar in an Iowa freight yard, their bodies having rotted for four months. In Maine, an ill-equipped van driven by an unlicensed, uninsured chauffeur would fall off a bumpy logging road, killing fourteen temporary workers from Guatemala employed by the companies who supply the companies who supply the paper industry. Most dramatic would be the seventy-four passengers—illegal aliens from Mexico—crammed into a semitrailer and abandoned by their driver in the hot sun of Victoria, Texas. Nineteen died of asphyxiation. None had been slaves, but none of them had been treated like American citizens.

It is hard to assess whether the abuse of foreign workers today is worse than abuse of workers in the past. It's important to remember that Chinese, Filipinos, Italians, Jews, Irish, even Germans, during the colonial days, were all discriminated against and mistreated upon arrival in the United States. It wasn't fair, but it was apparently the price of entry into a new country.

And yet, it seemed as if a whole new, systematic form of labor abuse was arising. Companies that could exploit workers abroad, in their own countries, were beginning to try everything they could to enjoy the same labor practices in the United States.

In December 2006, the EEOC would resolve a case against a San Francisco company called Trans Bay Steel accused of treating forty-eight Thai workers in much the same way Pickle had treated the Indian men. The company had won a contract to work on the Bay Bridge and decided foreign workers would somehow be preferable to Americans. The Thais—welders, like the Indians in Tulsa—had been brought to the United States under H-2B temporary-worker visas by Trans Bay and a third-party agency, which had charged them a high fee for the privilege of a job in America. Upon arrival in San Francisco, the men were held against their will, had their passports confiscated and their movements restricted, and were forced to work without pay. At least some of them were confined to cramped apartments without any electricity, water, or gas. To keep the men in line, the company told them that if they tried to leave the location where they were being forcibly held, police and immigration officials would be called to arrest them.

Another civil case, filed by a group called the Immigrant Justice Project, a branch of the Southern Poverty Law Center, alleged continuing massive exploitation of workers from Mexico, Guatemala, and Honduras, imported legally with temporary visas to plant trees, thin forests, and apply herbicides for timber contractors operating in national forests and on huge commercial tracts in the South.

The workers who perform this labor are little more than indentured servants. They pay large fees in their home countries to come to the United States. They routinely log sixty or more hours each week but earn substantially less than the minimum wage of $5.15 per hour. Some employers seize their workers' passports upon arrival, and many require workers to leave the deeds to their homes with recruiters in their home countries. Workers labor long hours, often six or seven days per week. It is physically arduous work, and the conditions are grueling. As one man said of working in a national forest on publicly owned land, "We were forced to camp in the mountains as temperatures approached freezing. There were no sleeping pads, mattresses, or sleeping bags. The only drinking water came from the creek." Another worker said that on many days, he was paid twenty-five dollars for twelve hours of work. At the end of a season of twelve- and thirteen-hour workdays, he'd saved all of five hundred dollars to send home to his family.

According to IJP director Mary Bauer, the nominal employers of the men are usually small-time labor contractors, but at the end of the money trail are typically large corporations such as International Paper, Weyerhaeuser, and Plum Creek. "Also huge," she told me, "are investment groups called TIMOs (timber investment management organizations) that invest in the land as a long-term investment. Some of the large TIMOs are such things as John Hancock financial and Harvard University. If you Google 'TIMO,' lots of interesting stuff comes up."

Her group has also filed a class-action suit on behalf of migrant farmworkers who were underpaid while working in South Georgia for subsidiaries of Del Monte. The setup, she said, was the same old same old. Penniless labor contractors, underpaid workers, high recruiting fees, deductions from paychecks—the whole nine yards. Del Monte is a Fortune 600 corporation.

During the long wait for the trial of the John Pickle Company, JPC's former "trainees" had fanned out across the country to Florida, North Carolina, Indiana, Michigan, and elsewhere, looking for jobs. As they made their way through the currents where Indian immigrants merge with the American economy, they quickly encountered additional pockets of abuse. Naturally, they relayed their reports back to Massey. And increasingly, Massey made it his business to do something about them.

Since he had met the Indian men and helped them "run away" from JPC, Mark Massey's life had undergone a series of changes. He lost his job. He surrendered one of his two houses to the bank. He saw another, a farmhouse he'd just restored, burn to the ground. Bottles had been thrown at his house in the night. He'd borrowed money from his mother that he couldn't repay. And his marriage, as one could probably surmise, was "stressed."

Most recently, he had learned of an alleged scheme involving dozens of Indian welders who were recruited to become steelworkers in Louisiana by a labor contractor named Chad Chandler, owner of a firm called Falcon Steel Structures. According to a lawsuit later filed in the U.S. District Court of Eastern Louisiana alleging racketeering, breach of contract, and fraud charges, Chandler had lured the workers to the United

States with promises of well-paying shipyard jobs in return for a recruiting fee of $7,000 to $20,000 per worker. Upon their arrival in Louisiana, Chandler allegedly deposited the men in low-cost hotels in poor conditions with little food. The men waited weeks before realizing that Falcon had no jobs for them. (Chandler denies the allegations and specifically denies that Falcon Steel received any recruiting fees.)

Massey drove to Houma and Morgan City in the spring of 2003, assisting the most recent group of Chandler's alleged victims (there had been several). Working with a local social worker and two volunteers from Catholic Charities, he helped to fill out visa-extension forms, find better housing options, and cajole donations of food from local charities. He enlisted Kent Felty's help to file the lawsuit and try to recoup the men's money. And he'd taken it upon himself to chauffeur the men wherever they needed to go; in just one year, he put more than a hundred thousand miles on his Dodge van.

According to Massey, on April 3, 2003, he'd received a phone call from a group of Indian men bunked at the Pines Motel in Houma. They'd been contacted by a newspaper reporter named Michelle Millhollon from the Baton Rouge *Advocate*. Millhollon had gotten increasingly curious about Chandler's operation. Chandler had told her that he couldn't find jobs for the workers because "the economy's been crap since September 11." He also said that the war in Iraq was a factor. Millhollon didn't seem satisfied. Worried that Chandler might attempt to deport the entire group, Massey volunteered to help relocate the men.

Massey arrived late at night and worked past dawn, rounding up the group of fifty men and sneaking them and their belongings, by van and taxi, out of the Pines Motel and into the DeLux Motel, some twenty-seven miles down the road, where he hoped Chandler wouldn't find them. Unfortunately, according to Massey, someone tipped off Chandler. At 7:30 in the morning, Chandler arrived in a Chevy Suburban to confront Massey.

Massey had never met Chandler face-to-face, but he knew enough about him to be wary. He had received several phone calls from Chandler telling him to mind his own business. And more significant, he had met Chandler's associate DeWayne, described by Massey as Chandler's bodyguard, "a muscle guy that you don't want to get in a dark alley with."

When Chandler arrived, Massey recalled, he angrily accused Massey of "absconding" with his men. Next, Chandler called DeWayne on his cell phone and began to give directions to the motel. Massey knew better than to risk delay. "I was not planning on waiting for DeWayne to come and block me in." So he bolted.

He and seven Indians piled into the van, and with Chandler in hot pursuit, they took off down Route 48. Massey was near panic, but he kept a cool head. All he had to do was get to a police station. Unfortunately, he had a small problem: he didn't know where one was. As Massey swerved in and out of traffic, turning onto Airline Highway, looking for a policeman, his cell phone rang. It was his wife, Dawna, calling to say hi. Massey tried to keep cool for her, but when she gathered what was happening, she became upset.

"She's a very emotional person," he said later. "From anger to whichever way—she responds to her emotions. So I let her know she called kind of at a bad time. I maybe even cut the phone call a little short. I just said, 'Chad's chasing us and we're trying to get away. Let's, maybe, you know, talk a little later.' "

Finally, Massey spotted a motorcycle cop by the side of the road and pulled over. He got out and explained to the officer that he was being followed. Chandler was by now nowhere in sight. The cop looked around him in vain for the alleged pursuer. When Massey insisted he was being menaced, the cop told him to follow along to the police station.

At the station, Massey launched into his epic, sprawling tale of recruiting fees and interest rates and Tulsa and dispossessed Indian families. The policemen seemed puzzled. "They had a very prejudiced attitude," Massey said. "They did not seem too favorable of me." They asked him why he had gotten so involved with a bunch of foreigners. What business was it of his what a Louisiana resident was doing? Was he crazy? Why didn't he just go back to Tulsa if he didn't like it here in

Louisiana? It wasn't the response Massey had expected at all. Finally, Massey said, the police decided to call Chandler and see if he could make sense of the whole mess.

Chandler arrived—with DeWayne—armed with a far simpler version of events: Massey, he charged, had assaulted *him*. Massey, he said, had "floorboarded" the accelerator of his van and tried to run Chandler down while stealing his men and trying to place them in jobs so *he* could collect the recruiting fees. Chandler had proof, he said. Was it okay with the police if he showed it? They agreed. Chandler loosened his belt. One of the cops joked, "Uh, Chad, you're not gonna get naked, are you?" Chandler continued sliding his pants off his rear end. Then, in the middle of the police station, he bent over and, with great fanfare, displayed a welt on the side of his butt. (Massey described it later as "a round indenture" with "no bruising or abnormal color.") This grievous injury, he said, was caused by Mark Massey, interloper, liar, and non-Louisianan.

Massey tried to get the cops to take testimony from the Indians, but by now, the cops were sick of him. They told him to shut up. One of the officers, Massey remembers, "told me that by the time they were through with me, I'd never come back to Louisiana again."

On April 4, Massey found himself spending the night in a twelve-by-twelve-foot cell in Baton Rouge's Saint Mary Parish Prison. He had been fingerprinted, handcuffed, and issued an orange jumpsuit, like any other criminal. He tried to pass the time making small talk with his fellow inmates. Most of them, he said, seemed like "pretty nice guys." But while they had been brought in on minor charges—mostly drug-related—Massey had been charged with a far graver offense: aggravated battery, a crime worth ten years. It was hard not to be consumed by worry.

Recalling his dark mood in the jail cell, Massey said that the fact that Dawna and the kids had no way of knowing that he was there, in jail, weighed as heavily upon him as the fact of his being there. "My mind was really going crazy. I'd been told it's like the Mafia down there. And I really felt like maybe I stepped into something far bigger than I could handle.

"I was starting to visualize being without my family and what it'd be like to have your kids get asked 'Where's your dad at?' while you're in prison. You know, you're sitting there thinking of everything you should have done and what you shouldn't have done and what you're gonna do—if you get out. So partly, I guess, in my mind, I'm thinking, 'If I ever get out of here, I'm gonna go back to Tulsa, work my job, and not do another thing.' "

As his regrets circled around, however, Massey's convictions redoubled. Ever since he'd first seen the frightened group of Indian men back at Hale Church and found them being abused, he had felt it was his calling to help them. "To me," he said, "this is Christianity. You know? Christianity is more than words and it's more than going to church and, you know, smile and shake hands and say, 'Hey, attend my church!' If I don't inconvenience my life for somebody else—then what's it worth?" Sure, Massey said, he would love to lead a steadier life and earn more money. He liked the fine things in life as much as anyone else. But not if it meant turning a blind eye to injustice. As he told me, "You've only got one life on this planet. Do you really want to spend it as a whore for whoever's paying? I can't do that. I don't see it."

After thirteen thousand dollars in legal fees and two years of worrying, Massey finally saw his criminal case in Louisiana dismissed. His family, he said, is "pretty well bankrupt." On the positive side, however, his eldest daughter was married, in September 2005, before a crowd of Oklahomans and Indians. He recently visited India with some of the Indian workers he met in Tulsa, and he is currently working with a group of Indian men in Mississippi, doing post–Hurricane Katrina reconstruction. His marriage, he told me with a nervous laugh, was still intact, despite the "different things in my life that I have done, you know, that has brought a little bit of problems in my family and in my life." As for Dawna, he said somewhat shyly, "she's beared through it. Maybe a lot of women wouldn't have put up with me this long. I don't know."

Said Massey of the Indians he helped, the ones he's helping, and the ones he'll no doubt try to help after them, "You know, as long as we can make it, I'll keep helping the guys." He looked down at his belly, which could perhaps benefit from a lap or two around the track, and laughed. "We're not going without."

At the time of this writing, John Pickle is retired. JPME, he says, was taken from him by the Kharafi family. He owns none of it. Even before the trial had begun, he sold JPC to a son-in-law, who changed the name to Port City Plate, then, just recently, sold it to a large conglomerate, which will soon go public. There is no further legal link between the company and John Pickle.

To this day he is adamant about his innocence, and never once in our conversations did it appear to enter his thoughts that I might be critical of his behavior. Of the conniving Indians and the stupid press, he said, "They broke my ass. I had a company worth about five million, and I'm worth zero. I got rid of everything in the company, paid all my debts off. I got zero money. Stocks, bonds—nothin'. I'm down to zero now. I get Social Security, and you know, that's about it. So if I sound a little bit vindictive, I prob'ly am."

I asked him if Canino was right, that he'd merely hidden his assets from the government, and he laughed. The government had declared him personally liable for what had gone on at his company. However, he said, speaking very carefully, "you can move money around. Just leave it at that. I don't even own the pickup truck I drive. My wife lives in a nice home. And I live with her. Let's put it that way." He laughed again.

When I asked him if he thought of himself as a racist, he said, "I was the most open guy. I'll lay it out to you: queers and dykes and fags and people still in the penitentiary and blacks and greens—all of 'em worked for me over the years. And they get paid to do a day's work, and that's my only criteria—period—about it. Only thing I had was about girl welders kissin' each other on lunch period on company time." He laughed heartily. "I said, 'I don't wanna see that shit here again.' If that's illegal, that's tough shit on my part."

Sounding a lot like Pérez, El Diablo's lawyer back in Florida, he said that the trial was an attempt by the government to find a scapegoat. He mentioned the 2000 anti-trafficking bill and said, "I'm the test case for the U.S. guvmint. They pumped millions in there against me. Prob'ly spent two million. That'd be a real conservative number." What he was saying didn't even make sense. The government hadn't charged him criminally under the statute he mentioned. Technically, they hadn't even charged him with slavery. Later he changed the two million to five million. Sometime after that, I asked Canino how much the government had spent on the case. He wrote back, "We spent $34,000 on the case, plus 4–5 months of my cumulative time over the course of almost four years, plus about two months of work by a Paralegal. The EEOC's entire budget to litigate around 400 cases filed per year nationwide is $3.2 million."

Pickle asked me if I'd figured it out yet, that he was being made an example. I told him that I really didn't know what to think of the slavery thing, but that I found it rather troubling to think of an employer taking his workers' passports and hiring an armed guard to watch their movements.

Undaunted, he defended himself. "I knew it was pickin' up steam and they was leavin'! In and out, in and out. The guard's duty was to see who was come to pickin' 'em up. The gate at the other end of the shop was not locked. They could leave anytime they wanted to. Now, Americans, we can carry a gun anytime you want to. You know that's the law here. And this guy is a ex-cop. Can carry a pistol anytime he wants to. That's nothin'. So the guys went out there and they saw him there and they started chattin' with him. He was the shippin'-and-receiving guy. He was there to find out who was helpin' them Indians leave my shop. But scare them? He didn't scare any of 'em."

Pickle reverted to default mode and began to rail. "Who gon' put up with this shit from the U.S. guvmint hagglin' you? You know, I'm the best—I'm a guy that flies the flag, U.S.A. all the way. But Jesus Christ, man. We're fixin' to go on a downslide. And anybody says different, they're lyin'. Y'know why? It takes one thing to make a country—it's called 'value-added.' You know how you make value-added? You grow corn, and you have new corn. You build stuff, you have new vessels. You have new cars. 'Bout ten, six, eight years ago, we had forty percent of the people in the United States was manufacturing value-added. The last three years, you know where it's gone to? Ten percent! How in the hell is the country gonna stay together, everybody's settin' on their ass cookin' hamburgers, being lawyers, fuckin' with everybody? You tell me how it's gon' stay together! Son, you on the downward slide, and it's gon' stay downward for anything.

"See, I'm not educated," he said. "I'm just a plain old country boy, see. But it's all leavin' the country. Now, we could stop it by having an equal-trade agreement, dollar for dollar. Like China—they don't buy nothin' from us. They go to Korea, Germany, France, or somewhere else. They're buyin' their stuff over there and they're not buyin' nothin' from here. And the trade deficit's growin' bigger'n bigger'n bigger'n bigger. You know we're borrowin' two billion dollars a day to prop up the American guvmint? Two billion dollars a day! How the hell we gonna keep doin' this? That is a problem that is gonna break the country. You hear that suckin' sound, all the jobs leavin' the country, gon' right down to the Third World country?

"Now, it's a very simple thing—see, I'm too simple. I'm a simple-minded guy. You know, I'm just one o' them 'mericans fuckin' around that don't make any difference. I'm just a, I ain't even a fly-shit speck on the roof, compared to what the problems the United States got. But we have a problem. All our money's leavin', and nobody's got the guts to do anythin' about it. Now that, you talkin' 'bout a book, now you got a problem there, that's what you need to write a book about."

I mention that he's the one who tried farming his jobs out of the country. Didn't that make him part of the problem and not the solution? "Well," he paused, stymied by a beat of what seemed like genuine frustration, "but I can't—I don't have the abilities to cure any of it."

# Ants

When I first started writing about slavery, a number of people asked me with great concern why I thought big-time employers, wealthy corporations made rich from modern American agriculture, would bother to exploit and enslave illegal immigrant workers when these workers' labor could already be had legally for a pittance. Why would anyone resort to such extreme and illegal measures for the sake of a few pennies? I didn't know the answer. What I came to believe, however, was that slavery and labor abuse in general have far less to do with economics than with emotions.

This is not, I imagine, an orthodox or obvious statement. It is certainly a counterintuitive one. After all, everyone knows that money makes the world go around. Adam Smith's "invisible hand" of capitalism *relies* on self-interest in order to work. I would argue that this is a skewed approach, biased and framed by the relatively enlightened age in which we live. What motivates human behavior more than simple greed or the desire for mere money is the desire for power—that is, power over other human beings.

Scholars have calculated that in antebellum America, under good circumstances, the rate of return on investment for the owners of male and female slaves between the years 1820 and 1860 averaged about 10 percent. To this day, white American families have, on average, seven times the family wealth of black American families. In a different setting, through the massive exploition of slave labor during World War II, both in and out of concentration camps, the Nazi industrialists Gustav and Alfried Krupp managed to accumulate a fortune worth $500 million. It is clear that under the right conditions, slavery can be exceedingly profitable.

But slavery has surprisingly often been a money-*losing* enterprise. While at first glance it would seem intuitive that free labor is an unadulterated boon for an employer, it's just not the way slavery has usually worked. Many slave owners in the American South, particularly smaller-scale farmers, went bust during years of bad weather or low crop prices. The drag of having to feed, clothe, and house slaves during lean times became too much for them. This problem—of what economists would call fixed costs—was only one of several structural shortcomings intrinsic to any economic system reliant upon slave labor. Another, of course, was that slaves tended to be reluctant workers. As Adam Smith wrote in *The Wealth of Nations,* "The work done by slaves, though it appears to cost only their maintenance, is in the end the dearest of any. A person who can acquire no property can have no other interest but to eat as much and to labour as little as possible."

But the problem—call it "bad attitude syndrome"—extended beyond slave labor itself, tainting every aspect of life in slave-based societies. When Frederick Law Olmsted spent three months in antebellum Dixie, writing for *The New York Times* about slavery and the Southern economy, he discovered that the mere presence of slave labor had a depressing effect upon labor productivity in general. Free white workers, competing with slave labor, were offered preposterously low wages, and in such an environment the very idea of work was degraded—something not worth doing, fit only for slaves. As a result, Olmsted found, white laborers were "driven to indolence, carelessness, indifference, decadence." The overall atmosphere of inefficiency and carelessness begat by a demoralized workforce led to a larger malaise and a general wasting of resources—broken tools, neglected livestock, and haphazard managerial skills.

Slavery wreaked havoc upon the possessors as well as the slaves. In the eyes of many, slavery was despicable not merely for being unjust and corrupt but for being inefficient, creating, as it did, an effete and useless owning class. As Benjamin Franklin noted in his *Observations Concerning the Increase of Mankind, Peopling of Countries, etc.,* the importation of "Negroes" to the Caribbean had "greatly diminish'd the Whites." "The Whites who have Slaves, not labouring, are enfeebled, and therefore not so generally prolific." Worst of all, he wrote, "the White Children become proud, disgusted with Labour, and being educated in Idleness, are rendered unfit to get a Living by Industry."

On a larger scale, the example of Portugal is often used to show how the easy profits derived from forced labor can stunt what we in the modern age like to call the entrepreneurial spirit, sapping an entire economy's impetus to seek "real," sustained economic development. After four hundred years of easy money from slave labor in Africa, Europe, Brazil, and the Cape Verde Islands, Portugal, formerly the dominant power in Europe, was in ruins, consigned to runt status among its peers.

Ultimately, the question of whether slavery "works," "makes sense," or is profitable indicates a profound failure to understand its essence. What, after all, is profit but a means to power? Any survey of different forms of slavery makes stunningly clear that prior to the modern age, slavery had absolutely nothing to do with profit. To focus on the rather modern, technical notion of profit and ignore the darker, cruder nature and allure of power is, in fact, almost quaintly naïve.

Slaves have throughout history been used as units of value, symbols of power and status. Some cultures used slaves as money itself, a way to pay back loans and make dowry payments. Slaves were also useful for religious ceremonies requiring a sacrificial victim. In China, Japan, Europe, and the Near East, slaves were often buried with their masters, en masse and sometimes alive, as good-luck charms for recently demised rulers. Other societies ate the flesh of slaves as meat—as both foodstuff and fodder for cannibalistic rituals. In other words, slaves were not used as a means to power but rather as ruthless expressions of it.

The creativity and variety of torture methods helps articulate how fully and even poetically the institution has been used not to turn a profit but to vent the violence apparently innate to the human psyche. Branding on the body or the face; genital mutilation; starvation; burning of feet; burning to death; roasting to death; the use of manacles, iron collars, slave forks; confinement in jail; confinement in tobacco sheds; confinement in "nigger boxes" (miniature prison cells with deliberately few air holes and very little room to move); time on the rack or on the cross; death by hanging; beheading—such are some of the more colorful techniques used throughout history to "manage" slaves. In Panama, escaped or rebellious slaves were fitted with iron collars and thrown to hungry dogs. In Mexico, they were tortured and beheaded. In Costa Rica, they were boiled to death. In Uruguay, they were dragged through the street and quartered.

The Greeks and Romans had three different types of whips with which to flog their slaves: the *scutica,* a whip with thongs of parchment, the *ferula,* a simple leather strap, and the *flagellum,* made of ox-hide straps weighted with lead. In Rome, innovators devised an instrument called the "brazen bull," a life-sized metal statue of a bull in which miscreants could be locked for misbehavior. A fire was built below the bull's belly, and with careful placement of musical pipes within the bull's head, the victim's screams of pain would be transformed into "music."

As Harvard scholar Orlando Patterson wrote in *Slavery and Social Death:*

Nothing in the annals of slavery, however, can match the Indians of the U.S. northwest coast for the number of excuses a master had for killing his slaves and the sheer sadism with which he destroyed them. Among the Aleut slaves were killed simply to placate the grief of their masters when a son or nephew had died accidentally. At such times, "they drowned them in water, threw them off a cliff in the sight of their parents, in whose despair and bereavement they hoped to find their consolation." Alternatively, slaves were killed to celebrate some special event such as a son's becoming a shaman. In almost all these tribes slaves were killed upon the death of their owners, especially when the latter were important persons: among the Tlingit, the selected slaves were bound hand and foot and thrown alive on the funeral pyre. When a new house was to be built, they were killed and buried beneath the posts; at ceremonies of initiation, especially into the cannibal society of the Kwakiutl (according to Franz Boas), the body was torn into little pieces and eaten by the initiates. But it was during the potlatch ceremony culminating in the ritualized exchange and destruction of property that the murder of slaves became a veritable carnage, in which "rival leaders attempted to surpass one another in the number of slaves killed."

Even today, the creativity of torture methods visited upon slaves boggles the mind. According to a Human Rights Watch report, the Beydanes, the ruling class of Mauritania, occasionally impose order on the Haratines, or slave class, by administering "the camel treatment," in which a miscreant slave's legs are tightly tied to the sides of a camel who has been denied water for weeks. The animal is then led to water and allowed to drink. As its stomach expands, the slave's legs, thighs, and groin are stretched apart and slowly dislocated. The slave is usually crippled and unable to perform further tasks.

Surely, such imaginative efforts go beyond the simple notion of making a tidy return on investment.

Most modern readers, to our credit, probably have a hard time "relating" to such barbaric activity. But in our world of cell phones, air-conditioned malls, satellite TV, and Nintendo, it is easy to forget that we, as a species, have spent a far greater proportion of our existence flogging and killing than sending one another text messages with smiley faces.

Upton Sinclair once noted, "It is difficult to get a man to understand something when his salary depends upon his not understanding it." But if you go back through history, it's easy to replace the word *salary* with the words *class, privilege,* and *position.* This is the way it's always been. If I don't know or believe I'm hurting you, I am not hurting you. If I somehow believe you're not as human as I am, it's not a big deal if I hurt you. If I believe that you have done something to hurt me, it is justice when I

kill you. If your class or race or tribe is inferior to mine, it is simply correct and just that I eat three meals a day and you eat one.

In the story about John Pickle, what was most interesting to me was
how he and many people around him managed to not see that what they
were doing was a problem. Pickle and his managers couldn't have hired,
housed, paid, or talked to American citizens as they had the Indians.
And if someone had told them about some white Americans who'd been
treated the way the Indians had been treated, they would have been
shocked. It didn't matter that American law says in very plain terms
how *any* workers on American soil are to be treated. When Pickle was
concocting his scheme, his eye merely fell upon the convenient fact that
India is a poorer country than the United States. And suddenly, Pickle
and his helpers were somehow able to fool themselves into thinking that
what they were doing was not a naked lunge for profit—profit being the
primary American, First World brand of and means to power over other
people. Instead, they convinced themselves that their moneymaking
scheme was an effort to "help" the Indians. *Voilà:* from abusers to good
guys, with a 70 percent cut in labor costs. Talk about value-added!

During the time I was musing about the extent to which Pickle's attitudes toward Indian men were analogous to those of a slaveholder
toward his slaves, I stumbled upon an interesting fact: the only other
species besides human beings that enslaves its own kind is ants. There
are subspecies of such ants around the world, but they tend to follow a
basic pattern. They have big, clawlike mandibles. And what they do is
raid neighboring ant colonies and use these big, clawlike mandibles to
chop off the heads of their neighbors. After driving off the soldier ants,
which defend the nest, the invaders enter it and eat as many eggs and
pupae as they can. The rest are scooped up and carried back to the home
nest. The stolen hatchlings are then deposited and dosed with a chemical that causes them to grow up thinking they are the same species as
their masters. The slaves grow up to perform all the colony's labor, including gathering food, cleaning house, nursing other larvae, and even
going to war against their own species on behalf of their masters.

Just this much comprises a fascinating, almost sci-fi scenario to contemplate, but what I found most interesting was the effect of the

arrangement upon the slaveholder ants. Charles Darwin, in *The Origin of Species,* described the findings of a scientist named Pierre Huber, who studied them:

> This ant is absolutely dependent on its slaves; without their aid, the species would certainly become extinct in a single year. . . . They are incapable of making their own nests, or of feeding their own larvae. When the old nest is found inconvenient, and they have to migrate, it is the slaves which determine the migration, and actually carry their masters in their jaws. So utterly helpless are the masters, that when Huber shut up thirty of them without a slave, but with plenty of the food which they like best . . . they did nothing; they could not even feed themselves, and many perished of hunger.

Reading this was the first time I'd truly apprehended the profoundly negative effect of slavery upon its beneficiaries. I tried for a long time to get it straight: Human beings have spent eons trying to enslave one another. We have spent much of our energy, most of our history, trying to subjugate one another. And in the end, we do all this so we can be crippled and useless?

It was only when I went to the island of Saipan, in the Pacific Ocean, that I learned why human beings would ever do such a dumb thing.

# SAIPAN

I f a person—say, someone beginning a book on slavery back in 2003—were to search around on Google and LexisNexis using terms like "slavery," "forced labor," "contemporary," and "America," an alarming number of results would come tumbling out about a mysterious place called Saipan. A U.S. commonwealth that few Americans have ever heard of, Saipan is an island in the Pacific Ocean. At forty-seven square miles, it's tiny. Yet somehow it has managed to generate an inordinate number of slavery cases.

Numerous reports of labor abuse and forced labor there surfaced throughout the 1990s. In 2000, a Korean family named Kwon pled guilty to forcing nine women, some of them minors from the Philippines and China, into prostitution. Mr. Kwon Soon Oh, aided by his wife and son, had apparently lured the women to the island to staff K's Hideaway Karaoke Club. To keep them in line, he threatened to harm their families.

In 2001, a small garment factory was found holding workers against their will and forcing them to work without pay. Later that year, a Chinese national named Zheng Min Yan would be charged with forcing three women to work for her as prostitutes. In September 2005, a female pimp, or *mama-san,* named Luo Xiuhong (aka "Sunshine") was arrested with a Saipanese man for recruiting two young women from the Philippines, promising them waitressing and massage jobs, then forcing them into prostitution. In June 2006, two sister strip clubs, the Starlite and the Stardust, were raided by local authorities. A local man named David M. Atalig and his Filipina wife were charged with luring dancers from the Philippines, some as young as sixteen, then locking them in their barracks during off-hours and illegally withholding at least some of their pay.

Like John Pickle in Tulsa, the Ataligs had a keen, if preposterous, sense of legality. Asking their hires to sign a "personal waiver," thinking it would somehow make things more legal, the Ataligs, while recruiting in the Philippines, videotaped the proceedings. The waivers stated that the dancers would remain in their barracks while not working, and that if they wanted to leave their barracks, they would have to pay $175 for the privilege.

Most of these cases fall closer to what I earlier called "sex slavery" than to what I would call "labor slavery." But nevertheless, I felt curious about an environment that created such ripe conditions for slavery. If Laura Germino of the Coalition of Immokalee Workers was correct that every slavery case represents a horrible labor environment, with possibly or probably hundreds or even thousands of poorly treated workers, what kind of conditions must exist on Saipan for workers in general?

According to the Equal Employment Opportunity Commission's Honolulu office, charges of labor abuse generated on Saipan represent some 30 percent of all complaints in the entire Pacific region. During the first ten months of 2005 alone, the island generated 701 complaints to the EEOC and other labor agencies. Most had to do with nonpayment of wages, breach of contract, wrongful termination, national-origin discrimination, nonpayment of overtime, and illegal deductions from paychecks. In a newspaper article, William Tamayo, the regional attorney for the EEOC's San Francisco district, would describe Saipan's high level of discrimination as "blatant and clearly intentional." It sounded like my kind of place. God knows I'd had a hard time getting anybody to admit that when they locked people up and didn't pay them, they were, in fact, slave owners. Maybe Saipan would be different.


After the Japanese defeat in World War II, the United States found itself the proud "administrator" of what was then called the Trust Territory of the Pacific Islands. Alternately known as Micronesia, the area consists of some two thousand islands with a combined landmass half the size of Rhode Island spread over three million square miles of ocean. Sprinkled across the territory were some 120,000 souls, deposited by the winds to such isolated chains and atolls as Yap, Palau, the Carolines, Majuro, Kapingamarangi, and the Marshalls.

Pacific islands hold an understandable allure for city dwellers dreaming of balmy, uncrowded paradise. But the images of sun, sand, slide harps, and crystal waters usually belie a Third World backwardness and low-intensity squalor common, almost by default, to such places.

Historically, Micronesians have gotten by on subsistence farming and fishing. Some islands have enjoyed sporadic booms in trade for sea slugs and copra (dried coconut meat) as foodstuffs, or seashells—trochus, for example—for making buttons. But for most of the region, trade and economic development were concepts historically as remote as snow. Despite the territory's picturesqueness, the fact remained that America's new Micronesian charges suffered from poverty, disease, illiteracy, and poor diet.

For thirty or so years after the war's end, federal efforts to administer the territory were characterized by infighting, factionalism, and indecision, with various branches of the government pursuing hesitant, shifting, and often mutually opposed agendas regarding its new conquest. The more idealistic participants in the debate felt that the United States had a moral obligation to rescue the islanders from the naked, sexually promiscuous, childlike ways of the past, endowing them with the educational and infrastructural wherewithal to participate in the world economy.

The opposing view, which many have disparagingly called "zoo theory," held that the islands of Micronesia were simply too small, isolated, and bereft to be worth helping. As Henry Kissinger would somewhat famously snip during a discussion of the islands' fate, "We're only talking about ninety thousand people, so who gives a damn?" "Development," it was argued, could only result in a system of handouts, which, even with the best intentions, would still be costly and insufficient. Why spoil the islanders with a taste for modern living that could never be satisfied? Better for all involved to leave them be, surviving as they had for centuries on coconuts, fish, and taro root.

One primary obstacle to "developing" such a region was the immense distance from place to place. As a 1964 United Nations Trust Territory mission would report, the territory was an area "whose geographical dispersion and remoteness makes every undertaking more costly, probably, than in any other area of the world."

Another obstacle was the weather. Many Micronesian islands stand in the way of typhoon trajectories. Inevitably, every storm season results in the devastation of buildings, power and phone lines, and sewage and water-treatment systems. Sometimes the same islands are hit twice in a season, or three seasons in a row. During typhoons, crops are doused with salty ocean spray, which kills off any but the most hardy, well-adapted species. Year-round, the moist ocean air and frequent torrential rains corrode virtually everything man-made: cars, hospitals, water tanks, pipes, and so forth.

Skilled laborers were largely nonexistent in the western Pacific, raising the question of who was to build and maintain anything like a modern infrastructure. If it did not seem polite for Americans to barge in and run everything for the locals, it did not seem feasible to propose any other plan. Western-style, First World goals had a depressingly consistent way of failing to materialize when left in the hands of islanders. Building materials often disappeared; schedules went unmet.

What Americans saw as tendencies to laziness, nepotism, graft, and corruption in the islands were, from the islander point of view, matters of long-standing culture and respect essential to enable people to get along in a small place. Tribal culture, to a degree Americans didn't— and still don't—usually understand, is entirely family-oriented. It's not just a neat thing—"Hey, you're my cousin." It's everything: it's me and my family and my cousins against you and your family and your cousins. Consequently, islanders given the power and authority to make hires frequently view the opportunity as a chance to support a family member rather than a mandate to search for the most qualified person.

Work ethic was another matter altogether. For centuries, islanders had managed to survive with relative ease. They fished or farmed, were often afflicted with arthritis, and died fairly young with a minimum of stir. With little to trade and not much beyond subsistence to hope for, why would anyone work a ten-, twelve-, or eight-hour day? Family celebrations, funerals, church ceremonies, and holiday gatherings were some of many valid reasons not to show up at work.

By the 1960s, it had become clear that the cost of maintaining the infrastructure of Micronesia seemed likely to surpass whatever economic momentum the islands could attain. It had also become evident that federal efforts to coordinate meaningful economic development for territories so far from the government's purview were proving futile. Two decades of sporadically, unevenly doled American largesse had taught islanders to consume American goods, and though education levels had been raised throughout the region, economies remained flat. With nothing to produce, the region had only been elevated to the status of an abject dependency. As Lazarus Salii, the longtime leader of Palau, would say despairingly, the lack of meaningful economic development and decades of welfare had produced "an economy that would soon be thoroughly dependent on imported goods, contracted skills, and annual outside aid."

Although the United States had never earnestly encouraged anything like true independence, by the 1970s, colonial possessions had become passé, and the process of encouraging Micronesian "self-determination" entered full swing. Citizens of the Trust Territory were now encouraged to determine their future status. Did island groups wish to form confederations with one another? What degree of self-government might they wish to retain? It was an intensely studied question, leading to conversations among islanders, their leaders, and Washington that went on for years. The indigenous leaders who came forward to lead these discussions appeared to be acutely aware of the stakes, and many of them were distinguished by their sophistication and shrewdness at the bargaining table.

In *The Edge of Paradise: America in Micronesia,* P. F. Kluge, a former Peace Corps volunteer and close witness to the period, described the islanders' choice as a stark one between modernity, with all its pros and cons, and the safer but lonely option of isolation, with the possibility of permanent regret. "You could almost see them weighing things," wrote Kluge. "What was good about America: health care, schools, federal programs, scholarships and travel, chicken and steak, cold beer and soda, ice cream and movies. What was bad about America: taxes, regulations, racial problems, federal agencies, auditors and prosecutors who didn't understand 'island ways.' " Did the islanders prefer to lose their land, autonomy, identity, and an entire way of life? Or lose out on the chance—perhaps the only one—to join the modern world?

Saipan is one of a group of fourteen islands known as the Northern Marianas. Its distance from the American mainland brings home the vastness of the Pacific—it is 6,000 miles west of Los Angeles, 3,900 miles west of Honolulu, and 120 miles north of Guam. During my many eventual trips to the place, I became frustrated with trying to explain where it was until I learned to say, "Well, fly to Tokyo, hang a left, and go for another three and a half hours."

The island is just a strip of land twelve miles long, three to six miles wide. It is beautiful, lush and green, peaked by the 1,550-foot Mount Tapochau, graced with six golf courses, and protected on the western shore by a coral barrier reef as brilliant a shade of turquoise as has ever beckoned from the cover of a travel magazine.

Isolated as it is, Saipan has had a long relationship with world powers. In the early 1500s, Magellan "claimed" the island for the Spanish throne, and for the next four hundred years the island served as a useful watering hole for ships crossing from Mexico to the Philippines. Attempts to govern the place were mixed; the Spanish presence was sporadic and volatile, alternating between military and religious governors unable to decide whether to shoot the natives or convert them to Catholicism. In the end, they managed to do a fair amount of both. After losing the Spanish-American War, Spain sold her Pacific possessions to the Germans for the fire-sale price of $4.5 million. The Germans stayed briefly, siring a few Hofschneiders, then left after their defeat in World War I. The League of Nations assigned the territory to the Japanese with one proviso: that the islands must remain unmilitarized. The Japanese, alone among Saipan's owners, were the only superpower to squeeze a profit from the place, a feat accomplished by planting every arable inch on the island with sugarcane, bypassing the locals altogether, and farming it with imported Korean and Okinawan workers.

America's role in the Northern Marianas began when military planners realized that possession of the islands would put bombers within range of the Japanese homeland. As it became increasingly obvious that the Americans were going to attack, the Japanese turned Saipan into a heavily armed bunker. The fighting began on June 15, 1944. Four days of sorties were flown and two thousand casualties were sustained on the American side before the United States established a beachhead. Subjugating the rest of the island would take another month.

The battle for Saipan, and the shorter, subsequent battles for Tinian and Rota (Saipan's less populated sister islands), were, coincidentally, the first time flamethrower tanks had ever been used. Three weeks into the fighting on Saipan, an estimated 20,000 bodies littered the battleground. Smoke mixed with the stench of decaying corpses rotting in the jungle heat. The island, formerly lush with cane, was a burnt scar. Survivors on both sides were tired, hungry, wet, and bruised. In the end, the Japanese would suffer 24,000 casualties in battle and another 5,000 by their own hand—suicides unwilling to surrender to the American barbarian. Dead U.S. troops numbered 3,400, while several hundred unarmed islanders would be caught and killed in crossfire.

By many accounts, the battle for Saipan was the most decisive of the Pacific theater. The United States immediately poured concrete for runways at the northern end of Tinian, an island five miles from Saipan. What had recently been jungle became the busiest airport in the world, with planes taking off every forty-five seconds. By March 1945, the firebombing of Tokyo had begun. On August 6, the *Enola Gay* took off from Tinian and dropped the world's first atom bomb on Hiroshima. Three days later a second bomb was loosed on Nagasaki and the war was brought to an end.

While most Micronesian islands voted to remain "freely associated" with the United States (a relationship that meant more independence and less cash assistance), in 1978 the Northern Marianas, including Saipan, after lengthy negotiations with Washington, voted to establish closer ties. The eventually agreed-upon designation was that together they would become a U.S. commonwealth, a self-governing body recognizing the sovereignty of the United States.

In the words of what would come to be known as the Covenant, the shared goal of the United States and the Commonwealth of the Northern Marianas Islands, or CNMI, was "to assist the Government of the NMI in its effort to achieve a progressively higher standard of living for its people." Islanders would become U.S. citizens but, since they had no representation in Congress, remain exempt from all U.S. taxes except Social Security and Medicare/Medicaid. The United States guaranteed the islands a certain income, money for sewers, bridges, hospitals, schools, and such, and the islands would be free to import skilled workers until such time as their economy could stand on its own two feet.

Legally, the CNMI would be obliged to conform largely to American law. However, it was agreed, it would remain exempt from American immigration controls and certain federal tariffs. Moreover, at least for a time, the CNMI would retain control over its minimum wage rate laws. In addition, at least for a generation, no one but the native Chamorro and Carolinian residents of the CNMI (and some from Guam) would be permitted to own land.

The self-control over immigration, customs, and minimum wage was intended to promote the development of the fragile island economy without the islands being "Hawaiian-ized," as it was known—taken over by foreigners, with the locals dispossessed and kicked off of their ancestral land.

It is at this point that Saipan's history took a turn for the sordid. In the early 1980s, trade representatives from the CNMI met up with garment interests from Hong Kong and Korea—"loophole shoppers," in the parlance of international trade—and encouraged them to set up shop on Saipan. From a manufacturer's perspective, the place seemed too good to be true.

Garment makers around the world had long been hamstrung by a set of trade barriers known as the "quota system," enforced by the United States since World War II. Under the quota framework, the United States allowed each country in the world to sell it only so many shirts, pairs of underwear, socks, and so forth. It was a classic means of waging diplomacy through economic means: if a country angered the United States, say, by voting against it in the United Nations, the United States could threaten to reduce the offending nation's quota. The kingdom of Jordan, for example, could sell disproportionately huge amounts of clothing to the United States as long as it played nice with Israel. African countries were often given sizable quotas as a humanitarian gesture to help foster economic growth.

The quota framework led to a wildly distorted global system of garment production. Clothing manufacturers not only needed customers, orders, factories, supplies, workers, and access to shipping, but if they wanted to sell to the United States, they needed the little piece of paper conferring the right to do so. A separate and unnecessary layer in the business was thus created. Trading companies commandeered the business of buying and selling quota from countries that had the document, then hiring someone else to manufacture the clothes in countries with cheap labor. In addition to increasing consumer costs, the quota system made garment manufacturing an unpredictable headache.

Foreign manufacturers coming to Saipan could forget all about quotas. Once incorporated on Saipan, they became American companies, working inside the quota system. Thanks to the CNMI's self-control over immigration and minimum wage, workers could be imported from Korea, the Philippines, Thailand, and China and paid about half of what workers made on the American mainland (the CNMI minimum wage was formerly two dollars and change; in 1997, it was raised to $3.05 an hour). Not only could the companies sell as much as they wanted to American retailers, they could now do so without paying the 21 percent American tariff on foreign garment imports. Best of all, however, was that clothes made on Saipan avoided the taint of foreign sweatshops. Each item could be legitimately tagged with the comforting label MADE IN THE NORTHERN MARIANAS (USA).

Apparel giants such as Gap, Target, J. C. Penney, J. Crew, Ralph Lauren/Polo, Jones Apparel Group, Lane Bryant, The Limited, Nordstrom, OshKosh B'Gosh, Woolrich, Tommy Hilfiger, Liz Claiborne, Brooks Brothers, Calvin Klein, Talbots, and Sears, Roebuck flocked to embrace the CNMI's favorable business climate. In no time at all, the island was host to thirty-six garment factories. Businesses' demand for temporary guest workers—more Koreans, Chinese, Filipinos, and Thais—skyrocketed. The CNMI government was overjoyed; thanks to a small tax levied on the garment industry, it finally had a source of cash besides Uncle Sam. Although some observers, both mainlanders and islanders, issued warnings about the social effects of the CNMI's new revenue stream, the warnings went ignored.

In 1976, the CNMI had been populated by 14,000 people—virtually all Chamorro and Carolinian natives. By the early 1980s, they had been joined by about 3,000 foreign guest workers. By 1986, the number of foreign workers had reached 10,000. A few years later there were some 18,000 guest workers on the island. Meantime, the garment industry vaulted from sales of $5.4 million in 1985 to $124 million in 1988 and nearly $1 billion in 1998.

Coincidentally, during this period the Japanese economy underwent one of the biggest booms in modern history. Saipan became Japan's Miami, a warm place to escape winter and a fun place to swim and scuba dive year-round. Saipan's hospitality industry exploded. In 1992, half a million tourists entered the CNMI and spent more than $500 million. The number of hotel rooms increased from a few dozen to nearly three thousand.

Japanese and, later, Korean investors began to snap up fifty-five-year property leases (the maximum that a foreigner could own). Property values on Saipan multiplied many times over as speculators bid up lease

prices. Many local families became overnight millionaires and proceeded to buy new cars and trucks and build immense, oftentimes gaudy
palaces. But even for those less fortunate, the late eighties and early
nineties were not just good years—they were amazing ones. The sleepy
little island that hadn't even had traffic lights ten years earlier had suddenly become the western Pacific's miracle of economic development.

But there was one problem. Well, actually, there was a whole bunch
of problems. As a congressional report would soon note, by the 1990s,
foreign workers accounted for 76 percent of the total working population of the CNMI—and 90 percent of private-sector employment. In
other words, almost all of the actual work in life—lifting stuff, doing
stuff, serving stuff, building stuff—was being done by foreigners. Local
people were getting skilled, all right—skilled at avoiding work and si-
phoning off federal funds.

Locals began to hire themselves for coveted—and cushy—government jobs, jobs that required little effort, forgave intermittent atten-
dance, and served as a pretend-work form of welfare. For many years,
on local censuses and economic reports, "government" would be listed as
the island's second-largest industry. About half of all locals had government jobs. As long as one or two people per family had a job, the rest of
the family could kick back and live off of food stamps. Meanwhile, 16
percent of the indigenous population was unemployed, and the poverty
rate among locals was an astounding 35 percent. Amazingly, since local
labor laws contained a special provision that maids and farmworkers
could be paid less than the minimum wage (only three hundred dollars
a month for up to seventy-hour weeks), many locals—including those
receiving food stamps—reportedly hired live-in Filipina maids. On
Rota and Tinian, Saipan's sister islands, people who farmed could now
hire farmworkers instead of doing the hard labor themselves.

The Reagan and George H. Bush administrations each expressed
concerns over what one congressional report termed "the overwhelming
and increasing CNMI dependence on an immigration and labor system
that requires the massive importation of poverty-stricken, low-paid, indentured alien workers." Ten years later nothing had changed. A letter
to the islands' leaders, signed by President Clinton, called labor practices

in the CNMI "inconsistent with our country's values." Administration concerns were met by what would, over time, become a familiar blend of denial, apology, and insistence that conditions were improving.

The predictable reports of abuse began as a trickle and quickly became a flood, driven by the same forces of exploitation we've seen in the Tulsa and Florida chapters. Virtually all foreign workers offered jobs in Saipan were charged fees, often enormous ones, by labor recruiters who controlled access to jobs. Many workers were lied to and cheated. Some were told that Saipan was a glittering island city like Singapore or Hong Kong. One man was told it was a mere train ride to Los Angeles.

In the 1990s, fees for a one- to two-year contract with Saipan's garment factories ranged from three or four thousand dollars to as much as seven thousand. As with the fees paid in India by international migrants, these sums were often borrowed at high interest rates; guest workers usually spent their first year working off the debt.

While CNMI labor law required health insurance and round-trip transportation to be provided free of charge by the employer, and for food and housing to be provided at minimal cost, many workers were forced to sign "shadow contracts" with their recruiters, outlining illegal deductions for airfare, housing, and food. Other provisions in such contracts prohibited workers from joining unions or attending church services. One two-year contract for a Chinese carpenter forbade him from engaging in "any political or religious activity." The contract went on to say he could not take drugs, watch "sex movies," fight, get drunk, or "fall in love or get married." Another worker's shadow contract stated, "This contract will not be shown to anyone else, especially the labor office." In all cases, guest workers in Saipan were (and still are) forbidden to change employers without their employer's consent. In essence, the best possible outcome for the average foreign worker coming to Saipan was a form of indentured servitude. Some employers might play nice. But many did not feel compelled to do so.

As stories emerged, scores of workers alleged being forced to work six and seven days a week, sixteen and eighteen hours a day, with no overtime; to live in hideous compounds, with eight or ten people to a room, with foul water, inedible food, not enough food, no water for showering, and intermittent electrical power. Those who complained about conditions were often fired and left to fend for themselves, unable to pay for food or lodgings. Reports surfaced of workers being raped by foremen, beaten, chained to their sewing machines, sexually harassed, and verbally and physically abused. Workers' passports were alleged to have been confiscated. Women were warned that pregnancy would result in deportation. At many factories, workers were told when they could and couldn't leave their barracks. At one South Korean company, for example, in 1997, workers were told that they could leave their barracks only twice a week for one hour. Violators, the company posted, "will be barred from going out of the barracks indefinitely."

Saipan's Department of Labor became a notorious seat of corruption, with supervisors accepting money from employers for favors and obstructing investigations into allegations of worker abuse. Some reports described Department of Labor officials assaulting workers for insisting on pressing charges of abuse. At one point, Saipan legislators tried to pass a bill charging workers two hundred dollars for the privilege of filing a labor complaint.

Aided by ersatz Saipanese employers, labor recruiters from all over Asia began convincing workers to pay huge fees for jobs in the CNMI that simply didn't exist. Bangladeshis were typically promised security-guard jobs; Filipinas were offered "waitressing" positions. Such workers arrived in the CNMI to find themselves bereft—homeless, desperately indebted, and extremely vulnerable to anyone who wished to take advantage of them.

The island became awash with prostitution, drugs, and lawlessness. Chinese triads, or organized crime gangs, and Russian and Korean mafia outfits set up shop. They were joined by wealthy, tax-allergic Americans such as Bill Millard, the CEO of ComputerLand, and Larry Hillblom, the "H" in DHL, the worldwide courier service that at its height employed 68,000 people.

Hillblom was a larger-than-life character, and a perfect fit for Saipan. After making hundreds of millions of dollars in his twenties and early thirties, he retired to the CNMI and cultivated an interest in underaged Asian girls. A licensed amateur pilot, Hillblom whiled away his early retirement flying around Asia, seeking sex providers to fulfill his special needs. Terrified by AIDS and yet unwilling to wear condoms, Hillblom found himself practically obliged to sleep with virgins. His collection of "partners," some as young as thirteen years old, came from Vietnam, Thailand, the Philippines, and throughout the Pacific.

Ever the entrepreneur, he commenced on Saipan construction of a project dubbed Cowtown, intended to serve as something like an assisted-living community for sex tourists. Partially modeled after Nevada's infamous Mustang Ranch, the once-legal brothel near Reno known for its friendly, "anything goes" atmosphere, it aimed to offer dwellings, hotel rooms, prostitutes, and a pornographic film studio, all under one roof. Japanese investors rushed in to complete a similar project.

Unfortunately for such endeavors, the CNMI declared prostitution illegal in 1993. And in 1995, Hillblom's plane went down in a storm less than an hour away from Saipan. His body was never found, and after a famously nasty legal squabble, his $600 million estate was split among four illegitimate children sired by Asian child brides. One of the inheritors was, rather touchingly, if inaccurately, named after his father: Junior Hillbroom.

By now, Saipan had justly earned an international reputation for Wild West–style lawlessness. No Wild Western town, of course, could be complete without its arch villain. Saipan's was an ethnic Chinese named Willie Tan, a naturalized U.S. citizen born in the Philippines. Tan's family owned numerous interests in garment, shipping, and hotels in Hong Kong, Cambodia, and the Philippines. At twenty-four, in 1982, Tan was dispatched to Saipan to establish the island's third garment company, American Knitters.

He very quickly emerged as the most notorious among Saipan's garment manufacturers. In 1991, U.S. Department of Labor officials would accuse Tan of stiffing twelve hundred workers on overtime and retaliating against employees who protested his actions. The DOL sued Tan for $9 million in restitution—the largest fine ever imposed by labor officials in U.S. history. Tan, without pleading guilty, agreed to pay the back wages.

Tan hit the news again in late March 1999, when nearly twelve hundred workers at his factories fell ill with food poisoning. "It kind of looked like a battle zone," said Frank Strasheim, a thirty-year veteran of the Occupational Safety and Health Administration (OSHA). "People were lying on the ground with IVs sticking out of them. I've never seen a food poisoning case of this magnitude."

Later that year, the firm Milberg Weiss filed a class-action lawsuit against Saipan's manufacturers and the U.S. clothing companies that hire them, alleging, among other things, that in 1998 "Mr. Willie Tan . . . drove up to a set of barracks on Middle Road in Saipan . . . and told the workers that if they talked to any foreigners, any press people, or any U.S. government agents, and revealed any secrets about the operation of the garment factories or any facts about the barracks' living conditions, he would have action taken against their families in China . . . and there would be physical retribution, including deportation."

In 1999, a bipartisan U.S. congressional commission noted that "only a few countries, and no democratic society, have immigration policies as open to abuse as Saipan's." In the same set of hearings, John Berry, assistant secretary of the interior, would testify that the need to apply federal immigration, wage, and trade standards to the CNMI was "inescapable." "The problem," Berry would state, "is the CNMI immigration and labor system itself, and the lack of will to change it fundamentally." As evidence, Berry cited "the unending stream of allegations, administrative determinations, court decisions, and statistics validating the fact that alien workers are routinely mistreated in the CNMI." In Berry's conclusion, what the system had generated was "a culture of disregard for the law and an expectation that corruption is the way to get business done."

Unsurprisingly, Saipan's experiment in economic development began to generate a barrage of negative press.

In 1998, ABC, CNN, the BBC, and *The New York Times* each confirmed reports of forced labor, sex slavery, and domestic forced servitude among the Marianas' so-called guest workers. The most scandalous report, perhaps, was produced by the ABC news program *20/20*, in a special about Saipan called "Is This the USA?"

Barbara Walters opened the segment:

Tonight, we take you to a tiny American island, a gem where the beaches are gorgeous, the palm trees sway, but an outrage against common decency and American values is going on in the shadow of the American flag. A *20/20* investigation has uncovered an explosive story behind the trusted label "Made in the USA."

Hugh Downs chimed in next:

How could this happen on American soil? Workers locked in squalid dorms, some cheated out of their meager salaries, women forced to choose between abortion and their jobs? ABC's chief investigative correspondent Brian Ross exposes a business deal designed for profit. Should it be labeled un-American?

Ross then took the viewer on a tour of Saipan, showing the squalid barracks where workers lived with broken toilets and contaminated showers and examining shadow contracts signed by Chinese garment workers. Ross interviewed a garment worker who claimed that her factory's management had tried to coerce her into having an abortion, then fired her when she wouldn't. According to ABC reporters and producers, their team was followed everywhere on Saipan by thugs they alleged were sent by Willie Tan. Rhonda Schwartz, who produced the segment, later told me that one producer's room had been broken into, evidently in a crude attempt to intimidate the crew into silence.

In perhaps the most surreal bit of footage, Ross interviewed former CNMI lieutenant governor Pedro A. Tenorio, enlisted by a Chinese garment-factory owner to talk to the media. Tenorio, famous locally for being a straight shooter, berated Ross and the media at large for never mentioning the *good* things about Saipan. Confronting Ross about the Americans' hypocrisy, he demanded, "What happened to the United States when you first got the colonies established and then bring people in? Don't you have slaves? Isn't it the American government that brought the slaves in and got the Civil War going? And Americans killed themselves because of that. You guys were killing each other because of that!"

Ross, somewhat stunned, sputtered, "Sir, this is 1998."

Undaunted, Tenorio retorted, "It doesn't matter!"


In 1995, Congress made the first of many attempts to "federalize" the CNMI, that is, to strip it of its exemption from U.S. minimum wage and immigration laws. As Allen Stayman, assistant secretary of the interior, argued, "Why should the U.S. suffer a continuing financial loss of $200 million a year in tariffs, a fifth of a billion dollars, for the dubious privilege of explaining to the rest of the world why it tolerates the C.N.M.I. human rights record?" President Clinton then recommended that Congress end the islands' exemptions from federal law.

Then-CNMI governor Froilan Tenorio, desperate to protect what, like a mantra, would perennially be referred to as "the fragile island economy," hired the law firm Preston Gates Ellis & Rouvelas Meeds to help block the measure in the House and "tell the island's story" to faraway mainlanders.

As has since become well known, Preston Gates was the employer of later-to-be-imprisoned lobbyist Jack Abramoff (he has been charged with conspiracy, mail fraud, and tax evasion). Abramoff, alone and in league with former aides to now-disgraced congressional House leader Tom DeLay, Republican of Texas, is on record admitting to bilking American Indian tribes of $82 million. It has been well publicized that he and DeLay were in the process of building an enormous political patronage machine, enriching and empowering themselves in the name of their ideological beliefs.

With President Clinton, Assistant Secretary of the Interior Allen Stayman, Congressman George Miller (D-CA), and Senator Frank Murkowski (R-AK) leading the fight to "federalize" the island by imposing mainland labor and immigration standards, DeLay and Abramoff rallied their conservative troops to block any such legislation, protesting that enemies of Saipan's economic miracle were funded by "big labor" and "the radical left," jealously trying to deny the islands' "shot at prosperity." In all, twenty-nine initiatives to curtail labor practices on Saipan were blunted by Team DeLaybramoff.

As a paid defender of "the island way," Abramoff explained, "These are immoral laws designed to destroy the economic lives of a people." Further positioning Saipan as an underdog, he noted, "What these guys in the CNMI are trying to do is build a life without being wards of the state." For conservatives, Abramoff said, the fight over how to govern the CNMI was "a microcosm of an overall battle." The commonwealth, he said, was "just what conservatives have always wanted, which is enterprise zones—tax-free, regulation-free zones where with the right motivation, great industry could take place and spill out into the general communities."

As DeLay, meeting with a group of Saipan dignitaries, would later crow, "You are a shining light for what is happening in the Republican Party, and you represent everything that is good about what we're trying to do in America and in leading the world in the free market system." On another occasion, DeLay would praise the Saipan Garment Manufacturers Association: "You represent everything that is good about what we're trying to do with conservative government and Christian principles." Later, discussing Saipan in an interview, DeLay would muse, "It is a perfect petri dish of capitalism. It's like my Galapagos Island."

DeLay even suggested that the United States take a cue from the CNMI and institute a similar "guest worker" program "where particular companies can bring Mexican workers in" to fill jobs that Americans won't take, paid at "whatever wage the market will bear."

In the next few years, Team DeLaybramoff would collect some $11 million from Saipan business associations and the CNMI government. Additionally, wealthy locals such as Willie Tan would be encouraged to donate money to political races under DeLay's direction. According to the Center for Responsive Politics, Tan would show up donating campaign funds to then-congressman Randy Tate (R-WA); Representative Bob Schaeffer (R-CO); Representative James Hansen (R-UT); Representative Benjamin A. Gilman (R-NY); Representative Kay Granger (R-TX); former representative Matt Salmon (R-AZ); Representative Jim Saxton (R-NJ); Friends of the Big Sky, the "leadership PAC" of Conrad Burns (R-MT); the North Carolina Republican Executive Committee; the Idaho Republican Party; and George W. Bush's 2000 presidential campaign. Last but not least, Tan would also pay hundreds of thousands of dollars to Abramoff toward "skyboxes"—luxury sport boxes leased in Abramoff's name at FedEx Field in Washington, D.C., and enjoyed by members of Congress, lobbyists, and friends of Abramoff's.

Abramoff designed a multiprong attack to protect the CNMI from "federal takeover." According to an e-mail from Abramoff to an executive of Willie Tan's, step one would be to either "defund" or "restrict" the activities of Assistant Secretary of the Interior Allen Stayman. (Stayman and his subordinate, David North, were subsequently fired for political activity while employed by the federal government. The man who dispatched them, Ken Mehlman, would go on to become chairman of the Republican Party.)

Step two was to prepare for upcoming congressional hearings about the CNMI, a process that involved "working with the garment industry to get friendly workers (one Chinese, one Filipino, one Bangladeshi)," "writing and reviewing testimony," and "preparing questions and factual backup for the friendly Senators and Congressmen."

Meanwhile, in step three, "Public Relations and Rapid Response Teams" would get to work "generating a host of positive letters to the editor," television coverage, talk-radio pieces, and articles by "friendly writers."

Dozens of conservative journalists and think-tank employees were flown to Saipan and fêted island-style. Lucky guests included staffers from the Cato Institute, the Traditional Values Coalition, and the Heritage Foundation. After a few days of beach, sun, and golf, how could one not sense the freedom? Thus enlightened, Ronald Bailey would come home and write for *The American Enterprise* that the CNMI was "a true free market success story." The Cato Institute's Doug Bandow would describe Saipan as a "laboratory of liberty."

When a mere five- or six-thousand-dollar junket wasn't sweet enough to make a writer "friendly," Team DeLaybramoff reached for their checkbooks. It would later be revealed that Bandow, a senior fellow at the libertarian Cato Institute, had accepted payments from Abramoff to promote the latter's positions in a syndicated column that went out to hundreds of newspapers across the United States. Op-ed pieces written by Peter Ferrara, a senior policy adviser at the conservative Institute for Policy Innovation, would also be rewarded with such undisclosed payments. (Later, an unabashed Ferrara would defend his behavior, saying with a shrug, "I do that all the time.")

Finally, the most important lobbying effort of all, step four, was to be executed by Preston Gates's CNMI "Travel Subgroup." "There is no doubt," Abramoff's e-mail continued, "that trips to the CNMI are one of the most effective ways to build permanent friends on the Hill and among policy makers in Washington. The importance of bringing Congressmen and Senators to the CNMI cannot be overstated."

According to an article in the magazine *Roll Call,* a complement of more than ninety congressional members and staff would eventually be flown to Saipan. So many of the delegations and "fact-finding missions" to the tropical island seemed to coincide with winter months on the mainland, and so many of the tours of working conditions seemed to end on the links, that *The New York Times* was moved to headline an article, THEY CAME, THEY SAW, THEY GOLFED.

One such taxpayer-funded mission took place in February 1999, when a congressional delegation of one Democratic and six Republican members of Congress (and nineteen staff and family members) set out for Saipan. The group's visit had been carefully arranged. The congress members would meet with local government officials, take the carefully arranged tour of Willie Tan's model factory (the one he always used for visitors), and perhaps, if there was any spare time, hit the links. The entourage then visited Guam and the Marshall Islands—also clients of Abramoff's.

To their surprise, however, upon arrival in Saipan, the delegation was met by a throng of some two thousand workers belonging to a group called the United Worker's Alliance. The group, composed of Filipinos, Chinese, and Bangladeshis, had already attracted the attention of the local newspapers and television stations. By all means, it was quickly decided, the delegation should meet with them.

According to one of the alliance's representatives, whom I met later and whom I'll call Brad, the meeting was a joke. Brad had paid nearly five thousand dollars for a job in Saipan as a commercial cleaner. He arrived to find he'd been conned. The room was crowded with other such workers eager to vent their frustrations. The congress members took their seats.

As the meeting began, Brad said, he was stunned to realize that the politicians had no knowledge of the issues raised by the protesters. The staffers hadn't seen fit to inquire and prep the congress members, nor had the congress members seen fit to inquire into all the negative press that had, by now, been spilling out of Saipan for years. "Their questions were kind of painful for us," said Brad. He imitated the politicians, looking lost and clueless. " 'Why do you complain? Who is doing you this?' " Brad looked incredulous. "They had traveled all the way here just to get some fresh island air. They were just killing time. Maintaining formalities.

"We gave all of these documents to the House Resources Committee," Brad complained. "We told them about all the Asian ladies being hired as waitresses and forced to be whores. Companies filing bankruptcy after not paying wages for months and months. I had a huge expectation in my mind that these learned, educated legislators would help these poor Third World people who had been abused and had all this goddamn shit happen to them. But all that hope went into the dump." Brad's face looked bitter as he thought back. "It just stinks." The meeting ended after twenty-five minutes, with the congress members promising to do something about the workers' problems.

Later that evening the workers, feeling that they hadn't been properly heard, held a candlelight vigil in front of the Hyatt Hotel, the island's upscale accommodation of choice. None of the delegation members would talk to them except an official from Insular Affairs and Robert Underwood, then the congressman from Guam. When Alaska's Representative Don Young appeared in the lobby, around eight in the evening, the workers tried to get his attention. "I'm sorry, I'm tired," he told them, breezing by.

Here, in his retelling, Brad began to laugh. What he had heard (one hears everything on an island as small as Saipan) was that tired or not, at least some members of the group spent the night at a party at Willie Tan's house. For entertainment, Brad claimed, Tan had invited the Filipina dancers from a strip club called Stoplight. "They had a warm celebration," Brad said with a smirk. I asked him what that meant, exactly, and he said, "What do you want me to say? A sexual—he just wanted to make them happy. Just to give them island-style special touch." (I was never able to confirm that such a party had taken place. A lawyer friend of a friend, when asked, admitted to being there but later denied it.)

Later that weekend, a group of at least three congress members took their fact-finding mission to a Filipina strip club called Orchids, owned by a local businessman named Benigno Fitial. The club was popular with local government officials and visiting VIPs looking for a good time. Later, the gang moved on to another club, called Russian Roulette, which featured Russian strippers. According to one source, who was professionally obligated to accompany the delegation around the island, "I've never seen grown men—they were just like kids!" He reported that he sat next to one congressman, who was neither drinking nor getting into the action, while the others "were running to the back of the place into these little stalls to get blow jobs. That's why they were there." I spoke with the congressman he sat next to. He admitted to being in the club but described it not as a strip club but as a karaoke bar. He assured me, "There really wasn't much going on." Neither the congressman nor my source were able to remember the names of the allegedly misbehaving congressmen.

To be fair, many congress members, Democrat and Republican, saw Saipan junkets for what they were. A press secretary for Representative Billy Tauzin (R-LA), explaining his boss's decision not to visit the island, insinuated that the missions seemed plainly bogus. "Staff members have been shielded from seeing and talking to people who would be able to shed some light on what is happening. You're only going to see what they want you to see."

Despite the public opinion of Saipan as a civil and labor rights abomination, however, Abramoff and DeLay successfully managed to keep their cadres in formation and to defeat all attempts to reform labor conditions on Saipan. Party affiliation didn't matter. When Frank Murkowski, a Republican senator from Alaska, moved to pass an immigration bill aimed at reforming abuse in the CNMI, DeLay blocked the legislation in the House.

In May 2003, after numerous holdups, a U.S. federal judge ruled in the Milberg Weiss suit that thirty thousand guest workers formerly employed on Saipan could proceed with their class-action suit against JCPenney, Gap, Tommy Hilfiger, twenty-one other corporations, and twenty-three garment factories. The case was eventually settled for $20 million in unpaid back wages and overtime. Yet again, Saipan received unwanted national media attention, prompting DeLay to dash off for another "fact-finding mission" to the island. Was he worried? "I didn't see any sweatshops!" he said. "Everywhere I went was air-conditioned."


The Pacific sky is unlike anything I've seen before, hard to get used to at first, so big it seems to bend—210 degrees of horizon instead of the usual 180. When I first visited Saipan, in the summer of 2003, I felt I didn't even know how to look at it properly because it seemed twenty times bigger than any sky I knew. Sometimes it seemed as if there were skies behind whatever sky I was looking at, and skies behind them. Completely separate weather systems seemed to slide past like herds of different species, unrelated animals, some loping, others galloping, crawling, grazing lazily across the sky, two patches of cirrus clouds, three rain showers out to sea, four patches of sunlight, shafting down with creamy blue and mercury linings behind them, a rainbow off to the side, with violets, aquamarines, and ocean gray reflecting everywhere, all of it moving west-southwest at a steady fifteen knots.

I had arrived in July, which happens to be when the flamboyan, or flame trees, are in full bloom. The name, if anything, undersells their brilliance. Wherever they line the streets, they visually sound like heraldic trumpet blasts, bright orange against the green of the palms and the blue of the sky. On the smaller dirt roads, where they sometimes arch overhead, fallen petals line the roadbeds by the tens of thousands, creating a top-to-bottom tunnel of fluorescence.

I'd been greeted at the airport by a white American from the mainland, whom I'll call Harry. While Googling "Saipan," I'd found a site called Saipansucks.com, which had some funny negative comments about Saipan, based on the author's personal memories of the place. I wrote to him to learn about his experiences, and he was kind enough to introduce me via e-mail to some of his acquaintances still living on the island. Harry was one of them. In what I would later learn was a kind of typical island friendliness that cut across all ethnic lines, Harry not only met me at the airport and took me on a tour, he was generous enough to lend me an old vehicle of his. (I also wrote to someone from the Marianas Visitors Authority, but that contact didn't seem too excited about my topic of slavery and labor abuse, and that was as far as it went.)

Jet lag surely played a role, but as we rattled along the sandy beach of the turquoise lagoon in Harry's rusty four-wheel-drive vehicle, the beauty of the place lulled me and made me feel careless. I'd been to beautiful tropical places before but never to a Pacific island. The particular combination of masculine ruggedness, feminine lushness, colors, cliffs, crashing waves, and simultaneous multiple ocean views cast a sort of ambient lyricism so overdriven it felt like falling in love. Near the beach, plumeria exploded like fireworks, big white flowers with yellow centers, beautiful and almost sickly pungent. Farther up the volcanic hills, acacia trees spread up and out a bit like live oaks in the Deep South, with fernlike epiphytes racing up all sides, covering the branches with a kind of green fur that made them look like creatures from a Dr. Seuss book. Every time we stopped near any kind of vegetation, butterflies seemed to chase one another about in pairs.

My first few days, I wandered around, mostly alone, just trying to get a feel for island life. The place is so small, I feared if I told anyone, worker or boss, that I was there, news would soon spread, and the powers that be would get their hackles up. (I later learned that an executive at Willie Tan's company had discussed whether or not to hire a private detective to follow me around.) I had decided that I wanted to take a different tack here than I did in Tulsa and Florida, and talk to the local spokespeople and power brokers first, then meet with workers to find out what was going on inside the factories. I didn't want to become prejudiced before I met with the businesspeople, then have to pretend otherwise.

I knew from my Googling that there were people from fifty-six different nations residing in the CNMI. According to a 2003 CNMI Community Survey, there were approximately 79,000 people living on Saipan, Tinian, and Rota. Of these, approximately 21 percent were "locals"— native Chamorros and Carolinians, as they're known. The Chamorro people are largely a mixture of Pacific Islander and Filipino, the latter of which includes a healthy share of Spanish and Mexican Indian blood. The Carolinians are descended from immigrants who paddled up from the Caroline Islands in the 1800s. The rest of the population is 26 percent Filipinos, 23 percent Chinese, 6 percent Micronesians, and the rest primarily a mix of Koreans, Bangladeshis, Japanese, Russians, and American mainlanders (known as *haoles* in local slang).

When I got there, "government" or "public administration" was still designated the second-largest "industry" on Saipan. While the average guest worker earned around ten thousand dollars a year, the average government job paid more like thirty thousand and up.

The CNMI was still a fairly primitive place in some ways, with two English-language newspapers, one cable-television company, five radio stations, and 10,178 telephone lines (Tinian had 499, Rota 524). The federal government had allocated the island enough money to build a sewage and water system adequate for the local population. Thanks to the population-distorting infusion of foreign workers, however, the planned-for infrastructure had become dismayingly inadequate. Power outages were still a frequent and irritating fact of life. Any business of importance relied on backup generators to get it through the gaps. Untreated sewage had a habit of spewing into the lagoon. Disease had begun to kill off or render inedible the fish inside the lagoon. The water table was dangerously low, as well as frequently contaminated by fecal coliform. The tap water was undrinkable, good only for showering and washing clothes and dishes. Islanders relied almost exclusively on bottled water or rainwater.

If all this conveys a Third World sense that indeed exists on Saipan, it would be inaccurate to describe the place as feeling entirely foreign. As poorly linked but official citizens of the United States, Saipanese spend dollars, buy Marlboros, usually speak English, and eat at Kentucky Fried Chicken, McDonald's, Pizza Hut, Tony Roma's, and Winchell's. (They used to eat at Wendy's and Church's Fried Chicken, too, but those franchises came and went with the boom years.) At the car dealerships, SUVs are available, and Shell and Mobil stations sell the gas, at a sixty-cent premium over mainland prices. Also taking a cue from the United States, perhaps, Saipanese tend to drive a lot, rather than walking or bicycling, as elsewhere in Asia.

Regardless of the wealth, poverty, developmental level, or culture of the island and its people, what interested me most about them was that Saipan was the only place in the United States with a legally segregated, two-tiered society. It was the only part of the country where some three-fourths of the population weren't entitled to vote or (since only U.S. citizens can serve on a jury) receive a trial by a jury of their peers.

Not only was Saipan nothing like a "democracy" as it's commonly spoken of in American discourse, but the conditions of unequal power that I'd found to generate forced-labor scenarios had been instituted as policy. In other words, unlike the environments I'd already looked at, where inequality and unfair conditions were an anomaly, in Saipan they were the norm.

In addition to wanting to see what ongoing forced-labor situations might be like, I was interested in studying people's attitudes. What was it like to live in "undemocracy," as Justice Brandeis might have formulated it, a world of lessened freedom and equality? What did it do to people's minds, their attitudes about class and race, their understanding of other people's humanity? I was also very curious about what Saipan's reliance on foreign labor might offer by way of analysis of the U.S. mainland's increasing reliance upon illegal Hispanic laborers. All in all, my main focus was to examine what it did to "normal people" to be around people with less power.

The writer E. J. Kahn, back in 1966, wrote, "The contemporary visitor to Micronesia's islands is likely to be struck less by their innate tropical beauty than by the shabbiness of their man-made embellishments." It's a sharp observation, though one that depends on where one spends one's time and the degree to which one is moved by beauty. Over the three years I ended up spending on Saipan, I came to feel like it was a rather even match, the wowing beauty of the place and the depressing tawdriness of everything human beings had done to it.

In his inaugural speech in 2003, CNMI governor Juan Babauta cited "blight and unzoned sprawl" as among Saipan's glaring problems. It sounds like an overstatement, inapplicable to such a small place. But true enough: where the island wasn't untouched and staggeringly beautiful, it was often disastrously and stupidly overbuilt, congested, overpaved, and hideously zoned.

Everything human on Saipan seemed to greater or lesser extents doleful: the people, the buildings, the signs, and the roads. Buildings were often made haggard by their cheapness, by their age, by unrepaired typhoon damage, by peeling paint, by the overall economic decline that characterized the place when I arrived. Many of the automobiles were rust buckets with misaligned wheels, jiggling fenders, and creaking trunks, held together by bungee cords and Bondo.

A strange thing I discovered early on was the number of buildings topped with rusting rebar (reinforcement rods used inside concrete structures), sticking up like stubble. Normally these are covered over, or sawed and finished. In Saipan it was like every fifth building needed a shave. One white government official later explained to me that under Saipan law, buildings considered unfinished were exempt from property tax. Building owners, I was told, left the rebar sticking up to pretend the building wasn't finished. This explanation, spoken with utter certitude, turned out to be wrong, like many, many things I would eventually hear on Saipan. (There is no property tax on Saipan!) The truth, I later learned, was that during the boom years of the late eighties to mid-nineties, people never dreamt that the good times would end. Buildings would forever rise, incomes would only grow, and the party would never stop.

Once, I was chatting with an old local guy, a landlord showing me an apartment. The woman who'd vacated was a Korean who'd borrowed money from everyone she knew, then skipped town. They used to drink together. Far from being judgmental of the woman's criminal conduct, he seemed sad that she was gone. He missed his drinking buddy. We went to the roof to check out the view. It was gorgeous, as always. Except for the rebar. By that time, I'd been on Saipan long enough to know I should take every chance I got to ask what it was for, just to hear yet another answer. The old man's was perhaps the most poetic of all. He looked at the rebar, downcast, referring to an expansion that never happened, a day with perhaps more hope. "It was de plon." He paused. "De plon."

The local newspapers featured daily staples about local corruption, endless intragovernmental squabbles, the declining economy, and occasional gems such as MAN NABBED FOR STEALING NINE ROOSTERS and THIEF CUTS COW'S LEGS. On a sadder note, there was a story about a CNMI house representative proposing legislation requiring treatment of people found sniffing butane. The majority of island residents and stores rely on butane for their cooking; locals who couldn't afford crystal methamphetamine were evidently huffing their gas tanks.

There are 1,414 licensed poker machines in the CNMI, and an estimated 800 illegal, unlicensed machines. They have names like Treasure Island 3, Tony's Poker, Gig Poker Parlor, K-3 Poker, and K-5 Poker, and they are perhaps the most depressing thing on Saipan, as they are wherever they're found on the mainland. There's nothing so reminiscent of an Indian reservation as walking into a lounge and seeing sad, wrinkled people, lit by the glare of the video, slumped over, chain-smoking, banging at the buttons in front of them like automatons and watching the video slot machines go round and round and round. The machines serve to effectively bleed a large portion of the local and guest-worker populations. It's common to read stories of mothers leaving their kids unattended while they gamble from 8 A.M. to 2 P.M. The lounges are favorite targets for robbers. You can expect to see headlines every few months in the local paper: BANGLADESHI GUARD STABBED, SHOT, KILLED BY POKER ROBBER.

But it's the sex businesses that seem to dominate the retail activity on Saipan. A cruise along the lagoon offers a wide array of "public-minded establishments" such as Sweetheart Massage, Kelly's, Red Heart Massage, Club Jama, Red Bar, A-1, Diamond Heart, Midnight Karaoke, Rose Bar, Hot City, 820 Club, Lucky's Karaoke, White Horse Karaoke, Marianas Club, No. 1 Club, Hana Karaoke, Nagona Club, the Stardust Lounge, the Jewel Box Disco, and the somewhat ramshackle Moon Night strip club. Adorning the exterior of the Moon Night are a dozen faded near-life-sized posters of the comely talent waiting inside every nightfall. After 9 P.M. two of said comely talent stand outside the entryway, in miniskirts and heavy pancake, swatting bugs and luring customers.

The epicenter of the girly trade is the sex-commercial heartland of Saipan, the relatively cosmopolitan area called Garapan. Garapan is ground zero for Japanese salarymen and college boys, American sailors, Korean sailors, merchant marines, and prostitutes. The Japanese tourists, perceived to be docile and flush, get charged seventy, eighty, a hundred bucks a pop, but the local white Americans and islanders know that fifty or even forty is enough for a quick romp on a sweaty cot. A cruise down streets with names like Orchid Street, Coffee Tree Hill, and Ginger Avenue feels like a combination of Bangkok and the Florida Keys.

Chinese prostitutes mill about, some successfully tarted up to look Japanese, others less so, and still others in garment-factory work clothes. Bored, smiling Filipinas in short skirts spill down stairs onto the street from neon strip clubs such as Club Mermaid, Club Starlight, Kings Club, and Happiness. For Asian men looking for non-Asian entertainment, there is Russian Roulette. And everywhere are unnamed karaoke joints and massage parlors with masseuses hanging around in front. *"Mita! Mita!"* they call from the doorway. "You want-a massagi?"

If anyone anywhere on Saipan who is interested in seeing dancing naked women or having sex somehow can't seem to figure out how to find the action, any taxi driver, for a fee, will be happy to take him to a secret back-room massage parlor or private home offering ladies' services. Then there's Hong's Free Shop, on Kadena di Amor Street, a sort of tenement hotel with a gambling parlor on the ground floor. All you have to do at Hong's is show up. Two or three girls should appear within thirty seconds. If they don't, honk. They'll come. If a customer in Garapan loses his way while peeing outdoors or throwing up, there is said to be at least one pimp who hides in the bushes and pops out to offer his human wares.

Another popular means of meeting ladies in Garapan is to get the number of a pimp. A wealthy Japanese man finding himself without a prearranged consort need only express his desire for one: a call is made, a van arrives, and seven, ten, or even a dozen five-foot-tall girls tumble out and dash across the street, clickety-clacking in their tiny plastic high heels, rushing to present themselves for the man's favor, wherever he might be. After he chooses, the lucky girl—or two or three—remains, and the rest go clickety-clacking back to the van or the next waiting customer. They make quite a scene, rushing about in their prostitute finery. Locals laughingly call them the "Garapan geese."

I met a lot of interesting people in my first few days on Saipan. Most of them seemed to enjoy living there, even as they expressed strong negative opinions about the place.

Harry had quipped that Saipan was like "a small Southern town that thinks it's a country." Another white from the mainland, a lawyer whom I met later, compared Saipan to the fictional hillbilly redoubt in Georgia: "It's like, fucking, the Hazzard County of the Pacific."

One white man I met, then unemployed, generously spent a few hours driving me around, showing me the entire island, north to south. He said that most white people on the island were lame and lazy. His own downfall he attributed to a change in the winds of local politics. He'd had a good position with a one-term governor. The governor was now out of favor—and so was he.

The man, like Harry, had a Filipina wife. He told me that he was an alcoholic, and there was certainly a strong whiff of desperation about him. He took me to Suicide Cliff, Bird Island, and the Grotto, sites with stunning views where the Japanese come to take photos or scuba dive. The entire time, he seemed numb to the beauty as he talked about past political developments and current gossip with a level of detail that went way over my head. It was almost autistically obsessive. This person had moved up to that job. This person had been pushed out but had gotten around that other person by using his connection to such and such a local ruling-class family. As an outsider, I had no idea who the people were that he was talking about. It didn't seem to matter. He wasn't really talking to me.

Noting that people on insular possessions often seemed forlorn, and, well, insulated, P. F. Kluge also described something he called "tropical depression." The man giving me the nice tour seemed to be afflicted with it, like he'd been on the island way too long. He seemed bright enough, but mired in an endless, inescapable cycle of resentment and self-doubt.

The people I began to meet on Saipan—regardless of ethnic group— often shared a sort of solipsism. Besides frequent reference to the evil federal government, threatening their evil takeover, it often seemed that there was no life elsewhere, beyond Saipan. Several times, when people learned that I'd come from New York, they asked me where I was during the September 11 attacks on the World Trade Center. Never mind that I lived three-quarters of a mile from the site of the explosions. Before I could answer, I would be interrupted to learn how emotionally devastating it had been for people on Saipan, nine thousand miles away.

As with the rebar explanation, assertions were constantly made that in fact had no basis whatsoever: Saipan had the highest per capita number of millionaires in the world. Saipan had the highest per capita number of lawyers in the world. Saipanese had the highest rate of Bud Light consumption in the world. None of these statements was true. I heard each at least a dozen times.

One thing I noticed was how often people on Saipan interrupted one another. It seemed like no one ever finished a sentence. If you were talking to a white or a local who spoke perfect English and understood you and your gestures perfectly, they interrupted. If you were speaking to a foreigner who spoke English as a second language, someone who didn't understand you at all, you were also interrupted. Many or most conversations between people who didn't speak the same language (English and Tagalog, Thai and Chinese, etc.) seemed to follow a soon-familiar pattern: one person would say "ABC," and the other person would say "CDE." Each person would hear the shared "C," ignore or fail to perceive the differences in what was being said, and part company, thinking that agreement had been reached or understanding had been furthered, when in fact the conversation had been an entirely failed undertaking. For example, I asked a Thai woman how many workers "stay" in the barracks at her garment factory. Using the universal pidgin English—or Chinglish, as it's often called—of Saipan, I asked, "How many workers stay you barracks?" Her answer: "I stay Saipan five years." Many times, it seemed impolite to ask the same question three or four times, so one learned to let things lie, even if nothing had been communicated. The acceptance that nothing meaningful had transpired, despite the effort, became a familiar internal note.

Soon I learned the two most significant facts about Saipan: life was pleasant—at least for citizens; and (differently than, say, in a typical Third World country) life was defined by a palpable atmosphere of disconnect. Things were always wrong, a little out of sync, unfinished, unrepaired, yet it seldom seemed to matter. People (again, I would learn, of every ethnic group) didn't tend to do much of what they swore they would, whether it was showing up at a party or calling you back or getting you the documents you were looking for. Smiling went a long way, promises not so far.


The first Europeans to make contact with the Chamorro inhabitants of Guam and Saipan described them as an extremely healthy lot: tall, handsome, and strong. They're still strong and tall, but it would no longer be accurate to call them handsome. Modern diet, automobiles, and the foreign labor force have taken a terrible toll on the population.

In the last two generations, diabetes has become epidemic. As on the mainland, but seemingly more so, a great many of the natives are not just fat but radically obese, knock-kneed, disabled to a degree that looks both humiliating and painful. Spam, as it does elsewhere in the Pacific, serves as a culinary mainstay. There are something like thirteen varieties in the local grocery stores. Perhaps one car in ten sports a bumper sticker proclaiming I ♥ SPAM.

There are many different types of locals. Some are completely "modernized," or Westernized. They've been to college on the mainland and traveled around the world and are as sophisticated as people anywhere else. The majority of them, however, as in most societies, are poorer and less sophisticated. Of this sort, it's common to see many sporting mullets, flattops, and fades, driving monster trucks and chewing betel nut.

Betel-nut chewing among locals is pursued as nonchalantly and avidly as Italians drink espresso and Bolivians chew coca leaves. The betel is a palm, and its nut is like a large acorn; it is often mixed with lime and inserted between one's tooth and gum. Chewing it produces a mild buzz and a prodigious amount of rust-colored sputum. It became a common sight, at stop signs and traffic lights: locals slowing down, opening their car doors, and sticking their heads out to purge liquid belches of spit. It takes only a couple of years for the habit to permanently stain one's teeth dark brown—an unfortunate result for a people who smile a lot.

Along the palm- and pine-fringed beaches, in the middle of the day, locals often parked their cars and hung out, whiling away the time, radio on, radio off, taking a snooze, chilling out. On weekends and holidays, extended families gathered for barbeques at covered open-air picnic areas with barbeque pits and benches and stayed all day, chatting and joking with car doors open, "island-style" music flowing from the stereo; or someone might even be strumming a ukulele.

Typically, as I saw, the litter from these gatherings ended up being tied into garbage bags and left at the picnic area. "Boony dogs," feral mutts that roam the island, would then break the bags open and spread the bones and trash about. The dogs were a vexing problem, producing litter after litter of puppies, which were often adopted, loved, cuddled,

and then at adulthood abandoned again to become another generation
of boony dogs. They were everywhere, and no one I met didn't resent
their presence. Many people had been bitten by them or at least attacked.
They also made driving a menace, standing in the middle of the road-
way when vehicles tried to pass, sleeping, licking themselves, balefully
scratching fleas and disfiguring patches of mange, until God or luck
arranged for them to get whacked by someone's monster truck.

At first the inactivity of the locals seemed appalling. Their gait, if
they could be seen to be moving at all, was slow-motion. Later I realized
some of this might be attributable to the fact that I'd arrived during
summer vacation. Some of the people outdoors, endlessly hanging out,
doing nothing, were kids out of school. Once, I drove by a teenager
standing out near the beach at sunset, next to his truck, car stereo blar-
ing out Eminem or Mary J. Blige or 50 Cent, just standing there, sway-
ing, dancing very gently by himself. Sometimes I'd see families hanging
out in the lagoon at sunset, cooling off. I could imagine the scene being
repeated backward through time for centuries, and it was beautiful. I
noticed a prodigious number of teenaged couples making out in the
shadows, reminding me of Gauguin paintings, only now the islanders
wore dreadlocks and listened to Fergie and Beyonce. What else was
there to get up to on an island without much to do but chill out and
enjoy the relaxed atmosphere? It began to make sense.

My first local friend was John the Loser. I couldn't stop myself from
calling him that in my head. He didn't seem like a bad guy; it was just
that his face palpably registered so much loss. Whenever he smiled or
laughed, even that was vividly rueful. He gave the impression of someone who would never again enjoy life.

John worked at the cheap hotel where I was staying. It was apparently all but abandoned, which left him ample free time. One day I cor-
ralled him into helping me decipher some Chamorro graffiti behind the
hotel, on a park bench near the beach. (Chamorro is the language of the
Chamorro people, though most Chamorros can speak English.)

Some white people I met later would comment negatively about the
sound of the Chamorro language. I always liked it. To my ear it was like

funny, drunk birds joking around. It wasn't exactly musical, but it was pleasantly unhurried, full of lilts and lurches, punctuated by incredulous, opinionated pops and clucks. Chamorros and foreigners who'd been "on island" long enough often said the word *lanya,* a term whose meaning varied from one context to another, from mean, angry, or profane to something more benign, perhaps akin to Americans' use of the terms "fuck" or "fuckin' A." Chamorro and Carolinian elders didn't use it, viewing it as a crude swearword, but younger people peppered their conversations with it, conveying fairly lighthearted notions like "Oh, man!" or "Wow!"

Between the hotel and the twenty-five yards to the park bench, we got off track in a typically Saipanese way and never got around to the graffiti. Instead, John told me his story.

He used to be married to a local woman and had six kids. He had a business that went broke in 1986 or '88 or so, at which point he started using and dealing crystal methamphetamine, known locally as "ice." This went on for about ten years until finally John got caught and sent away for about nine months to a minimum-security prison somewhere near Bakersfield, California. To my surprise, he said he felt lucky to be sent there. Prison on Saipan, he said, was really boring. "You're just in your cell. There's nothing to do. 'Cause it's like, they don't have any facilities, recreations." In Bakersfield, he said, there was "plenty to do."

One reason I found the story interesting was because it was another window into how boring or static life on a Pacific island can be, another version of "tropical depression." Here was John, separated from his wife, currently shacked up at a free room in the hotel with a twenty-four-year-old Filipina. He was forty-two. (As he explained, "You know, the Filipinos, they don't mind if it is older, especially if you can get them a green card.") And here we were, sitting in front of a beautiful lagoon, with turquoise water and an amazing sun setting behind four of five ships (military supply ships, semipermanently anchored about a mile offshore), and yet, in John the Loser's head, I could see what looked like regret, running like a hamster on a wheel, round and round, forever. *Fuck fuck fuck fuck.* Everything sucked. *Lanya.*

My first meeting with any kind of official in Saipan was with Jay Jones, then head of the Saipan Chamber of Commerce. Jones is a tall, thirty-something white man with gentle brown eyes, a baby face, a soft chin, and a doughy neck. He grew up on Guam, where his family settled and prospered after World War II, then attended college in North Carolina, where he met his wife. When I met him, he and his family owned the Triple J car dealerships on Saipan and Guam and numerous businesses on islands throughout Micronesia, including grocery stores, hotels, restaurants, construction companies, a freight-forwarding business, and a consulting service.

Jones didn't seem particularly eager to meet with me. I couldn't blame him. Media descriptions not paid for by Jack Abramoff had been harshly critical of Saipan. Though my initial hunch was that Jones, personally, didn't seem like the kind of guy who owned a barnful of slaves, he was guarded and uncomfortable.

I asked him what he did as head of the Chamber of Commerce. He said it was just a volunteer job, but basically, he did what other chamber heads do throughout the country: he facilitated opportunities for his constituent businesses. I asked him what this meant locally. He said it meant that his goal was to maintain optimal relations between the CNMI and the U.S. government.

To my surprise, Jones went on to disparage the garment industry. Yes, he said, the industry generated about 25 percent of the commonwealth's economy, and it was important for the CNMI to generate its own income instead of relying on the federal government. However, he felt, the strain it put on the island, in terms of reputation and infrastructure, wasn't worth it.

Jones felt that Saipan should find cleaner industries to develop— schools, for example, for Asians wanting an American experience but who didn't want to travel or couldn't get visas to the mainland. Retirement communities for Japanese and Korean elderly were also an excellent notion to explore. This was the kind of future he and other business leaders I would later meet envisioned for Saipan. They were good ideas—if they could be made to work.

I'd woken up early that morning and had driven around aimlessly. I'd passed through a neighborhood of blocky, affluent-looking houses, shady and cool but gracelessly made of thick concrete, with air-conditioning units jutting out into the jungle foliage. Then I drove past a few garment factories and saw thousands of Chinese women milling around, filing in and out by the hundreds. Some lingered in the shops, pecking at the three-dollar outfits in the bargain clothing bin. Others walked arm in arm, shading themselves with parasols as they crossed the street. Some wore detachable sleeves to keep the sun off their skin. Their shoes could not have cost more than two or three dollars.

I explored a neighborhood near the airport, a neighborhood I later learned was called As Lito. It appeared to consist of poor local families. The kids were like kids from guest-worker ethnic groups but fatter, playing and maneuvering their bikes around speed bumps, boony dogs, and one another. Many wore raggedy shorts and no shirts. Most of the houses were typical Third World shacks—improvised affairs with walls of cracked cement brick and roofs of corrugated tin weighted with bricks and rocks. Some were steel boxes—literally shipping containers with a window or three blowtorched out in jagged rectangles.

When I asked Mr. Chamber of Commerce what this neighborhood was called and described what I'd seen, he looked blank, as if I were describing some other Pacific island. Nothing rang any bells. He shook his head. I repeated that it was a poor neighborhood, and it was near the airport. He tried to help. Nothing came to mind. He frowned, unable to figure out what neighborhood I might be talking about. I explained again. It was near the airport. There were only a couple of roads around there. I knew this on my fourth day in Saipan. How could he be so confused? "You know, in Saipan," he said, "there's really no lower class to speak of."

I almost laughed. What fun! I would repeat Jones's words over and over as I explored the island.


On Saipan, many interviews, formal or not, ended up at strip joints or karaoke clubs. It's not like everyone I met with made me go to them. Typically, it was with younger men and poorer men—and sometimes women. It wasn't something that had ever come up before in my work. Generally, if I'm reporting, my task is to be agreeable. If someone I'm interviewing wants Italian food, I eat Italian. If they want Indian, it's Indian food for me. And if someone suggests Club Chicago or the Korean-owned karaoke place near the Payless grocery store and they happened to be telling me something I want to learn about the garment factories or labor situation on Saipan, then that's were we go.

The difference between the two types of clubs is that at a strip joint, one finds one or more women dancing—first with clothes and then, after a little while, without clothes. And then there's the whole writhing-around-for-one-customer-or-group-for-a-dollar thing. At a karaoke place, the hostesses are clothed, seldom if ever writhe, and merely encourage their patrons to drink and sing along to old hits.

Typically, a man walking into either sort of club on Saipan orders a drink and is immediately approached by a young woman who offers to sit down and lend her company. If the first few conversational gambits go well, the hostess will ask the man to buy her a "lady's drink." A lady's drink usually consists of something like iced oolong tea or Kool-Aid. In Saipan, a male customer usually has the option of buying a cheaper lady's drink, for, say, seven dollars, or a more expensive one, for, say, fourteen dollars. The cheaper version buys the company of a "hostess" for about fifteen minutes, and the more expensive buys half an hour. Conversation of this sort typically opens along the same lines. "How long you stay Saipan? Where you from? You handsome man. You buy lady's drink?"

I took these "reporting" opportunities to ask women employed at such clubs how they'd gotten there. Were they enslaved? Was anyone forcing them to do what they were doing? Obviously, I didn't ask these questions quite so baldly; I was more subtle. What I learned in most cases was that the women had worked in garment factories for a time, then migrated to this kind of work. Many had worked hard, saved a lot of money, and then lost it in underground gambling dens.

On Saipan's sister island Tinian, I visited a karaoke bar and met a Chinese hostess who called herself Coco. Her hair was done in two tight little buns, Princess Leia–style. Coco seemed to be in major de-

cline. She said she'd worked in the garment factories for two and a half
or three years, saved up a bunch of money, then blown it all gambling.
Forty thousand dollars. Then she'd gotten a short-term garment-job
contract in Tinian, but that had ended after a few months. She'd been
at the karaoke place for four months. Coco said that working in the
garment factory was a good job. She had hated it, but it was a good job.
Here, at the bar, you had men grabbing you everywhere. You had to
hang out with Bangladeshis and Chamorros and Filipinos. She made a
face.

Coco was glad that I came and that I was white. She said that white
is very good, and that she loved me. She kissed me a couple of times to
prove it. She rubbed my leg. She seemed drunk. She was worried about
someone from Immigration finding her there. "You aren't going to give
me a hard time, are you?" What she meant was to ask if I was an undercover agent with the Department of Labor or the FBI.

She started laying it on thick. "This is my sixth beer of the night," she
whispered sloppily into my ear. "Make me get—I get too crazy in bed!"
I couldn't help thinking that fate was not on her side, that she would get
caught soon. She was twenty-seven. She kept talking. Her father was a
big playboy. Why were men such playboys? She took a swipe at my
crotch; she really hoped I wasn't going to give her a "hard time." Haha-
haha! Did I get it?

On a small, isolated island with precious few outside stimuli, gossip
becomes a casual blood sport—constant, pervasive, vicious, and glee-
fully nonchalant about accuracy. There was no one of any station I met
on Saipan about whom I hadn't already heard numerous personal details, harsh criticisms, and flagrant lies. Opinions about Richard Pierce,
then spokesman for the Saipan Garment Manufacturers Association, or
SGMA, ran almost universally negative. I'd been on the island for no
more than a few days, yet before I'd even met him, I'd heard Pierce dismissed as a former bag boy (he'd worked years ago at a Safeway store), a
liar, "a whore for the garment industry," and, stain of all stains, a man
who cheats at golf. As the representative of an industry loathed by many

people of all stripes, Pierce was, to many, the embodiment of everything wrong with Saipan.

The first time I met him, he complained, "I'm probably the most misunderstood person I know." We'd met at the Coffee Care restaurant, on top of beautiful Capitol Hill, overlooking the breathtaking lagoon. Not only did people outside the garment industry resent Pierce, he said, for defending something so seemingly indefensible, but because he was constantly harassing his own clients to reform their ways, "most of them hate my guts."

One reason Pierce may have been so misunderstood is that his mind leaps around in a way that many people would find maddening. He seldom finishes even a half-thought before flitting on to the next—and the next and the next. After initiating a few new threads of conversation in quick succession, he often loops back to topics dropped earlier, carrying them a few steps further, and sometimes toward an eventual conclusion. Without a tape recorder and the chance to analyze his words in slow motion, it is difficult to piece together what he's saying, and easy to suspect him of dissembling.

Pierce has thinning hair, a gray, trimmed beard, bright green eyes, and a healthy, attentive, slightly elfish face. When I met him his forearms were noticeably tanned from long hours on the golf course. He'd come to the island in the early eighties with a girlfriend. As he joked, "Things didn't go so well with the girl, but they went well with the island." He'd been on Saipan twenty-five years. Like many other whites attracted to the place, he found the casualness of island culture a pleasant alternative to life on the mainland. After a period of wild partying and drug use, which he freely admits to, he sobered up and settled down. He'd been married to the same woman, a local Chamorro from a prominent family, ever since.

Pierce offered what amounted to three distinct lines of defense to questions about Saipan's garment industry. One of them—call it Defense A—runs parallel to that offered by Team DeLaybramoff and Saipan government officials: Saipan is not the United States. It has no resources, and as impossible as it is for mainlanders to understand, the guest-worker program is necessary to foster the island's fragile economy.

Without the taxes and ancillary income produced by the garment industry, the local government would be forced to rely on the U.S. government for handouts. According to Pierce, virtually all of the attacks on Saipan were politically or economically motivated. Liberal opponents of Saipan's labor relations, such as Congressman George Miller, were simply representing the interests of their labor-union constituents. (According to the Center for Responsive Politics, during the late nineties, when Miller first began leading the charge of opposition to Saipan's guest-worker system, some 25 percent of his funding came from labor. Since then the level has risen to about 45 percent.) The bad press about Saipan, Pierce said, was nothing more than a massive smear campaign orchestrated by agenda- and profit-driven media outlets.

Pierce's Defense B took a more confessional tack. In the early years of Saipan's garment industry, Pierce insisted, no one—not the islanders, not the Chinese and Korean factory owners, not the U.S. government—knew what they were doing. The manufacturers were simply running things the way they would have run them at home. In the old country, Pierce explained, employers had a much more paternalistic relationship with their workers. Factory owners went to the parents of young, migrating workers, he said, "and promised to take care of them. 'We're going to take your son or daughter to Saipan. They're going to be there probably two or three years. This is how much they're going to make. We promise to take care of them. Nothing's gonna happen to them.' "

What this meant, Pierce continued, was that the bosses guaranteed workers a certain income per month but that each worker would be responsible for processing her share of whatever work the factory was facing each day, whether it be 200 shirts or 150 pairs of shorts (since orders fluctuate enormously in the garment business, especially before the Christmas shopping season, the number of garments to be sewn each day and each week can vary enormously). Many workers, said Pierce, were able to finish their workload in less than eight hours. Others took longer. In any case, Pierce insisted, when you averaged workers' hours, they were earning at *least* minimum wage—Saipan's minimum wage, if not the mainland minimum wage—and many times more than they would have earned back home.

The problem, Pierce said, was that this "Asian" way of doing business meant that yes, for some periods, for some hours, some garment workers were temporarily paid less than the legal minimum wage. As some Asian accountants realized what was expected of them from U.S. Labor officials, they began to keep two sets of books, one designed to average out workers' wages and make things look nice for inspectors. Naturally, said Pierce, when U.S. Labor Department officials found the dummy set of books, they became suspicious. But then they took it too far. "And this," Pierce told me with evident frustration, "was one of the examples of—this was called labor abuse. This was called violations of labor laws. This was called all the other stuff that got wrapped around it, including people being locked up and forced to do things they didn't want to do and all this nonsense."

In Defense B, Pierce admitted that there had been *some* forced and abusive labor situations on Saipan but said that the situation was far less egregious than had been portrayed in the media. Most of Saipan's garment workers had been and were currently perfectly happy to be there.

Yes, he said, "some factory owners were saying to their workers, 'You have to be home by twelve o'clock.' And they said that because they want them to get a good night's sleep. Yeah, there was some of that stuff. They had supervisors saying, 'Yeah, you better be back or else you're gonna get in trouble.' There were some restrictions back then. They don't occur now."

In any case, the motivation behind them was strictly paternal. No one—no one, he said—in the garment business had ever behaved in anything like the harsh, quasi-slaveholder manner portrayed in the media. Laughing a little bitterly, Pierce said, "I remember we told people at our factory that they had to stay in the factory one night when there was a typhoon coming. That was the extent of our locking anyone up."

Defense C consisted of explaining the effect Willie Tan had had upon the reputation of Saipan's other garment manufacturers. The genesis of many of Saipan's problems, both real and perceived, he said, lay in Tan's feud with the DOL. The DOL had offered Tan a chance to settle, but Tan, by defying them, had made it personal. "The DOL," Pierce said, "never forgave him, and it really set the tone between the CNMI and mainland labor officials for years to come. The majority of our guys"—the garment-factory owners—"they've always felt that they've had to live with this stuff that came as a result of what he did, the things he did in the early days. There's a resentment." It was understandable but unfair, Pierce said. Since the days of scandal, both Tan's and Saipan's other garment manufacturers had made serious, genuine, and successful efforts to reform. But the enmity against them—and especially Tan—never seemed to dissipate.

When I asked Pierce about Tom DeLay and Jack Abramoff, his eyes widened and he visibly checked himself. As one of the main liaisons between the island's business interests and Abramoff's firm, Pierce suddenly found himself keeping powerful company. "In the beginning," he recalled, "when I started getting mixed up in the middle of it, I thought it was . . . exciting. Wow! I sit in Jack's office, he calls DeLay and tells him what to do, you know? I went, 'Jesus Christ.' " In Pierce's recollection, it wasn't necessarily that Abramoff was the boss, but he remembers conversations between the two in which the former gave the marching orders to DeLay: " 'Here's where I want you to be, here's what you have to do'—*physically*."

DeLay, Pierce said cautiously, was "very good at his job. He remembers everyone he meets, and he can sit there with the same smile on his face for a hundred photos in a row." He also said that DeLay was a surprisingly fun guy who lived up to his nickname from his days as a Texas state representative, "Hot Tub Tom." On the golf course, said Pierce, "you pretty much never saw him without a beer in his hand."

Pierce said that at some point, he began to feel turned off by the workings of power. Recalling the scene at DeLay's annual charity golf event in Texas, at which he surveyed the links and observed all the people and businesses that needed a friend in Congress—only ten thousand dollars a foursome—Pierce said, "It seemed like that scene in *Blazing Saddles* where all the bad guys are waiting in line. Here I was, representing garment factories, and then there were oil companies, big auto, big tobacco, the NRA, power and utility companies, alcohol companies, Indian tribes, you name it." With all of the money such events funneled to

DeLay, his foundations, and his family members, Pierce said, part of him felt jealous. "Who wouldn't want to be a politician?" he quipped. In the end, he said, hanging out with guys like DeLay and Abramoff began to feel unhealthy for his sobriety.

Even after the fall of DeLay and Abramoff, however, he maintained that Team DeLaybramoff deserved credit for doing its job. The federal government had never been very adept at looking after the needs of far-away Micronesian constituencies. Now it was threatening to break the Covenant it had signed with the CNMI. Team DeLaybramoff had stopped them from doing so. They did what they promised to do and preserved the island's right to self-government.

What Pierce resented, however, was the way that Saipan had been used by mainland factions, prey to a process he called "getting sucked onto the Beltway." Explaining further, he said, "Once your situation goes from just a situation to being a big political football in Washington, you've got Democrats and Republicans using it as a way to clobber each other. And it has really very little to do with you. You never get out of it."

He paused, musing over the furor that Saipan had caused on the mainland. "Where else," he asked, "could you find a place with this small of a population that would get U.S. politics involved like they are here, where you've got people up in Congress yelling shit about it?"

In the end, in Pierce's estimation, everyone—the politicians, the media, the lawsuit-mongering lawyers—had used Saipan for their own interests, knowing little and caring less about the place. And yet, para-doxically, things had gotten better. Labor conditions on the island had definitely improved. Slavery was a thing of the past. And here he sur-prised me again. If all the hullabaloo and lawsuits and overstated charges were what it took to make the island change and learn and grow, he said with a small gulp, "you know: okay!"

The day after I met with Pierce, I met with Pamela Brown. After a bit-ter and prolonged fight, Brown had just been confirmed as the CNMI's attorney general. The AG post is a fairly new, and seemingly untenable, position. While virtually all other positions in the CNMI's government are held by islanders, the AG slot seems lately to be filled most often by mainland Americans. Tacit is the understanding that in a population as small and a culture as family-oriented and corrupt as the islands', a local appointee can't reasonably be expected to hold the post.

According to local gossip, Brown was loathed as roundly as Pierce. Not only was she a liberal and a non-golfer, but she was perceived by many as being irrationally out to get the garment industry. As one local probusiness, antiregulation guy complained to me, "She's got a hard-on for the industry that happens to be the only source of revenue on the island!" Others saw her as a stand-in for Congressman Miller, who in turn represented the meddlesome ways of the federal government.

Brown, like nearly every member of the white, Japanese, or local elite whom I'd interviewed, had suggested we meet at the same restaurant where I'd met Pierce—Coffee Care. When we took our seats, we noticed that Pierce sat at the table next to ours. This was island life; your enemies were never far away.

Brown is a pixie-ish, freckle-faced woman with red-plastic-rimmed glasses. She conveys a keen intelligence and an appealing "been there, done that" attitude. After having been a criminal defense attorney in Seattle, Brown arrived on Saipan in 1989, when the island was still in its Wild West period. "In those days," she recalled, "it was waitresses forced into prostitution and things like that. Things were bad. Chinese construction workers had been brought over and literally dumped into the boonies." "The boonies" are the woods, usually overgrown with thick vines and vegetation concealing treacherous holes and sharp spikes in the limestone underfoot.

She recalled an episode that occurred once when Congressman George Miller was visiting. Miller, Brown, a few aides, and some Chinese workers and translators were chatting. Suddenly, one of the translators seemed to get flustered. Brown asked what was wrong, and the translator answered, "Oh no, you don't want to know. It's too horrible." The group pressed her to answer, and finally the translator said that one of the workers was asking if perhaps Congressman Miller might want to buy his kidney. He could see that the congressman was very powerful, and, well, with the price of kidneys being what it is these days on the black market, it seemed worth asking.

The last big slavery case related to the garment industry that Brown could recall took place in 2001, when she was still federal ombudsman. There was a group of garment workers from a small factory who had been locked up and forced to work without pay. Brown said she had to assemble "a flotilla of relief" to spring the workers from their abusive employer. "Literally," she said, "my pickup, our van—we enlisted all these people to just drive over there and rap on the gate. We were doing this like at six o'clock at night. They wouldn't let them go."

While Saipan was still rife with problems, she said, the kind of horrendous, physically abusive exploitation of the 1990s was very much on the wane. Charges still arose frequently about workers being paid late or not at all, employers writing bad checks, and so on. But the number of workers who sought help from the federal ombudsman's office was down from 1,221 in 1999 to 549 in 2005. And the number of complaints filed annually during those same years has dropped from 962 to fewer than 500.

The problems now, Brown said, were more about attitudes. Employers on Saipan still suffer from what she called the "Asian mentality" problem. "They don't understand that people have rights. They're still arguing with me about why they can't terminate pregnant workers. And I keep trying to explain to them: we have these federal laws and we just can't do that. That's discrimination. That's the risk you take when you bring twenty-two-year-old women to a foreign country!"

Moreover, she said, despite repeated efforts by the garment industry and Saipan's government to put a stop to the practice, foreign workers were still having to pay recruitment fees of several thousand dollars to get jobs on Saipan. There were also continuing scams in the construction and security businesses, with local company owners stringing foreign workers along, month by month, paying nothing, then declaring bankruptcy.

"The industry"—meaning the garment industry—"really has attempted to self-police and correct things. Things have been cleaned up so radically," she said. There were many factories where workers were quite happy. Even as she said this, however, as on several occasions when I met with Brown, she alluded to the fact that there was a lot more she'd like to tell me—a *lot* more. But, she mentioned, her husband had a valuable business in Saipan (he ran a company that supplied the merchant marine ships anchored offshore), and, well, both of them had to live there. If she told me everything she knew, she said, "they'd kill me."

**O**bviously, if I wanted to observe labor conditions on Saipan, it seemed critical to get a tour of a garment factory. I wasn't so keen on tangling with Willie Tan or seeing the same factory tour he offered to visiting U.S. politicians. Through Pierce, I was able to meet Paul Zak.

Zak was not a factory owner but helped run two different garment companies, Advanced Textile and Rifu Apparel, for a Korean named Choi. Together they employed about seven hundred workers, which, Zak said, made him "maybe the fourth-biggest guy or fifth-biggest guy on the island." He was also the only native English speaker among the garment-factory managers, which, I figured, would greatly ease communication.

Zak looks like a combination of the late actor Norman Fell and Donald Rumsfeld, the former secretary of defense. His face has an unhealthy, greenish pallor, yet he becomes surprisingly lively and expressive when he talks. Zak is a gesticulator. He's fond of putting his hand to his temples and screaming "AAGHH!" like his head is about to explode. "How do you make a million dollars on Saipan?" he asked me. "Start with two!" He laughed, then up went the hand. "AAGHH!" He roared. Did I think he was joking? That was his story. He'd lost a million dollars since coming to Saipan. AGGH!

Before bringing me to his factory, Zak suggested we have dinner. Did I want to meet at the Coffee Care restaurant on Capitol Hill? By now, I knew my way around the place fairly well.

Zak has had a number of careers. He claimed with a straight face to have invented the concept of MTV (he was ripped off). He had another close brush with moguldom after that, which, frankly, I didn't catch because I was still musing about him inventing MTV. He'd come to Saipan to help a Hong Kong firm manufacture surgical towels, and ended up falling in love with the place. When I asked why, he mentioned the fact that it was free-market heaven—taxes were low, labor costs and regulations minimal. And yet, he said, it was almost like living in Asia. Despite the cheap living and the foreignness, a person in Saipan was still protected by the Marines. "You're safe," he said with a wink. "You're protected by all the rights of the United States."

The day after I met him, Zak agreed to take me on a tour of Rifu's main factory building. While Brown and others had mentioned Tan's "show factory," I was pretty sure Zak and his operation were nobody's idea of a show *anything*. By this, I merely mean that Zak was not someone I would describe as a real pro at personal image management. My most memorable meeting with him—well after interviewing him—was a Sunday-afternoon grocery store run-in. He seemed a bit disheveled and spent an hour telling me about how crushed he was because one of his factories had recently caught on fire. The local fire department was slow to arrive, and the darn thing burned all the way to the ground. As Zak told (and retold) me the story, his girlfriend, either a transvestite or transsexual—I'd heard about her—hovered by the pastry rack, too shy to come join us. My point is merely that Zak was clearly not someone who had been recommended to me to con me into believing everything was perfect in Saipan's garment industry.

What I can say from direct observation is that Rifu seemed like a decent place to work at an unappealing job. All my adult life, I'd read and heard about sweatshops and eighty-hour weeks and the horrors of the garment industry. While Zak's workers weren't exactly waltzing about with watermelon grins, they did not seem unduly dour, bruised, or chained to their machines. A few of them smiled. And to cede a point to Tom DeLay, the factory was indeed air-conditioned.

Zak took me around a room with four production lines. Each consisted of covered tables about ten feet wide and perhaps a hundred feet long, lined on both sides by predominantly female sewing machine operators. Each line was devoted to making a single garment and employed about twenty-five sewers, all Chinese. They raced rapidly and mechanically to keep up with a two- or three-foot pile of partially assembled shirts behind them, awaiting their attention. Indeed, the work seemed monotonous and stressful. *Rrrrrr.* Each sewer would stitch a sleeve, a piece of trim, a label, and so on, then yank the garment from the machine, cut the thread, put the garment onto the pile of the sewer next to her, grab another from the pile behind her, and—*rrrrr*—sew the next one. Supervisors, some Chinese, some locals, moved up and down the line, watching for production bottlenecks and, presumably, hustling along any worker falling behind. At the end of each assembly line, an inspector checked every hem for irregularities.

The process made me wonder about the term "unskilled labor." Sure, it didn't take an Einstein to learn to perform such menial tasks. But to do them well, quickly, without getting sleepy or distracted, seemed very much like a skill to me. The combination of tedium and the need for precision seemed like a brutal one, and by no means easy to sustain. We moved on to the cutting table.

Cutters are almost always men. (Men make up about 20 percent of Zak's labor force.) Their job was to maneuver a disturbingly sharp, hand-powered razor along a tracing drawn over dozens of identical pieces of cloth. Each cut marked a sleeve, a pant leg, the back panel of a shirt or turtleneck. It looked like an extremely skilled job. If a cutter makes a mistake, the factory is in big trouble: they no longer have the materials they need to complete an order.

"This business is not simple," Zak explained. He pointed to a container—the kind that trucks and freight trains carry. It had just come from a Korean trading company. Inside the container was everything that Zak's factory would need to produce the order, whether it was skirts, pants, sweaters, or pantsuits. Everything was included, from instructions and fabric to buttons, collars, trim, thread, even price tags. There was very little extra material to allow for mistakes, and from the moment the container arrived, the company usually had three to five days to turn out the order. With a schedule and supply mechanism like this, you could understand why, if a cutter screwed up, an entire order would be scotched.

Sales for Advanced Textile and Rifu Apparel combined, Zak said, were about $35 million a year. Sounds like a lot, he said, until you real-ize how insanely competitive the business is. Nobody in apparel manu-facturing made as much money as the public imagined they did. For a manufacturer on Saipan, or at least Zak, you then had to subtract the 71 percent he paid for labor, 7 percent for federal Social Security tax, the local CNMI 3.7 percent tax on garment exports, plus electricity (which costs much more than power anywhere else in the United States). "If nothing goes wrong and everything works like a Swiss stopwatch," Zak said, "what I get out of ten dollars in sales is three cents. That's what I put into my pocket. That's my profit. It's three cents out of a ten-dollar bill."

It wasn't just garment manufacturers who had it rough, he said. Re-tailers also found it hard to make money in today's clothing business. "Take, for example, Sears. Sears is only making—look at their annual report—is making 2.8 percent of that net. My biggest customer is Jones New York, and they make—after all is said and done—they make 5.3 percent."

The problem, according to Pierce, was competition. "Walk into any clothing store," he said to me. "How many things are cut way down? How many things are on sale? Nothing is full price anymore, because of all the competition in the garment industry. Nobody pays retail any-more." Pierce had told me that many of the retail clothing companies ac-tually order price tags to be made and attached to clothes with two prices written on them, one, say, for $29.95 and another for, say, $19.95, with the higher price slashed over by a marker.

During the time of the big media exposés about Saipan, in the late nineties, Zak said, much was made of the fact that Saipan's garment manufacturers weren't paying U.S. tariffs. Zak recalled a conversation he had with a "fact-finding" congresswoman.

"How much do you think I make?" Zak asked her.

As he remembered, she said, "Well, since you're not paying duty to the United States, you must be making twenty-one percent."

"Yeah . . . right," Zak told her. "I'm not paying U.S. duty. So who's getting it? Must be me!" He laughed again.

"Okay," he said to the congresswoman, "let's do a little bit of role-playing. You play the buyer and I'm the supplier. You come to negotiate with me, and I'm making twenty-one percent. And now you go back home to your boss, letting me make twenty-one percent. You're fired!"

He laughed uproariously. Up went the hand. "AAGHH! It's discounted! The American consumer made the twenty-one percent. If I paid the duty, it would be twenty-one percent higher. Because he's not paying, who do you think got it? The American consumer got it, because he's buying it at Wal-Mart for nine ninety-five!"

Zak, like Brown and Pierce before him, acknowledged that labor conditions had been awful in the past. "Was this the Wild West? Yes. Were people taken advantage of? Yes. Things were fucked up. There were no rules. OSHA wasn't here. Nobody was here. We didn't know what the rules were. There were no manuals. Buildings weren't built to any codes. And all of a sudden, civilization comes in, guys with badges come in."

Like Pierce and, to a certain extent, Brown before him, he said that you really had to look beyond the sensationalized media horror stories to see that most garment workers on Saipan were doing—and had generally done—very well for themselves. They came to Saipan in their young twenties. They worked for a few years, maybe four on the average. They made ten times as much money as they would have back in China. And then they left. "How much do you think my average worker after four years leaves to go back to China with? Twenty-five to thirty-five thousand dollars cash. What would you do if you had your entire retirement in cash at twenty-eight years old? They open up businesses. Stores, karaoke, dress shops, small manufacturers."

Zak laughed at the portrait of labor abuse that had been painted about Saipan. Conditions had changed so drastically, he said, thanks to the media attention and the intrusion of mainland ways, that by now it was the employers who were being abused. "Workers' rights?" He cackled. "What about employers' rights? Why doesn't anyone talk about that?"

Employers on Saipan are required to buy an airplane ticket home for any worker who wants to leave. If Zak spends a lot of money bringing a worker to Saipan and the worker wants to go home, tough. If the worker just arrived and hasn't served his or her contract, too bad. The employer still has to pay.

Employers on Saipan are also responsible for their workers' medical costs. While I would later hear complaints from workers about bosses who were too cheap to take their workers to the doctor, the problems went both ways. Zak told me about a new employee who arrived and turned out to have mental problems. "Three weeks after she gets here, my security guy calls up," he said. "She's outside the company area with two bags waiting for a helicopter. She's nuts. What are you going to do? Put a nut on the plane?" He said he had to send the woman to the local psych ward for ten days of observation at five hundred dollars a day. AGHH!

Pretty much everything I learned from Zak would turn out to be true. Employers on Saipan did have responsibilities that mainland employers didn't. The fact that it wasn't a real free-market system with people free to come and go, where almost all labor was performed by foreign guest workers, made it a completely jury-rigged setup for both workers and employers.

The most perverse story I heard about this complicated paternal dynamic came from a hearing officer with the Saipan Department of Labor. Under the law, as the inspector said, employers are responsible for repatriating anybody who dies while in their employ. One Bangladeshi man got so angry at his employer that he burnt his boss's business to the ground. Unfortunately, he forgot to run out of the building on time, got caught in his own blaze, and died. The employer, obviously, shall we say, chagrined at the loss of his business, was even more so when he learned he would have to pay for the man's coffin to be flown to Bangladesh.

Since the scandals of the late nineties, Zak said, he'd learned to deal with the retail clothing companies' compliance teams. But it was a nightmare. "They come in twice a year," he said—all of them, Polo, Liz Claiborne, Sears, JCPenney, Gap, everyone. The compliance teams spend anywhere from three to five days compiling ten pages of forms. "Ten pages of shit. Safety, human rights, working conditions, payroll." Sometimes, he went on, two compliance teams would show up at the same time. "One wants to see my time clock. So I give 'em all my time-clock things. I run from that office, give it to the other guy, and he does the same thing. Nuts! Nuts! And then the garment association, once a year, has PricewaterhouseCoopers come in and they do the same thing. Nuts!"

What people don't understand, he said, is that even in a world with no government regulation whatsoever, a garment-factory owner would have to be out of his mind to mistreat his workers. First of all, he explained, to set up a factory, an employer had to erect buildings, dormitories, toilets, and water tanks, and buy equipment like pressing machines and hundreds of different types of sewing machines. He had to spend all of that money before making his first dime. In Zak's estimation, each worker represented a ten-thousand-dollar investment. A ten-thousand-dollar liability.

Did I get it? "I live by these workers," he said. "If a worker goes, what do I do with that machine? If you've got twenty-seven people lined up doing various parts of one garment and three of those people leave, what do you do? Do I send the other twenty-four home? Each one's got a different skill. Each one does a different function. I can't take my ironer and make him a sewer. So what do I do?

"Do I want to fuck with a worker? Why? He's my partner. Do you know what it takes to have a wise guy—God forbid—put a needle in the collar of a shirt you made? Do you want to know what sabotage is all about? Why would you fuck with somebody who could sabotage you?" Worker abuse, he said, just didn't make sense. He wasn't being antagonistic toward me. But he was obviously fed up with the way people had portrayed his industry—while knowing nothing of the guts of how it worked. "Why fuck with somebody when they're making $3.05 an hour?" A worker, he said, "he's your racehorse. He's your thoroughbred. Make sure he's fed well. If he gets sick, what the fuck am I up? Shit's Creek!" He put a hand to his temple: "AAGHH!"

Zak showed me his workers' barracks. They weren't bad, as barracks went, and yet, at the same time, no worker accustomed to American standards would have considered spending even a single night in them. They were clean, recently painted, relatively free of the mold that eats at so many cheaply constructed buildings in a humid place like

Saipan. Fluorescent lights, linoleum floors, painted, cement walls. Most rooms had four bunks, some had five. On the floor, attached to the bed—everywhere they could fit—were plastic buckets, baskets, and covered bins for storing clothes, scraps of fabric from the factory, objects made from scraps of fabric from the factory, stuffed animals. Many of the bunks had curtains drawn around them, for privacy. The curtains often had photographs of family members and celebrities pinned to them. Beside the beds were little plastic wardrobes for clothes and little rows of shoes. Most women seemed to have four pairs.

Zak took me to the shower area, a group affair with ten spigots and no privacy. The cafeteria was similarly adequate—not horrible, just plain, utterly unadorned, definitely below a college dormitory in terms of luxury, possibly hovering around lower-class youth-camp accoutrements. Zak said that he subcontracted the food preparation to a catering service. "I don't want to be in that business," he said.

Referring to the big, headline-generating lawsuit by Milberg Weiss against Saipan's factories and the retailers that hired them, Zak said, "When the class-action happened, six workers complained against me. Six. Out of—total number of workers that I had during that time? About six hundred." Was this evidence of the massive mistreatment of workers reported in the press? Up went the hand: "AAGGHH!"

He went on. "You know, John, I betcha I could go to any organization and find someone that doesn't like what they do. I once had as one of my investors a guy who was making eighty thousand dollars a month as an eye surgeon. He pulls up in his twelve-cylinder Jaguar, and he's got his Gucci shoes, his Rolex watch, camel-hair jacket; he comes into my factory and says he hates what he's doing. He hates operating on people with glaucoma. 'I hate it.' I looked at my man and I took him to the window and I showed him my manufacturing floor with forty people and said, 'You know what, Terry? They don't like what they're doing either.'"

At the top of Saipan's pecking order is fifty-year-old Willie Tan. Tan is the chief executive officer of Tan Holdings Corporation. Tan Holdings, according to its website, in turn owns sixteen companies. Combined operations exceed $300 million each year. The corporation is tied to Luen Thai Holdings, a Hong Kong–based company focused on apparel manufacturing with twelve offices in seven countries throughout Asia. Luen Thai, which went public in 2004, is headed by Tan's father. According to its website, it has 17,000 employees.

In 2004, Tan Holdings owned three garment factories employing 2,500 workers. In February 2007, Tan shut down all Saipan garment-manufacturing operations. Before divesting them in 2006, he also owned an estimated one hundred of the island's ubiquitous gambling machines. He still owns the *Saipan Tribune,* one of the island's two English-language newspapers, and four hotels on Saipan and Guam (the Fiesta Resort Guam and, on Saipan, the Fiesta Resort, the Saipan Grand Hotel, and the Century Hotel). Further holdings include a travel agency, multiplex theaters on both Saipan and Guam, a regional freight airline, a marine shipping company, an insurance company, a regional distribution firm, the local FedEx outlet, a regional fishing company, and an ice cream parlor. Although Tan is a U.S. citizen, maintaining a home and business address on Saipan, anecdotal evidence indicates that he is actually in Saipan a few weeks a year or less, preferring to spend his time in Hong Kong.

Pierce had told me that huge operators such as Tan probably made slightly higher profit margins in the garment business than someone like Paul Zak, but still, in 2004, even Tan was making only about 1 percent on sales of garments manufactured in Saipan. It was enough to survive but not to thrive. What made Tan's money, Pierce said, was the fact that he owned so many other businesses on the island. His shipping line took a cut for moving his fabric and finished product. His insurance company took a cut for insuring his workers. His local FedEx outfit shipped his documents. As Pierce said of Tan's garment business, "He can lose money and still make money."

I asked Pierce repeatedly to get Tan's people to talk to me and was several times refused. Pierce told me that Tan had simply felt he'd been burned by too many reporters. Tan's people continued to be wary of me for a long time after my arrival. Once, a friend I'd made on Saipan had invited me to accompany him to Willie Tan's Christmas party. I found the idea rather amusing. But when word got out that I was coming, the friend called me and nervously said he'd changed his mind and had to go to another party that night. I wasn't invited. He later told me he'd gone to Tan's party after all.

All I could really do was snoop around Tan's operations. The now-closed Concorde factory was situated near Beach Road (one of Saipan's two main drags, the other being Middle Road), past the tourist hotels, close to the port. It employed about one thousand workers. The main facility was an enormous structure made of corrugated metal painted a faded-custard color with rust-red trim. Massive vents throbbed day and night, emitting steam into the sunlight and roaring loudly. Behind the factory was a moat of filthy water, the banks of which were lined with graceful casuarina pines.

Most garment factories are ringed by barbed-wire fences. Media accounts usually make much of this. The implication—and sometimes the reality—is that workers are locked in. Certainly, the gates and the guards make an impressive visual aid. What is seldom mentioned is that *most* factories around the world are ringed by barbed-wire fences. The reason, of course, is to keep out thieves.

At any rate, the Concorde factory was not surrounded by a gate of any sort. Anyone who wanted to could, as I did, drive right up and peek inside the factory through any one of several doors that were, at least during my visits, left open. Inside, operations seemed similar to those I'd observed at Zak's factory: sewers leaned over sewing machines or stood at cutting tables or inspection bins beneath a massive latticework of fluorescent lights. Managers cruised the floor, up and down the line.

When a shift ended, hundreds of workers—mostly female—streamed out of the building into the parking lot. Nearly all wore shirts with the letters TH, for Tan Holdings, embroidered on the breast. Some were plain white or solid colors, others horizontally striped in blue, red, light green, pale yellow. Each color designated a different section of the factory floor: buttons, collars, cutting, trim. On perhaps a half dozen different visits, the general mood seemed to be one of wan exhaustion. But it would be a wild exaggeration to imply that every worker seemed miserable, and disappointing as it may be for any writer, I would resist the urge to deploy the word *Dickensian*.

The dirt parking lot outside Concorde was dotted with mud puddles. In front of a few cars and a row of shuttle buses were a dozen or so male produce vendors, each in front of a truck. They had laid out their boxes and plastic buckets in rows among the mud puddles. All of them were Chinese, and their vegetables—bok choy, kangkong, long string beans, hot peppers, okra—came from local farms.

Around the factory were several barracks. One of them, a block away, had a sign over the entryway:

TAN HOLDINGS CORPORATION
HAVING THE BEST CARE FOR WORKER IN THE WORLD!

Next to the words was a cartoon character: a heart with a face and little arms with white mitts. Over the character were the words WE CARE FOR OUR PEOPLE!

This public relations effort betrayed a problem. In the same way that people who repeatedly call you "my friend" are seldom your friend, why would any business have to announce such a thing? Imagine a store in a shopping mall or a Starbucks putting up a sign that said WE TREAT OUR WORKERS JUST GREAT!

On a personal level, several people told me, Willie Tan was a very nice guy. Totally unpretentious. If you met him, one person told me, you'd never think he was *Willie Tan*. Another person told me that he'd heard Tan shouting and swearing at one of his business associates over a speakerphone like a petty, bullying tyrant. Some people blamed Tan for everything wrong with Saipan, referring to him as "Willietan," as in: Satan. One resident who didn't like him much explained his alleged ethical lapses, saying, "Willie's like a lot of businessmen. They get away with as much as they can. If you give him room, he'll abuse people. If you watch over him, he'll comply. Whatever he can do to make money, he'll do." Some people went into a familiar litany one often hears about ethnic Chinese in Asia: they're "the Jews of Asia." The thought occurred to me several times that Tan probably took a certain amount of heat by default; as the richest guy on the island, he made an awfully convenient target. This didn't make him innocent of all charges. It just meant that charges against him deserved as much scrutiny as those against pretty much everyone else on Saipan.

Once, on a bar stool, I happened to meet the former head of Saipan's Social Security Administration, a white guy named Mike Newman. Newman had been on Saipan twenty-five years. He was one of the many people I met who felt that the island had been treated unfairly by the media. His feelings about Tan were mixed. Like several people I spoke with, including former Tan employees, he said one reason workers complained so roundly about his operations was that he was so efficient at managing them, his workers got little overtime.

This is something that many well-intentioned accounts of poor workers and guest workers get wrong when they bring up "workers forced to work seventy-hour weeks." My experience was that the foreign laborers who came to Saipan were almost always eager to work longer hours than they were currently working. Perhaps they did not want to work ninety hours per week, but they got very pissed off and cagey when they were only given forty or forty-eight hours. They hadn't come to Saipan to play or to have a nice life. They had come to make money.

According to two cousins I met, one a garment worker and the other a former garment worker, failing to get overtime was the worst thing that could happen to a guest worker. "You are not going to make any money on twenty-four dollars a day, so you need overtime," one explained. "That's where you are going to get the money that you are going to save." Garment workers "come here for no other reason but to work. You've paid all that money; you bankrupted your family to borrow the money to come here, take a big risk, and make an investment. So you are sitting there thinking, 'I paid all that money to come here and I am not making money,' and it literally can drive a person crazy." They didn't seem to be exaggerating, they seemed to be stating plainly that workers obsessed so intensely about their failure to get overtime hours that some became mentally ill.

Of course, the fact that workers wanted more hours needed further parsing: if they were paid a higher wage, they could work forty hours a week and still have a decent life.

One wrinkle I discovered in Saipan's jury-rigged labor system was that somewhere between many and most workers on the island filed labor complaints against Tan and other employers in order to get a special dispensation from the Department of Labor called a TWA memo. TWA memos allowed them to seek another job—this time, perhaps, with an employer who offered more than forty hours per week. The effect was to create a huge incentive for workers to file complaints—bogus or not. Since each worker complaint required an investigation, the Department of Labor was constantly overwhelmed and less able to focus on complaints meriting the most attention.

This needs parsing as well. As mentioned earlier, guest workers who came to Saipan were contracted to work for the employer that hired them. Unlike workers in a real free market, they were not free to look for another job until their contract had ended, they wanted to leave the island, or they obtained a TWA memo. In a sense, whether benignly or by consent, guest workers on Saipan really *were* a captive labor force.

Almost offhandedly, Newman noted that while he didn't think the Tan operation was as horrible as it had been portrayed in the media, he did remember once paying a visit to the Human Resources Department at Tan's company. He happened to notice an entire wall lined with black plastic binders. Out of mere curiosity, he asked what they were; he was told, "Oh, those are the runaways."

When I visited the Saipan Department of Labor, I was shuffled around and referred from one officer to another. Eventually, someone let me sift through a couple of three-ring folders clogged with adjudicated labor complaints. The most common of them concerned unpaid wages, workers being illegally forced to pay their own processing fees and medical-exam fees, and so on. I didn't see anything about slavery. But I found it difficult to interpret what the complaints meant, or what they implied. As with the Indian men in Tulsa, I did not want to dismiss the possibility that workers would use every tool in their arsenal to improve their already meager lot. Why shouldn't they lie if it would do them some good?

Eventually I was referred to a hearing officer named Jacinta Kaipat. Cinta, as she was known, was a massive, fierce, haughty Carolinian who'd been educated on the mainland. When I asked her a question or two about the workers' complaints, she launched into an endless tirade. She was tired of hearing bad things about her island, she said. It wasn't really all that bad. She was sick of all of these foreigners who just came to use the place. She went a solid forty minutes without letting me get a word in, then insisted that I watch a documentary film she had made.

The film was self-centered, self-pitying, and delusional in the extreme, in a way I would later find to be characteristic of a certain type of islander. Ignoring the fact that it was Saipan's own government and business leaders who had encouraged the quadrupling of the local population with foreign guest workers, the documentary repeatedly bemoaned the "foreigners flocking to our shores to find work." It really was something of a joke, especially considering that the Carolinians had only come to Saipan in the last couple of hundred years, fleeing the Caroline Islands. In the end, Kaipat barged past every one of my questions, answering none. She has since been elected to Congress.

Eventually, I would begin to better understand how to view labor complaints. Here are some examples.

> Labor complaint 1, signed, 8/14/2003
> COMPLAINANT: XXXXXXXXXXX
> DATE OF ARRIVAL 12/19/98
> FIRST DAY OF WORK 12/20/98
> OCCUPATION: Commercial Cleaner / Masseuse
> GENDER: Female
> LAST DAY OF WORK 08/12/03
> RESPONDENT: Ko Woon Corp
> DBA/AKA: Sabana Aroma Massage
>
> Re: Labor Complaint
>
> My name is XXXXXXXXXXX . . . employee of KO WOON CORP . . . I would like to complain my employer as follows:

1. I clean for my employer with no pay, my boss agreed me work as a cleaner is $700 per month, and working for massage is $800 per month by cash, but I never got paid for cleaning.
2. My boss always sexual assaults me while I was at work, if I defend, I might got fired. My manager yells me and she slapped me one day in July, because I was late 30 minutes from the previous day's over-night working.
3. I am not allowed to have boyfriend, though I am off after work, I still couldn't go out from my barracks.

The complaint ends by requesting that the Department of Labor grant the complainant a transfer to work at another company—a TWA memo. It also requests payment for five weeks of unpaid wages plus unpaid overtime of three hundred dollars. There's no reason to accept or dismiss out of hand the issues addressed in the complaint, but it would be helpful to know, for example, if the worker's contract was soon due to expire, to assess whether the worker filed the complaint merely to stay longer in the CNMI. One would also have to consider how a worker could possibly stay at a job for nearly four years before complaining about something as serious as continual sexual assault. Such a worker would either have to be extremely tough or extremely desperate.

A second complaint, signed on October 7, 2003, by a male Chinese garment cutter, asserted:

My name is YYYYYY, an employee of Top Fashion Corp, I came to Saipan on October 4, 1997, and I worked for the company, but I felt so much unfair things at my work and with my supervisor so I want to
    Complain to labor as follows:

1. Working with no pay, we have to clock in 5 minutes before the schedule, 2 times a day; if we have to over time work, we clock in 3 times a day. Since this year I have 50 hours no pay at all.
2. Deduction of our food monthly $90, but our food taste so bad, our breakfast always served with the left over from previous day.
3. Our line manager always yell at me with no reason, I have to watch his emotion at work; one time after I came back from using the restroom, I got scolded, when I tried to explain, instead, I told to be stop working. It makes me very nervous every morning when I go to work.

4. We have to get permission for sick leave, but we have to leave for 3 days even though I only got minor sick. That made me have no 40 hours working in one week and I don't get paid for 40 hours.

A third complaint read: "Our food taste so bad, we were always unhappy with the meals, sometimes I don't have enough to eat, but when I went to ask more food from the kitchen, they responded me there's no more food. I have $94 deduction for living, but the living condition is not good." Still another noted, "We have a pass-card for leaving the barracks, each time I have to sign out and write down the car license plate number when I went out after work." And so on.

When I first tried to approach garment workers directly, I would find them leaving a factory and ask them through a Mandarin-speaking translator if I could speak with them. They almost always turned away. Later I realized that many workers would happily talk—under the right conditions. It was stupid of me to think that they would talk to a complete stranger, an American, no less, on company property, in full view of managers and guards—and even other workers. One didn't do such things.

On several visits to Saipan over three and a half years, I spent enough time and found enough ways to approach garment workers to get a true picture of their lives. It was mixed. I learned that the largest number of worker complaints were directed at Tan. Some workers said he gave them too much overtime. His barracks were crummy. They lacked hot water. They lacked water, period. He never upgraded them. He never repaired them. He didn't always pay overtime. He made his employees wait in long lines to be frisked on their way out of work—wasting several minutes per day. One claim, alleged in a complaint made to the CNMI Department of Labor and Immigration, was that Tan had been profiting from the rent he charged his workers for their meager housing—a no-no under CNMI law. The suit made its way through the appeals process and then stalled, for no apparent reason.

Another consistent and repeated charge, according to findings made by the CNMI Department of Labor as part of a complaint filed against two of Tan's factories, was that even as Saipan's garment industry began declining in 2005, Tan's Saipan operations continued profiting from fees charged workers recruited from his family's Hong Kong companies. Saipan and federal authorities had worked diligently to limit such recruiting fees to fifteen hundred dollars, but in practice, regardless of their efforts, workers I talked to who were new to Saipan kept reporting they'd paid fees of three and sometimes four thousand dollars for their jobs. In support of the allegation that Tan was profiting in this way, I found it troubling that he was allowed to bring workers from China to Saipan as late as one month before the announcement that he would be closing his factories. Why else would an obviously shrewd businessman do such a thing?

One woman I met, a self-employed Chinese translator who had seen many labor disputes, told me that she was well aware that many worker complaints were baseless, filed merely to gain more time "in America." When two or three people complained about something, she said, she seldom believed it. But if twenty, thirty, or one hundred people complained about the same factory, talking about the food and insects in the vegetables and nothing but finger bowls of meat for eight people and hardly enough soup and workers going hungry, then that was enough to indicate a real problem. This translator said that the majority of such complaints she had seen came from workers employed at L&T, one of Willie Tan's factories.

Think about the vegetable vendors one saw outside many of Saipan's factories, she said. If employers were feeding their workers so well, why would there be food vendors outside? Why would poor, frugal workers spend what little money they had on supplementary food? The food in most factories was disgusting, poorly prepared, lacking in vegetables, and frequently infested with insects.

This translator had no chip on her shoulder whatsoever about the garment industry in general. When I asked her about Advanced Textile and Rifu to get her opinion of Paul Zak and his Korean partner, Choi, she recognized the latter's name and said, "Oh, he's nice." She, like other sources intimate with factory conditions, said that the worst conditions were usually at the smallest factories, the ones that were barely surviving.

Other workers echoed this. Smaller companies, it was voiced, were often stressed and underfinanced, so they routinely paid workers a month or two late. This translator mentioned that some of these factories were so stingy they didn't buy toilet paper for their workers. Workers in such cases resolved the problem by stealing scraps of fabric, using them for toilet paper, and throwing them into cans near the toilets.

Workers at bigger factories faced different problems. According to one garment worker, Chinese floor managers extorted floor workers to pay bribes. "You have to give the 'red envelope,' " she said, referring to a common Chinese euphemism for monetary gifts often used as bribery, also known as "lucky money." If a worker expects to get her contract renewed for another year, she has to pay up. The bribes vary in size, but some said that a thousand dollars was typical.

Big factory or small, complaints about supervisors were nearly universal. One of the two cousins I interviewed said that her supervisor would circle around her and hiss, "You are slow, like a pig."

I heard several complaints from a garment worker I came to think of as "Loud Girl." When she talked to me, she almost barked, in a haughty, self-amused voice. I had met her at the home of a Vietnamese man who would later be investigated for defrauding garment workers, selling his assistance in translating and processing fake labor complaints. His company's name was Freedom, Inc. Loud Girl met me wearing her pajamas. She was a friend of the Vietnamese man's Chinese wife and had gone to their home to take a shower because, she said, the shower at her factory barracks was disgusting. Often there wasn't even water with which to shower. She had midlength black hair and was taller than most Chinese women I'd met. Despite bags under her eyes, she was nevertheless attractive, perhaps because she seemed extremely strong-willed. When I asked her if she liked anything about her job, she snapped, "What we don't like? We don't like our jobs, that's what. Because we have real talents, and we can't use them. At home, I used to study management. Now here, I work sewing on a system where I have to do so many things in an hour, and if I don't, I'm in trouble. People without an education, maybe they like standing there on the line all the time. People like me, we need targets, goals."

She complained about the sameness of the work. The type of garments changed, but the routine of what she did never, ever varied. When I asked her if the work was routine enough to allow her to space out and think of other things, she said no. "You have to concentrate or you won't finish, and you won't reach the quota."

I asked Loud Girl if she and the others had much chance to talk during work hours, and she barked, "Talking is not allowed. It's only good for you to work. We can only talk secretly, when the line manager is not around."

Like others I met, she noted the difference between the industrial pace on Saipan versus that in China. As one worker explained, "Factories very different here and in China. In China, they work slow. Saipan, very fast, much more stress. In China, when you're working, you work a lot, but it's more playful. Saipan, you work a very short time, but you produce much more. One hour in China, fifty garments. One hour in Saipan, one hundred garments. At L&T, you can never stop. There is no rest. In China, you can go to the bathroom, get a drink of water, or chat. Saipan, just you working here, you must stay where you are."

After her nightly shower, she said, "I hurry back to the barracks and go to sleep because I'm tired to death. My mind is like an empty sheet, I can't think of anything."

She was anxious that I not mention her name, she said, "because everybody is friends, and I don't want to cause trouble."

Loud Girl, like virtually every other garment worker I met on Saipan, described her co-workers as unhappy, but then she added that that made sense since they were in Saipan to make money, not to have fun.

As an American, a citizen of a country devoted to life, liberty, and, most avidly perhaps, the pursuit of happiness, I was shocked to see the extent to which many workers viewed their time on Saipan as utter sacrifice, during which thoughts of happiness were almost entirely deferred. One woman told me that some garment workers cared only to work at the busiest factory they could find, "so they can just running themselves like machines." She told me that her factory was currently running from 9 A.M. to 2:30 A.M. and that there were many girls voluntarily working this shift seven days a week, all year round. "They just

prepare in their mind," she said, describing their thoughts, " 'I will suffer three or four years and when I go back I will be comparatively
wealthy.' "

"You know," the cousins told me, "Chinese people are very save their
money, they don't spend money, frugal." They proceeded to tell me
about a woman who worked in one of the cousin's factory. Her job was
mainly to clean the bathrooms. It was the most horrible job in the
factory, and it meant being on her hands and knees much of the time, in-
haling stinky cleaning compounds. The bathroom was enormous, with
many stalls, enough to accommodate something like fifteen hundred
workers.

As discussed, workers had housing and food and Social Security deducted from their pay. A critical decision for any worker, then, was how
to spend the rest of the money he or she earned. Send it all home? Bank
it all? Enjoy just a little bit of it? The woman who cleaned the bathrooms—both cousins got bright-eyed with admiration as they told me
about this—was the most frugal person they had ever seen. At the end of
every month, she allowed herself one luxury: She allowed herself to buy
three red apples. One cousin recalled, "I think it was those red apples
from the States. Maybe at the time you could buy three for a dollar.
Yeah, I think they're those big round ones from the States."

It took dozens of stories like this to get me beyond the simple question of whether or not Saipan's garment workers were being mistreated
or enslaved. During the day I spent with Paul Zak, he told me a story
that was wacky and factually all over the place but that remained nevertheless the best metaphor I'd heard for why Saipan was interesting.
Twenty-six miles offshore from Saipan and six miles below the surface
of the ocean, he said, lay the Mariana Trench. The trench, he explained,
was a well-known site of intense tectonic activity. And what was happening, and what one could observe with a unique vantage point on
Saipan, was the collision between what he called "the U.S. tectonic
plate" and "the Asian tectonic plate." The process, he explained with
some glee, illustrating by sliding one hand beneath the other, was that
one of these plates would be sliding over and covering the other. One
would be on top. The other would be at the bottom. Here on Saipan, he

said, "you're on the leading edge of the future. This is where the old world is going down and the new world is going up. This is where it's cracking."

Many if not most of the garment workers on Saipan are peasants from rural villages in China. Although the Communist government is finally making noises about loosening the system, as of 2006, Chinese citizens were required to live and work where they were registered, which is to say, the village, town, or city where their mother or father was registered. Travel or relocating outside of one's *hukou*—or permanent registered residence—is forbidden. The *hukou* system is enforced by the dreaded Public Security Bureau, the nation's police bureaucracy.

China's current population is about 1.3 billion. Of these, an estimated 780 million are considered rural peasants. While the Chinese economy has grown miraculously and with much fanfare over the last three decades, the growth distribution of wealth has been almost entirely limited to the coastal cities and special economic zones. Until recently, the peasantry has been deliberately excluded from the rising prosperity, and 180 million to 350 million of them (numbers vary wildly) are currently estimated to be in "excessive" or "dire" poverty.

The *hukou* system does not mean that China's peasants obey the law and stay on their farms. It means that if they want to leave, they are forced to pay numerous bribes and live the life of illegal aliens within their own country. There are an estimated 114 million migrant workers within China's borders who have illegally left their homes to seek work in the cities. Their situation is roughly analagous to undocumented Hispanic workers in the United States, but in the case of China, it's not only employers who exploit them but also government officials, who at every turn demand endless numbers of documents, deposits, and bribes. Peasants are forced to purchase personal-identity cards, "border-region passes," certificates demonstrating their marital status, and to obtain temporary residence permits, pay transportation costs, and shell out substantial sums to leave on deposit with new employers for the privilege of being hired.

Migrant workers employed by large firms are under constant surveillance. Most workers live in cramped spaces on company-owned
compounds. Many are not permitted to leave the grounds or are permitted to leave only for brief periods each week. Many log twelve-to-
eighteen-hour days, seven days a week, without a day of rest for months
at a stretch. Death by overworking—or *guolaosi*—has become a commonly used term in contemporary China.

As Anita Chan, an Australia-based expert on Chinese labor, writes,

> The young people have traveled long distances to get to these facto-
> ries, but once inside, their physical world shrinks. When there is
> work in the factory, their days are divided between the shop floor
> and the dormitory. When there is no work, they have no use for their
> free time because they have no money to go anywhere.
>
> Leisure and entertainment are not part of their lives. The high-
> light of an occasional day off is no more than window shopping (not
> buying). Having a soft drink in a café is far beyond their financial ca-
> pacity. For the duration of their years in a factory, their physical and
> mental horizons barely extend beyond the compound.

Clearly, China's labor environment was worse than Saipan's. But
what did this mean about Chinese workers' understanding of life on
Saipan or their place in the world? In China, migrant workers were like
a herd of "virtual slaves." Regular nonmigrant workers were only a step
above. What about on Saipan?

I met a Filipina who had been on Saipan for many years, working
first as a maid for three hundred dollars a month and later as a freelance
(legitimate) masseuse, a job that paid about five hundred or more per
month and offered much more freedom. I asked if she thought Saipan
was a good place. She beamed. "Ah. You know, it is so good to be in
Saipan. Everybody is so nice. I used to work in Kuwait, I went on a two-
year term from 1992 to 1994. Oh my God! That was horrible. I lived in
this one house that had five floors and had seven of us working, all from
the Philippines. They didn't feed us anything. My God! You know how
Filipinos are, we like our snacks. In the Philippines we ate three meals a

day with rice. And there, in Kuwait, we just had this—like a pancake thing in the morning. It was just this dry pancake. And no rice. And then the only real meal of the day was at ten o'clock at night and basically they would put all the rice on a big plate and eat it with their hands and give the leftovers to us. It wasn't very good. And the pay was only three thousand pesos [fifty-five dollars] a month. Plus you had to pay the recruiter—the 'agency' as it was called—at home."

She said some girls couldn't stand it. They'd run away. But inevitably, they'd get caught and sent to jail. Once in jail, they were raped by the police. "And so," the masseuse concluded, "it is so much better here in Saipan. People are nice."

The Chinese on Saipan had the most palpably low status of all the ethnic groups. One reason was that they were the newest, most recent group to arrive on the island. Also, unlike the Filipinos and Bangladeshis, who traditionally learn English in school, the Chinese seldom spoke much English. They were well aware of their status on the island. As I heard from two different Chinese women, simmering at how others, especially Filipinos, perceived them, "They think we're like ants."

There were many different social niches on Saipan, between and within ethnic groups. A Chinese garment worker with four years' experience on Saipan knew the ropes better than one with one year's. Many had little side jobs, translating or participating in one scam or another. One woman I became friends with had come to the island many years back, worked as a prostitute, paid a local guy to marry her, then worked her way into a legitimate job translating at the court. Later she moved to Guam, and then Hawaii.

She and other Chinese translator acquaintances had climbed a few steps up the socioeconomic ladder and gained a better understanding of the idea of rights. Most Chinese on Saipan, fresh off the plane, had little notion of human rights in general. In many ways, their lives simply counted less than those of workers from other ethnic groups on Saipan. During my time on the island, it seemed that they got hit by cars an awful lot. I saw one get hit myself. It seemed like you heard about accidents or read about them on the average of once a month. The reason for so many accidents was that no one had ever bothered to make sidewalks or crosswalks—an interesting choice for an island with about twenty-five thousand pedestrians. The rate of accidents had become something of a joke on the island. Before I came to Saipan, a vogue had passed where clever motorists posted a bumper sticker that read I BRAKE FOR GARMENT WORKERS.

I met a white American who told me about the night he'd seen a local guy hit-and-run a Chinese girl on a bike. A cop had come, and his first question was "Who did it?" When he found out the driver was a local, and looked over the wounded Chinese girl on the ground, my source said, he felt he witnessed the cop closing the case. When the American called the police station a few days later to inquire about the police report, he was met with stalls and excuses. Evidently, it hadn't been necessary to file a report. Another American acquaintance, a prosecutor, told me of prosecuting a rape case on Tinian. She'd had more than ample evidence; in fact, she described it as "the best rape case I've ever had." Nevertheless, the jury found the suspect, a local, innocent of raping the victim, a Filipina. When the judge later polled the jury, he asked them if they hadn't been convinced of the man's guilt. Oh no, they answered. They'd just felt that the sentence—twenty years—was too long. After all, the accused was a buddy of theirs.

It wasn't just locals who thought like racists. One time, a Filipina friend and I were talking about the Chinese prostitutes one saw everywhere on Saipan. More precisely, we were wondering what it must be like to hawk your wares on the street, offering yourself for sale as you pass families with kids. My friend was raised on Saipan and knew well Saipan's sexual and social mores. I was a little surprised when she said of the Chinese, "You know, I don't think they really feel the same about prostitution as *other* people." I almost laughed at how racist this sounded. She said, "I just think that in their culture it's not that big a deal. I don't think they know what it means. They don't think the same way we do."

Constantly on Saipan I heard stories about Chinese exploiting other Chinese. In the memorable words of Paul Zak: "No one can fuck a Chinese like a Chinese can. It's just the way it is." And that is the way it was.

I heard stories of triad operators running illegal gambling parlors whose job it was to lure innocent village girls into gambling so that they could become addicted. Some triad members' job was to drive a van around to all the garment factories at closing time to pick up workers wanting to go directly to the gambling den. Such workers didn't last long in the garment industry. Their debts piled up too quickly, and they were forced to turn to crime. I heard of prostitutes so addicted to gambling that they would perform a trick, run back to the casino, lose their money, run out, do another trick, and so on.

I heard and personally saw evidence of Chinese attempts to lure old friends, former co-workers, and even cousins to jobs that didn't exist, in order to make a few thousand dollars on the "recruiting fee."

None of this meant that there was massive or industry-orchestrated slavery on Saipan. And none of it contradicted what many Saipan employers and fans of Saipan's guest-worker society kept telling me: that these workers were lucky to be there. Such workers typically tended to leave with ten thousand or twenty thousand dollars, often in cash, withdrawn from the bank the day before they left. Still, as anecdotal evidence of life in a structurally unfair society began to mount, I found it hard to fall in love with Saipan's model of economic development.

Another comment I heard that helped describe the strange limbo between abuse, freedom, and desperation on Saipan came from a white guy I met who was married to a Chinese woman. Saipan's guest workers were mistreated, he said, but they preferred mistreatment in the CNMI to what awaited them back home. "You know," he said, "ask 'em if they like the housing: No. Ask 'em if they like the food: No. Ask 'em if they like the work: No. Ask 'em if they like the pay: No. Ask 'em if they wanna go home: No."

The forebears of the modern Saipanese were an impressive lot. The courage and ability required to set out in man-made canoes across the wide-open Pacific, braving days and nights of storms and surf, charting course for pinpoint destinations, is nearly impossible for a modern person to imagine. In the old days, only the sons of noble families were taught the complex navigation techniques that guided islanders across the waves. During their apprenticeship, future navigators were taken out to sea and floated on their backs to learn the feel of the waves. Each type of wave had a different name. With enough experience, an apprentice could sense from the roll of a boat and the appearance of waves that rocked it how far away they came from and from where. It is said that ancient navigators could see the wake made in a wave that had passed by Hawaii, four thousand miles away.

What is most noticeable about the modern indigenous population of Saipan, however, is how precisely unskilled it is. It would be fruitless to argue which share of the blame belongs to the islanders themselves and which to the succession of colonizers that has blasted away at their culture. It would be ridiculous to characterize in any blanket fashion an entire people. I met many types of islanders, some ignorant, some educated, some uneducated but clearly shrewd, some insightful, honest, and critical, others deluded, dishonest, defensive, and prideful. Many were conflicted and confounded about themselves and their people, friendly, eager if somewhat guarded, and, quite often, extremely funny. Usually, if I presented myself amiably and openly, I was treated the same way in return and invited to hang out, to attend social gatherings. But my point was not to ascertain whether Saipanese are "nice," or to describe what they were like or to what extent I liked them. It was to analyze the effect of the labor regime that had evolved on Saipan and characterize how the unfair labor and immigration system had formed their attitudes about work and race.

To live on Saipan was to witness a place where locals, however poor, were largely absent from virtually every public form of labor. Large employers, such as garment-factory owners, were obligated by law to hire 20 percent locals, and they did, but grudgingly. I never heard of a garment factory with *more* than 20 percent local employees. In general, locals were seldom found performing jobs that required rigor of any sort. It was impossible not to be continually reminded of Frederick Olmsted's description of the labor environment in the antebellum American South: work as a degraded institution, something avoided, something low and despicable to be pawned off on foreigners.

As Samuel McPhetres, a professor of history at Northern Marianas College and long-term CNMI resident, explained, "What we have done with immigration is create a society that's totally dependent on foreign labor. Sixty to seventy percent of all local families have a live-in Filipina maid." This, he said, forced (or perhaps liberated) both parents to work to pay the maid. Not only had it hurt the relationship between parents and kids, but it had denigrated the local culture. "You have neglected children who speak Tagalog"—the predominant language in the Philippines—instead of Chamorro or Carolinian, he said.

As McPhetres saw it, islanders were still in transition between tribal and modern mentalities. On the one hand, one saw gracefully maintained traditions such as the genuine respect for old people. Young people will often take the hand of an older person and kiss it or touch it to their foreheads, and the elder will make a cross there. Once, during the Christmas season, I was at a local family's house. Guests were sitting around, drinking and talking, when my host's mother arrived. She was ninety-two, and wheelchair-bound with a broken hip. All conversation stopped. She was unquestionably the star of the show. The obeisance paid to her, the unforced, respectful way in which the family rose to greet her, kiss her, shake her hand, and wish her Merry Christmas, was touching and in direct contrast to mainland attitudes toward the elderly.

In some ways, however, much of "the island way" hadn't changed so much as syncretized with modern consumer culture, taking the form of idiotic status objects and playthings, displaying an old-fashioned power structure and world orientation. For example, members of the island's ruling class whiz around the island in souped-up Japanese imports with stickers displaying the family name: SABLAN, GUERRERO, TENORIO. The more humbly born get into the game as well, proclaiming what they can with stickers that read CHAMORRO POWER. I wondered what kind of reaction I'd get driving around on the mainland with a WHITE POWER sticker.

Despite the adoption of Western dress, Monday-through-Friday workweeks, MTV, modern slang, and many other American habits, McPhetres said, most islanders he knew "still have genealogy charts in their heads." By this he meant that every islander knew everyone in his family, down to his fifteenth cousins, and that family and ethnic identity were still the most important things to locals, just as they always had been.

McPhetres felt it was unreasonable for mainlanders to expect an entire culture to transform itself in thirty years. Change on a small, remote, undeveloped island was harder to achieve than elsewhere, like the continental United States. Islanders who had embraced modern, democratic, meritocratic ideas couldn't simply move to a town down the road where those ideals were celebrated and lived; nor could they force these changes upon others who disagreed with or feared them. They were stuck, forced to compromise constantly with entrenched powers and others reluctant to embrace the concept of fair play.

The flip side of this kind of preferential treatment is that the locals were almost universally despised by every other ethnic group on the island. Foreigners came and worked hard, and even when they got paid as promised and were unabused, they couldn't help noticing that their hosts benefited from an unfair and inexplicable privilege. It was very rare to meet people of any other ethnicity on Saipan—Chinese, Filipino, Thai, Nepalese, or mainland American—who had local friends. It was unpleasant to imagine what the world must look like through local eyes: everyone hated them, so why should they be nice?

It seemed the locals had been led—by themselves, by their leaders, and by the U.S. government—with good intentions, with shortsighted strategies, and by greed, into velvet handcuffs. They had wanted the modern world. They had wanted its goodies. They had wanted "development." But they had gotten guest workers instead.

As McPhetres described it, underneath attitudes of machismo, indifference, and racial superiority, locals were overwhelmed. Modern American ways and the waves of foreigners had created among them a sense of panic, he said, of "the erosion of everything traditional and a very real sense of insecurity." In the mind of the locals, the only world they knew was disappearing. 'The feds are going to take over. The Chinese are going to take over,' " McPhetres said. "It's a very pervasive feeling for a large portion of the population."

The teenagers of Saipan seem to have it worst, in terms of attitude

and preparedness for modern life. No longer skilled at fishing or farming, viewing themselves as outsiders in their own homeland, they have
gravitated toward the most predictable American commercial culture,
that of the rap and R&B world. Slouching, greeting one another with
gangsta-style handshakes, wearing baggy jeans, low-slung underwear,
and knit caps, even in temperatures of ninety-five degrees, local kids
sneer, pose, and profile like teenagers anywhere on the mainland. Like
teenagers everywhere, they are terrified and insecure. But in their case,
the terror and insecurity are justified. In contrast to kids from the States,
few CNMI teens have an available route to a life that would be considered successful anywhere but in their own, jury-rigged, "entitled" system. Most are unlikely to travel beyond Saipan or Guam.

I met perhaps two dozen teachers, mostly whites and Filipinos, during my time on Saipan. Universally, they shared the opinion that the
Chinese, Filipino, and Korean students in their classes were far more
eager to learn and work hard than the locals. In fact, fewer than a quarter of the local students entering eighth grade in the CNMI's public
school system currently go on to earn bachelor's degrees.

According to one health-education teacher, the ignorance of the local
teens was astonishing. Teenaged boys in this teacher's high-school class
believed that Yellow no. 5, the food-coloring agent in Mello Yello and
Mountain Dew, had the capacity to temporarily kill sperm, thereby allowing unprotected sex. The girls in this teacher's class professed to believe that drinking a gallon of vinegar would abort an unwanted
pregnancy.

Physically as well, local youth were under siege. Over 46 percent of
third-graders in the CNMI are either overweight or at risk of becoming
overweight. According to a recent survey performed at the University of
Hawaii, kids from the Northern Marianas Islands suffered from
"alarming" intakes of sodium, carbohydrates, and protein. The Food
and Drug Administration recommends that one-to-four-year-olds consume approximately eleven grams of protein per day. Local three-year-
olds consumed fifty-five grams per day. Where the FDA recommends
no more than twelve hundred miligrams of sodium per day, local seven-
year-olds consumed close to two thousand. Calcium intake in some age

brackets was less than a fifth of what it should be. The culprits are all too visible in the grocery stores: Spam, snacks, chips, and other junk food.

The bad diet and inactivity are taking a radical, tremendous toll on the local population. In 1993, Commonwealth Health Center, or CHC, the main hospital on Saipan, saw 709 diabetes patients. By 2006, the number had shot up fivefold. Diabetes now affects 25 percent of Saipan's adult, indigenous population.

I met no shortage of locals willing to discuss the plight of the CNMI. (Almost all of them were keen to remain off-record. Since an enormous part of island culture stems from the need for people to get along in such a small, static environment, getting caught shooting one's mouth off to a mainland reporter is not a bright idea.) However, it didn't mean that among locals there wasn't wildly divergent, keen dissent about the island's economic development. As one man told it, he'd left the island one semester back in the early nineties to return to college on the mainland. The island he departed, he said, was a place where "you knew seventy percent of the population. Everyone waved at each other. And then, all of a sudden . . ." He almost winced. He explained that the then-governor, Froilan Tenorio, had, against the wishes of many locals, authorized a near doubling of the number of Chinese guest workers. The next time the man came home from college, the island seemed like a foreign country. Corruption and labor abuse had skyrocketed. The entire feel of the community had changed. He felt that the commonwealth and its people had been sold out by special interests.

The garment industry and, by the same token, the political and business elite, had always received special treatment. The garment industry was taxed at a paltry 3.7 percent "garment tax" rate, even though its presence had required massive subsidization by public funds for health, safety, policing, labor, and immigration processing. An entire dump had been filled with garment-industry trash, and then closed, at the public's expense. And then there was the oft-mentioned impact on the island's dilapidated infrastructure. This man, like many other locals, resented moguls such as Willie Tan and another named James Lin, "with their mansions and their new Lexuses." Continuing, he asked, "How much of that is trickling down to the regular people? People are sick of being left out. Every year the negative response is growing." When I asked if he thought most people would prefer that the foreigners leave, he maintained a polite silence. I realized I was one of the foreigners.

A local friend with whom I became quite close laughed roundly at the antiforeigner sentiment. Locals, he said, complained incessantly about the foreigners and the meddlesome mainlanders. Yet year after year, he said with a laugh, they remained unwilling to work. "They don't do anything! They just stay home." He shook his head. He understood the rationales for local indifference: It was hard to get motivated about work in the private sector when the minimum wage was only $3.05. It was hard to attract bright locals to get an education and work for the local government when, regardless of their qualifications, the jobs they sought always went to someone else's less qualified cousin or sister-in-law. But still, he said, "we wouldn't need anything from outsiders if people just got off their ass and started working. Some of them, their pride is so high—they don't have any skills, they don't finish school, they don't work hard, but they think they should go right into management. They don't want to learn anything. They just want to get paid."

The CNMI government is modeled after the three branches of the United States federal government. A full-time bicameral congress is composed of eighteen representatives and nine senators, three from each island (Saipan, Tinian, and Rota). A governor and lieutenant governor make up the executive branch. The judiciary is composed of a superior court and a supreme court, with courthouses on each island. As if insufficiently equipped to preside over a population comparable to that of a small mainland town, each island's government is further augmented by its own mayoral office and a dizzying array of trusts, authorities, directorships, divisions, councils, offices, departments, and commissions, each requiring office space and full-time staff.

By unanimous agreement, the CNMI government is and always has been the mother lode of corruption and dysfunction. A local business-man once aptly described CNMI government employees "as alternating between laziness and vacation." According to a 2002 security assessment written by a security specialist from the Department of Justice to the U.S. attorney on Guam, Frederick Black (who was removed from office just after issuing subpoenas in an investigation concerning Jack Abramoff), "The political environment on Guam and in the CNMI is largely controlled by a few well-placed families and wealthy business-men in each location. Nepotism and financial advantage are a distinct part of island politics. Some office holders use their influence to appoint their relatives or associates to government positions or to funnel lucra-tive government contracts to their relatives and business associates." To this point, the report cited the examples of a police captain convicted in 2002 of embezzling drug-enforcement funds and a former speaker of the CNMI legislature then under indictment for stealing half a million dollars intended for emergency student classrooms.

Virtually every edition of Saipan's two newspapers charts the peren-nial pettiness, ineptitude, and rapaciousness of local officials. Public lands are stolen, government travel allowances are abused, unqualified relatives are appointed to important jobs, bids are rigged, kickbacks re-ceived, cars "misappropriated." Local politicians hire "special assistants" from the mainland to perform their jobs, freeing them up to focus on symbolic duties such as attending barbeques, drinking Bud Light, and taking trips anywhere they can. Lawsuits are in perpetual blossom. Peo-ple sue the government over public land that was supposed to be given to them for a homestead but that was given to some other family. In-dividuals sue companies, government agencies, and one another for nonpayment of wages, debts, and contracts. Different branches of the government often sue one another, frequently as a way of extending family or political rivalries. Since so few people either understand the law or obey it, legal maneuvering is the island's way of perpetuating a veneer of U.S. legal respectability. Lawyers stand by, ready to help by skimming contingency fees from every botched, misunderstood, or mis-managed transaction.

Today, after years of reckless deficit spending and mismanagement, the CNMI government is insolvent. The publicly held Commonwealth Utility Corporation, or CUC, can't collect its bills, repair its generators, or even pay for fuel. Its generating engines are capable of running at only 41 percent capacity. Twenty percent of this is then lost through line loss and theft of power. Power outages are a regular and frequent fact of island life. Thirty years after the islands became part of the United States, Saipan's tap water remains undrinkable, overtreated with chlorine and tainted at times with fecal coliform. Sewage continues to spill into the lagoon. Tourism is in decline, down 14 percent in 2005 and further in 2006. In 2005, Japan Airlines announced that it would discontinue flights to Saipan. According to an article from February 2007 in the *Marianas Variety,* eight thousand children and adults in the CNMI now rely on federally funded food stamps, up from fewer than a thousand in the early 1990s.

In short, for a place designed to be a celebration of free enterprise, Saipan has a record that is by virtually any measure a disaster. It's hard to find a better gauge than the reaction of investors themselves: in 1995, there were 173 new foreign investors opening businesses in Saipan. By 2003, the number had shrunk to six.

It is Saipan's garment industry, however, that has delivered the greatest blow to rhetoric about free-market principles. At midnight on December 31, 2004, under rules promulgated by the World Trade Organization, the quota system was dismantled, and something like true free trade has finally become the law of the land. While the U.S. government has maneuvered frantically to slow the onslaught of Chinese competition, few observers believe any American factories will be in the garment business beyond 2010.

The effect of real free trade upon Saipan was immediate. Between 2004 and 2005, garment sales from the CNMI dropped 39 percent, from $826 million to $501 million. The number of garment factories on the island dropped from twenty-five in January 2005 to nineteen in October 2005. Later that year, Saipan Garment Manufacturers Association president James Lin said that at least seven more factories might shut down their operations by the end of 2006, a prediction that was optimistic by one. In February 2007, even Tan Holdings threw in the towel, closing all three facilities left on Saipan.

The current governor of Saipan is Benigno Fitial (the former owner of the club called Orchids, where U.S. congressmen went to relax during their fact-finding missions to Saipan). A former consultant to Tan Holdings, he was elected to the CNMI House of Representatives; in 1999, he became speaker of the house.

The means by which he did so provide an interesting glimpse into the involvement of Team DeLaybramoff in CNMI affairs.

In a letter to House Resources Committee chairman and California representative Richard Pombo, and later in another letter, to U.S. attorney general Alberto R. Gonzales, Congressman George Miller outlined his concerns about DeLay's actions, accusing him of breaking laws against illegal interference in territorial affairs.

The letters, citing stories in the *Los Angeles Times* and the *Marianas Variety,* explain that in 1999 the CNMI had suspended its contract with Jack Abramoff. At the same time, Fitial was running a losing race for speaker of the house. To obtain the two votes he needed to win, Fitial met with two individuals associated with both Abramoff and Congressman Tom DeLay: Ed Buckham and Michael Scanlon. At the meeting, Fitial recommended that the two lobbyists meet with two of the congressmen opposing him, Alejo Mendiola and Norman S. Palacios.

Scanlon and Buckham met with the two legislators and promised to help secure them money for local projects in exchange for their votes for Mr. Fitial. The legislators agreed, Fitial was elected speaker, and in short order, Mr. Abramoff's contract was subsequently renewed. The legislators—at U.S. taxpayers' expense—got their pet projects, a breakwater on the island of Tinian and the repaving of an airport in Rota. Fitial's gubernatorial campaign platform? Pro-business.

His election was something of a wonder on Saipan, given that he is a Carolinian and married to a Filipina, both negatives on an island that reflexively votes along racial lines. But in a three-candidate race, Fitial earned two hundred votes more than his competitor and won with 25 percent of the vote.

Fitial's record after a little over a year in office is mixed. He inherited a rapidly dwindling economy and a bloated, bankrupt government. To his credit, he has bravely proposed the politically unthinkable: to fire and reduce the salaries of government workers. That said, he has spent about half of his time as governor off-island and has also continued the island tradition of hiring unqualified friends and family members to head government departments.

I met Fitial in July 2006, during one of his weekly press conferences. He sat next to his lieutenant governor, Tim Villagomez, in a room on top of Capitol Hill. The occasion was formal but, like most things on Saipan, pleasantly relaxed and unpretentious. Both officials wore untucked short-sleeved Hawaiian shirts. Fifteen or twenty people, including the Filipino reporters and photographers from the local newspapers, attended the affair. Only one or two white functionaries bothered with suits and ties.

As people settled down so the conference could begin, I couldn't take my eyes off the governor's mouth. In repose, it turned down more sharply than any mouth I'd ever seen, becoming at times almost an inadvertent sneer. During photos, Fitial produced a wooden dummy's grin (I discovered later that he wears dentures). When he was amused, however, which seemed to be often, the dummy grin smoothed out to an infectious, charismatic beam.

The first order of business that day was the official recognition of Miss Marianas Universe 2005, Shequita Bennett. Miss Bennett wore a tiara and gave a short speech. The CNMI speaker of the house congratulated her and declared that a congressional resolution would be passed to congratulate her again.

The remainder of the conference was devoted to an agonizing shorthand litany of the island's decline. The lieutenant governor discussed the power utility's strategy to ensure that power would be guaranteed for the upcoming Micronesian Games, a sort of regional Olympics. In order to protect the games from blackouts, the governor had asked the island's largest hotels and garment factories to disconnect from the island's power grid and use their own generators while the games were in town. They had agreed.

Next came the utility's budget. CUC needed $11 million to fix at least some of its generators and, most desperately, to keep paying for oil. The company had exhausted its credit line, and Mobil had refused future fuel deliveries unless the island could pay in cash. No fuel, no electricity. The education budget had already been slashed by two million dollars. Now the governor's office was trying to borrow the money for the oil from the local retirement fund. It was an extreme measure; and the retirement-fund officials were resistant. On a small island where everyone knew one another, how could you show up at a party and hang out with people whose pensions you'd stolen? The governor seemed frustrated by the stalemate. He favored plundering the retirement fund. When it came his turn to speak, he took long, comfortably heavy pauses. He said he understood that the retirement-fund officials wanted to look after the retirees, but they were being shortsighted. After all, they were all citizens of the same island. He smiled and concluded with a threat to the retirees: "Their retirement won't be so great if they don't have power."

No one needed to acknowledge that each one of these problems was loaded to bursting with frustration and embarrassment. As Villagomez continued with a highly technical report about engine 1 and engine 4 at Power Station 1, which engines were online, off-line, disabled, or repairable, what percentage and how many megawatts they were generating, you could look around the room and see heads of every race shake in disbelief. How depressing and inept could one island get?

The governor announced that in the meantime, to raise the necessary eleven million dollars, the government would begin laying off employees—not tenured locals, it was understood. The first layoffs would be mainland and Canadian nurses and doctors. How many nurses and doctors would be laid off? a reporter asked weakly. One hundred and forty, the governor answered. How many more employees would have to be laid off? Well, said the governor, as many as it took to get to eleven million dollars.

There was a long silence. The fact that the island was messed up didn't mean everyone on it was stupid. What was happening was plain. Modern medicine, education funding, retirement pensions, things that led toward the future, toward comfort, toward safety, were being traded for air-conditioning and a refusal to improve "the island way." But even the governor, well intentioned as he might have been, could not possibly force the entire island to change its behavior. To conclude, he asked, "Any more questions?" He flashed his big beam, the charmer. "Any suggestions?" The room broke into laughter.

Since the late nineties, when Jack Abramoff and Tom DeLay last exerted influence to protect the CNMI from federal minimum wage and immigration laws, both men have been dispatched from U.S. politics. DeLay has declined to run for office while he faces a growing array of legal charges. He is under indictment in Texas on money-laundering charges, and his two former aides, Mike Scanlon and Tony Rudy, have pled guilty to corruption charges related to the investigation of Abramoff. In the 2006 congressional elections, the Democrats took control of the U.S. Congress. It appears likely that with Saipan's protectors deposed, the faction led by California representative George Miller will enact its agenda from the 1990s: the "federalization" of Saipan. In January 2007, Congress raised the minimum wage on the mainland, including quick incremental hikes of Saipan's minimum wage as well. By 2009, the island's minimum wage will be the same as the mainland's. The local business community is predicting doom.

What remains unclear is how or when or to what extent the United States will exert control over CNMI immigration. Local opinion about the issue was mixed. My most conservative friend on the island—a self-described Ross Perot libertarian—was all for the takeover. As he put it, "This place has to decide: Do you want to be part of the United States, or not?" Liberal Pam Brown, on the other hand, was largely against the idea. She, like others, felt skeptical that federal officials could ever do a good job of making decisions regarding a complex, faraway place about which they knew little. How much credibility could the feds claim when there were ten or twenty million illegal residents on the mainland? Many rank-and-file islanders I talked to were surprisingly pro-federalization. They'd been living for so long with the stigma of the island being known as a bad place, it seemed better to go ahead and be done with it. Others— whites and locals—felt federalization would be a violation of the notion of CNMI self-government, as agreed to in the Covenant. Still others acknowledged that while the guest-worker program had led to abuses, the island simply didn't have access to a labor supply like the mainland did— therefore, it would have to continue relying on the program.

It was an extremely complicated issue: The system was broken and needed fixing. But what would happen, exactly, if you removed from a population, a polity, an economy, the people who do the actual work?

Some people's rationale was that reliance upon the undemocratic guest-worker system was the only possible way Saipan could function. Never mind educating the locals. Never mind starting over. Never mind the fact that the system didn't work. In the minds of many, the only way Saipan's economy could survive was for it to preserve the right to live off of the 75 percent of the population who weren't citizens. It was amazing to watch people—whites and islanders alike—defend a system that had kept so many of its intended beneficiaries ignorant, unhealthy, and unprepared for life in the modern world.

When I told Governor Fitial that in my estimation, some degree of federalization seemed both imminent and inevitable, he smiled and said, "Well, that's gonna be a problem." He said that if the feds tried to make a move, maybe Saipan would consider cutting its ties with the United States. He said that the United States, with all its rules and regulations and labor unions, made it impossible to do business. The locals wanted to build a factory, but the feds wouldn't allow them, because of some stupid endangered warbler or hummingbird or something. The guest workers had to stay.

As he rather dramatically told the local newspaper, "If they do not listen to me, they better come up with a solution because I think it will be genocide for the federal government to impose something that will devastate the livelihood of the people of the Commonwealth."

Around the same time I met the governor, in June 2006, a friend of mine from the attorney general's office suggested I might be interested in watching the police raid two strip clubs mentioned earlier. The owners of the Starlite and the Stardust had been accused of locking their dancers in their barracks during off-hours and placing a padlock on the gate.

In addition, the dancers alleged that contrary to promises made in the Philippines that they would be required only to dance, they were frequently fondled by the men who came to watch them. Sometimes the club put on shows for large groups of American sailors, at which dancers were expected to wear edible underwear.

While the bosses paid the dancers the legal CNMI minimum wage of $3.05 an hour, they then made deductions from their workers' paychecks for items like bedsheets, carpet, costumes, and jewelry. In a two-week pay period some dancers made as little as ten dollars. Lest the bosses be confused with bad or mean people, it should be noted that they threw a birthday party for one of the girls at the "compound" where they stayed. Avoiding the inconvenient fact that the girl was still below the age of legal employment, instead of calling it her seventeenth birthday (which it was), they simply called it her eighteenth.

My friend had told me when the busts would happen. At around seven, I went to the Garapan and sat down on a bench outside the Starlite. The club is on the Paseo, a blocked-off pedestrian zone created a couple of years ago to make the area more tourist-friendly. A sign in front says:

WELCOME US NAVY

LIVE EXOTIC SHOWS

Next door is the Wonderful Chinese Restaurant; on the other side is another strip joint called Macau Club II. Two or three doors down is Taste of India, which was pouring tabla and sitar music into the night.

As I waited for the bust to happen, the nightly fireworks went off at the nearby Hyatt Hotel. Suddenly, about eight officers from the immigration, police, and attorney general's investigation unit appeared and entered the club. It was strangely uneventful. After an hour or two, the women still hadn't been led out. The problem, it seemed, was that no one knew where to take the "freed" dancers. It didn't seem right to bring them back to their barracks. Finally, it was decided to take them to a battered-women's shelter.

While all of this was being deliberated, several cops relaxed outside, chatting. A group of Chinese tourists walked right past us, oblivious to the drama going on inside the building.

One of the officers saw me with my notepad and politely inquired as to what I was doing. When I said I was a writer, he became extremely uncomfortable. "You're writing about the improvements, right? I really wish sometime they would write about the improvements." Although the police had conducted their raid professionally, the fact remained that I'd heard of many other strip clubs and karaoke joints on Saipan that locked up their workers in the same way. If I knew about such cases, why didn't the police? The cop looked at me, frustrated and almost forlorn. "You know?" he said. "Things are getting better."

N ot long after I arrived on Saipan, I'd gone out with Harry for a drink. Driving home afterward, we passed hundreds of garment workers walking along the road. "Tonight," he said, "there are ten thousand girls without men here. There are ten thousand Chinese women walking around Saipan. So do the math."

The math meant that anywhere you looked there were women, unaccompanied and looking very—I don't know how else to put it— hungry. Sometimes flirty or interested in sex but just as often bored, poor, lonely, powerless—hungry. There were literally thousands of them. Do the math: sixteen thousand garment workers times 90 percent female. Add to that the Filipina masseuses, maids, waitresses, strippers, and nurses. Multiply that by American income per capita divided by the per capita income in the Philippines, China, and Bangladesh.

The result was palpable: everything normally subsumed under such notions as love, romance, feelings, trust, mutual interest, became, in the words of one white man I met, bemoaning his relationship to a Thai woman, "transactional."

For most of the men on Saipan, regardless of race or nationality, it seemed there was little difference between a garment worker and a prostitute. A local official told me that if you looked outside the factory gates at quitting time, "you'll see a lot of cars will be at the outside. Mostly, you'll see Bangladeshis and Filipinos. They park outside and honk the horn. A lot of them will have a regular girl that they pick up when they want some. Not girlfriends, just a regular girl that they pick up when they want to screw."

One group of men I became friends with were basically nice, respectable, normal guys. Several were lawyers. All had Thai wives. What made them stand out was that there didn't seem to be any overt exploitation or manipulation between themselves and their wives. Their relationships seemed old-fashioned and perhaps different from relationships on the mainland. During parties, after dinner, the men tended to smoke and drink on one side of the room while the wives, who never smoked, gathered on the other side or in another room. Often the women would turn on the boom box, get tipsy, play Thai music, and start dancing together. Their husbands weren't girl-crazy cheaters like many men on the island, and the power dynamic in these relationships seemed fair and comfortable. I also met a group of men married to women from the neighboring island of Palau. Those marriages, too, seemed to be based on mutual respect and affection. But most relationships I saw between foreigners on Saipan were to greater or lesser degrees predicated on the crummy bedrock fact that the women needed citizenship and the guys needed to get laid.

The math meant that many men on Saipan became silly playboys. Guys who to my reckoning sometimes seemed like abject losers became heady with their newfound power. White women who came to Saipan, alone or with their husbands, were usually subjected to a horrible experience, consigned to sexual oblivion for the duration of their stay. Few, if any, seemed to choose Asian or local men for boyfriends. Their husbands and boyfriends, however, were almost unanimously overcome by the attentions suddenly being offered up by numerous and much younger Asian females, which often proved irresistible to the average male from the mainland.

I don't mean to suggest that men on Saipan—whether locals or foreigners—were worse than men elsewhere. Korean, Chinese, Bagladeshi, local, mainlander—their behavior simply paralleled that of employers. In a vacuum of civil and economic rights, bad behavior thrived. One girlfriend was nice, but three was better. The island, as Richard Pierce once commented, neither praising nor condemning it, was simply a place where life was "more naked."

For my birthday a Chinese friend bought me a gift certificate for a massage at the Hyatt Hotel. During the massage, I asked the masseuse about her life. She was from the Philippines. She was thirty. She had spent the last ten years living with her "auntie" to save money and send every peso possible back home. The money had enabled her two brothers and a sister to attend college. All three were married now, but my masseuse was all alone. We didn't discuss it; the subtext was too obvious: at thirty, in the Philippines, she was an old maid. She had no complaints about pay or her work experience in Saipan. But how was she ever going to meet someone on Saipan, shut in all day at work or at her auntie's? I asked her why she didn't go home to have her own life after all this time. She said that's the way it was in the Philippines: the older sister takes care of the younger siblings. When I met people like this, I felt incredibly powerful. She was worth so little. I have little doubt that if I had proposed to her on the spot, she would have accepted with few questions. I had not become worth more. I simply realized for the eighteen hundredth time how much poorer others were. I didn't like the power, but I had it.

I met a woman named Da Yang from Harbin. She worked as a translator for a large garment company. Da Yang told me that she didn't think Saipan was so bad. Women came here and put their happiness on hold for three or four years to return home relatively wealthy. There was nothing so wrong with that.

She said the worst problem for her and the women she knew was loneliness. There just wasn't much to do on the island. Women from her factory sometimes went to the Monte Carlo discotheque in Chalan Kanoa, or else they took the illegal, three-dollar Chinese taxi service to go sightseeing. Still, she said, the numbers were indeed against them. Her factory employed four hundred people, fifty of whom were male. Again: the math. Most of the women she knew had boyfriends. It's just that most of the boyfriends had more than one girlfriend. What could the women do but accept it? "Nothing entertainment," she complained. "You need someone to support. Everyone is alone. You feel lonely." In other words, women in Saipan would do pretty much anything for some companionship, even if it was humiliating.

As she told me, "There's a phrase for the kind of love you will have on Saipan." She drew the Chinese characters:

塞班情, 塞班了; 上了飞机就拉倒

Translating, she recited them almost like a poem:

*Saipan love*
*Saipan stop*
*When you get on the plane, abort*
*That is over*

My friend Eric took me one night to the Lucky Snack Bar Night Club. He speaks excellent Mandarin, and as a result he had full access to the back alleyways of the Chinese world of Saipan, which was more or less off-limits or unknown to most non-Chinese. He explored it with relish.

He'd met a woman who worked there who told him she used to play for the Chongqing Opera. She played the *erhu,* a two-stringed instrument with a bow. She'd studied since she was eleven and majored in music at a big state art university in Chengdu. When we walked in, she and the other three or so women working there were sitting at the bar, wearing sheer, cheap-looking polyester dresses. Typically, as described earlier, karaoke hostesses' job was to hang out with male clients and encourage them to buy "lady's drinks." I don't know if sex was also on the menu at this particular club, but I wouldn't be surprised if it was.

Eric was polite to the woman. He'd been to the club and seen her play several times. He didn't act like her patron, he simply urged her to play with the rationale that Saipan was boring, and anything one could do to raise the cultural bar was worth doing. He ordered us beers and chatted with his acquaintance. She kept trying to beg off, saying she was ashamed to play and that she was out of practice. Finally, she went into a back room and returned with her instrument. As she began to play, it was immediately clear she was a gifted and highly trained musician.

During her song, which was heartbreakingly beautiful and emotional, a television mounted high in a corner played a Hong Kong action movie with lots of overdriven karate-kick noises: *KSH! KSH! KSH KSH KSH!* A tall American man sat at the bar with each arm around a woman. The one on his right looked at us longingly, as if she wished she could come sit with us. The man was rubbing the other woman's ass. With each rub, her cheap dress rose and fell a couple of inches. Occasionally, the man turned his head from the movie to try to kiss the one who was watching us. She flinched and continued to gaze at us.

In a booth behind us were five sailors, stunned into silence for once in their boisterous lives by the music. The song ended. Our table and the sailors' clapped. Eric asked what the song was called: "Remembrance of Three Doors to Heaven."

How else could you explain the moment but to think of it as another example of the Chinese tectonic plate meeting the American tectonic plate? The woman could earn a hundred dollars a month in China as a highly skilled musician or eight hundred dollars a month as a karaoke hostess in a Saipan dive. Bingo. Do the math. I saw her a year later. She'd become a freelance prostitute.


Most mainlanders who come to Saipan are professionals, contracted to inform, teach, advise, heal, and otherwise guide the unworldly locals toward the democratic and technical ideals of America. They come in many types: whites, blacks, drunks, sports enthusiasts, religious zealots, tax avoiders, dropouts, burnouts, and the just plain curious. It would be as silly to categorize them with a single swipe as it would be to do so with the islander population. Many seemed like normal, well-adjusted people, looking for adventure or perhaps for a place to enjoy life away from the hustle and strife of the mainland.

There are many reasons besides easy sex why mainlanders often underwent rapid personality changes upon arriving in Saipan. The pace, the beauty, the necessity of learning to be patient with the sheer amount of dysfunction—all of these accounted for a slowing down, a chilling out, an acceptance that yes, this is no longer Kansas.

But for many of the mainlander men I met on Saipan, a particular type of clock had apparently started ticking the moment they had landed. With each tick, they got more puerile, more self-centered. If they'd ever been big on learning, the process stopped. Their interests shifted to sports, women, and drinking. You saw it with the guys who'd been on the island for a long time. Each year, they knew less and were in most cases less capable of competing back on the mainland. And each year, to compensate, they pronounced from bar stools with greater and greater vigor, "I am a man who knows things." And many of them actually did know things, but smart or dumb, the main thing they'd learned is that life is good when one finds oneself at the top of the sexual food chain.

Suddenly, it was okay that three-quarters of the population lived as second-class citizens and were frequently abused, even though this was supposedly the United States. Three or four blow jobs into Saipan, most white men's reactions to the island seemed to evolve from "Gee, this is wrong" to "Well, it's complicated."

Every time I fussed about labor abuses, I was met with a fairly standard set of explanations. "But they're making ten times what they make in China." As one man, "a lifelong Robert Kennedy Democrat," told me with a sigh, "You know, I wish someone would write the story about the thousands and thousands of women who've come and built a new life, thanks to this place. That's the story someone needs to write." And his story was true more often than, say, cases of forced labor. But to my ear, his and other whites' inability to look honestly at what was wrong, un-democratic, unequal, and un-American about the Saipan status quo sounded a bit like how Southerners must have sounded explaining plan-tation slavery to Yankees: "Oh, I'm shuah it must all seem rathah strange, but you couldn't possibly understand." Sure, not a single slaveholding state in antebellum America had laws defining the rape of a slave as a crime. But what did that have to do with anything?

It would be hypocritical to deny that I had some silly affairs on Saipan myself. I just couldn't understand how an emotional life cobbled out of serial sexual hijinx didn't get old. I sat in on countless and endless conversations comparing the sexual merits of Thais versus Filipinas, Russians versus Chinese, replete with body parts and the likening of women to various breeds of dog and sex acts to animal behavior. Were people so bored by the smallness of island life that they had nothing else to talk about or do? I asked a friend of mine—a white guy from the mainland whom I'll call Fred—about this. He admitted to being a play-boy when younger but seemed pretty domesticated by the time I met him. He laughed at my confusion. What was it about Saipan that made everyone, particularly the men, obsess, dream, and talk about sex all the time? He grinned and barked like an old man, "It's kulcha!"

It took me a year to get what he was talking about. During that time, I met a Bangladeshi who, in his own words, spelled out the same patently obvious thing: Saipan's primary appeal, he said, wasn't that you could merely exploit poor Asians. It was that you could fuck them. What was going on with the men on Saipan if not a sort of ravenous cel-ebration of enhanced sexual power? Did I see it now? the Bangladeshi asked. "It's not really about dollarland. It's all about sexland."


During my stay on Saipan, a young freelance reporter named Rebecca Clarren came to work on a piece for *Ms.* magazine. She had come for the same reasons I had: to write about what a horrible place it was. She stayed five and a half days.

When the article was published, in the spring of 2006, the headline screamed in crimson letters, SEX, GREED, AND FORCED ABORTIONS IN PAR-

ADISE. Clarren and her editor, Katherine Spillar, were featured on NPR's *Fresh Air,* where the sensational charges were repeated. The article was reprinted in several other publications and on websites, and I noticed that the word *forced* had been downgraded to *coerced.*

On the radio, Clarren seemed to hesitate about which term to use. Spillar kept emphasizing the word *forced,* while Clarren seemed to pull back and guide discussion toward the more cautious notion that the abortions were coerced. As she characterized it, women on Saipan weren't so much forced by their employers into having abortions but were, rather, compelled by economic necessity.

I don't imagine many of the show's hundreds of thousands of listeners were obsessing about the nuances like I was. Most of them probably walked away from the broadcast with the simple impression that Saipan was an evil place where brutal, brown-skinned islanders took poor Chinese girls and dragged them into abattoir-like abortion mills. It must have made a very potent image.

By then, I had spent about two years on and off Saipan, speaking with dozens of people on all sides of every issue and thinking about everything I'd heard. It was a complicated, rumor-driven place. People talked all the time and alleged the worst sorts of things about one another. But I'd never heard of a forced abortion. No one I had ever talked to had heard of one, either. I tried to imagine an employer forcibly dragging a worker to the abortion table. A nurse, a doctor, and perhaps one or two others would have to witness such a thing. Did they do this all day, as a matter of routine?

As Pam Brown had said, yes, there was a lot of pregnancy discrimination on Saipan. Employers with thin profit margins were understandably put out if their employees—whose medical costs they were responsible for—became pregnant. I have no doubt that many such employers used their power over employees to avoid paying for such expenses. But where did one—or should one—draw the line between "forced abortion" and pregnancy discrimination?

I called Spillar, the editor, to hear her thoughts. "We never claimed that anyone had ever been forcibly abducted," she told me. "We talked to a number of garment workers who had become pregnant. They were told, If you continue the pregnancy, you have no job. They know what that means. They're threatened, because they're trying to pay their room and board and repay their traffickers. They want to keep their job, keep earning money. They have no choice." It was more than mere discrimination, she said. "In the U.S., an employee has recourse. She can go to the EEOC, she can get an attorney. They enforce the laws—sort of. But those women, they have no place to go. They have no alternative. It is coercion."

As it turned out, Spillar was wrong. Workers in the CNMI have access to the EEOC and file complaints with them hundreds of times per year. Appropriately or not, however, "forced abortion" would be the term that characterized the island for the next journalist looking up information on Saipan. Politicians from the mainland would refer to the article when they were deciding what to do about Saipan's future. Garment companies such as Ann Taylor would cancel their orders and stop doing business with Saipan, placing their orders, no doubt, with countries with lower pay and even worse working conditions than the CNMI's. And the islanders would have to live with the shame of knowing that that's how people on the mainland probably thought of them. It didn't seem very fair or nuanced enough to capture the subtlety of what was messed up about Saipan.

The discretion missing from the discussion of pregnancy discrimination was equally necessary to explain the reality of the sex workers on Saipan. To what extent was it fair to say they were forced into their jobs? It took a long time to gain their trust, but eventually I would get many opportunities to meet, know, and speak with Chinese prostitutes about their lives. If I didn't learn every detail about their thinking, I gathered enough to get one thing straight: few shared the American, postfeminist, university-incubated notion that sex work had anything to do with "empowerment."

One Chinese prostitute told me that back in China, she and her new husband spent their entire savings—about eight thousand dollars—for her, but not him, to come work in a Saipan laundromat. When she arrived, like so many others, she learned she had been scammed. She turned to the streets. She gets about forty dollars for each sex act, half of which she gives to the storefront operation she works for. Her husband has no idea what she does.

A Chinese friend of a friend said that she'd run away from home at about age sixteen because her parents wouldn't let her go to college. She went to Shanghai to work, saved her money, and bought a house in her hometown. The land value dropped precipitously, and she lost most of her investment. She came to Saipan. By living frugally, she saved a lot of money, went back to China, and opened a store. Some friends of her parents ripped her off in an investment deal and left her poor again. Finally, she came back to Saipan and started to work in the bars—first as a hostess (available for chitchat and lady's drinks only), later as a prostitute. For a while she earned sixty dollars for each sexual act, with her *mama-san* taking twenty. After half a year, she quit. She still gets offers from her *mama-san*—four just last night, she said. It was a constant temptation.

Li Lan was a Chinese prostitute I interviewed at length. Twenty-eight years old, she came from a rural village about a hundred miles south of Shanghai that has since been subsumed into Shanghai's immense sprawl. Her parents were "kind of like farmers." She doesn't know how much money they earned, but according to statistics, per capita income for farmers there these days averages $207 per year. Li Lan had one elder sister and one younger brother, running water, and a two-story house. "We had some money," she told me. "But everything is so expensive." Her parents grew rice, vegetables, and wheat while raising a few pigs, chickens, and dogs. She attended primary school, which is like high school in the United States, and graduated at seventeen.

Li Lan is exactly five feet tall. She has high cheekbones and a serious-looking face that sometimes slips to betray a sly sense of humor. Like many Chinese women I met, she described her face, rather hopefully, as being a very *shanliang,* or kind, face.

At first, she seemed detached and possibly not too bright—or perhaps just uninterested in things. She was the plainest kind of Jane one could ever meet. Not too pretty, not too smart, not too loud. The Mandarin word is *shuncong,* or obedient. She seemed like someone who accepted whatever came along, who tried to be pleasant, to put a good face on things, and, on the whole, not to trouble anyone with her needs. When she cracked a smile or a laugh, it became easier for me to see that there was an observant person hiding behind the obedient, easygoing exterior.

Ever since she was a little girl, she said, "I just wanted to be free, to do something exciting. To be somewhere where there were a lot of people. I wanted to be in a crazy place." She used a common Mandarin term, *renao,* which literally means "hot-loud"; it's a word used to describe cities, parties, and crowds. "I always dreamt of places like hair salons," she said, "places where you would come into contact with a lot of people."

When she turned eighteen, Li Lan began to work as a sewer for a government-owned garment factory, making jackets and suits. The job paid two hundred yuan, or twenty-three dollars, per month. "Sometimes we work until nine or ten at night, until the quota is done," she said. She worked there about seven years and didn't seem to have minded. "It was okay. I like to make clothes."

Then one day, at work, she saw an advertisement for sewing jobs in Saipan. After passing a skills test, she was charged a "fee" of thirty to forty thousand yuan—$3,500 to $4,700—a sum she borrowed from relatives, and which covered her visa, plane ticket, and physical exam.

Li Lan left China in November 2000. She was thrilled to go. Unsure of what would be available in Saipan, she packed an extra suitcase full of her favorite foods: dried fish, marinated chicken, dried mushrooms.

She hadn't thought much about what Saipan might look like, but she'd seen images of America—"pictures of cities, nice cities, of Chinatown." She mentioned a Chinese television show set in a Chinese restaurant in America. "I thought it would be like on TV." She laughed at how mistaken she'd been. Breaking into English, she said, "From velly first time arrive a China, I don't see the nice house. I start to cry." Reverting back to Mandarin, she continued, "It looked just as bad as poor parts of China." She laughed some more. Everything on Saipan was so crappy! The houses, the roads—even little sixteen-hundred-foot Mount Tapochau looked cheap. It wasn't even a real mountain!

Willie Tan's L&T factory barracks were as much of a letdown as

Saipan. When she arrived, it was late, everyone was already asleep, and the man who showed her to her room wouldn't help her carry her heavy food bags up the narrow staircase. She started crying. In English again, she described the crowded sleeping arrangement in the barracks: "Six ladies, one to one to one." Reverting to Mandarin, she said, "And dammit! I even had to sleep on the top bunk."

Li Lan didn't have as many specific complaints about her work as some other sewers I talked to, but like nearly all, she said it was bad, and that the bosses were abusive. They didn't hit her, she said, but they were "just talking bad, saying, 'Work more. Work more.' " The salary was too low, she complained, and there was little if any overtime. Every month her employer deducted a hundred dollars for rent, another hundred for food. There was always a line for the shower, no hot water. "For food," she said, "we would be six to a table and they would only bring one of each dish; we had to share it." If you arrived just a minute too late or were a slow eater, forget it—your favorite dishes would be gone.

She'd borrowed the money to come to Saipan from her family, she said, and all she could ever think about was repaying it. In China, people had warned her about the Chamorros on Saipan, telling her to be careful with them because they were kind of "out there." Since she was trying to send all of her money to her parents, she pretty much stayed put in the barracks. The most exciting thing in her life was cutting other girls' hair. She soon got good enough to charge for it. But she was bored and lonely.

One day at work, she said, she had an idea about how to improve production. She told the supervisor her idea, and to her surprise, instead of rewarding her, the supervisor got mad. She later realized that the supervisor had probably felt threatened that Li Lan was angling for her job. The supervisor stopped assigning Li Lan what little overtime hours she had been getting. Things got more boring, and her paychecks got smaller.

After her one-year contract at L&T ran out, she went to another factory, named Mirage. Mirage, she said, was better, except there she encountered the opposite problem—too much overtime. The factory was busy six, sometimes seven days a week. She earned enough to rent an apartment with some other Chinese women and get away from the barracks.

All this sounded like an improvement to me, given what I knew about garment work, but Li Lan lasted only three months at the Mirage factory. After that, I gathered, she had had enough. I asked her several times to describe how it was that she made the transition to prostitution, but I never got a straight answer. One explanation was that she had met an American man who became her boyfriend; the man forbade her to work anymore in the garment factory. Later, however, she told me that she'd met him only after becoming a prostitute. The stories didn't add up, and in the end, all I knew was that she didn't blame her decision on Willie Tan or Saipan or the garment business or anyone else.

Li Lan went to work at a place called the Yellow House Karaoke Bar. It looked like many of its cousins on Saipan, a typical lounge on a second-floor balcony over Beach Road, not far from the Grand Hotel and World Resort—and their supply of Japanese customers.

Patrons of the Yellow House entered a lounge area with a few couches, a karaoke machine, and a TV. Small Christmas lights lined the corners of the walls, floor, and ceiling. Typically, guests tended to hang out in the main lounge, ordering drinks, chatting or singing until the mood was right. In back, five or six cheaply constructed "massage rooms" offered means to address any sexual needs that might arise.

The *mama-san* of the Yellow House was a forty-one-year-old woman named Ding. By pure coincidence, I had met Ding independently of Li Lan. Her story was one of the most ironic I'd heard from any Chinese on Saipan. She'd come to the island in 1997 to work as a waitress. After paying a recruiting fee of $5,000 and another $550 for her plane ticket (despite CNMI laws requiring the employer to pay for transportation), she was met at the airport, deposited in an apartment with two other women, and left to wait. She waited for days, but no one came.

Soon her suitcase was stolen, and not long after that her savings ran out. A group of women she'd met on Saipan pooled some money and offered to buy her return ticket to China. She said she would be too ashamed to go back without any money. Her new friends introduced her to the karaoke-bar scene.

Ding told me that at the beginning, she felt stupid because she was considerably older than the women she worked with. She looked into her options and decided she had no choice but to give in.

Her new boss extorted a two-thousand-dollar "deposit" from her for helping her obtain legal papers to work as a hostess. According to Ding, he also tried to force her into prostitution. She refused. He tried to beat her. In a slightly different telling, she said that the two had an argument that became a physical fight.

I should mention that by the time I interviewed her, several years after these events, Ding practically had the words "hard case" tattooed on her forehead. She had, at that point, already been jailed twice for promoting prostitution. I definitely felt when she spoke that she was "adjusting" her story for me. I found it interesting nevertheless, especially when she told me that her boss eventually got murdered, that she had nothing to do with it, and that she soon teamed up with another woman to take over the club as the new *mama-san*. Give or take a few discrepancies, Ding had demonstrably gone full circle: from victim to prostitute to pimp.

When Li Lan showed up at the Yellow House, Ding remembered, laughing, "she looked awful. They always do. They come in from the countryside, they're shy, they don't know how to dress." She said it usually took a couple of months for the girls to learn how to use makeup and do their eyebrows and lips.

Girls tended to split into two types, she said: those who eased into the job, realizing it was better to hurry things along, be friendly, but think only about the money, and those who tended to think too much and feel bad about themselves. Li Lan seemed pretty obviously to fit into the second category. When I tried to get her to describe her feelings about her work, to tell me what aspects of her job she liked or loathed, she looked pained and ashamed. "You know," she said, "when you do this kind of work, it's pretty much all bad. It's just one long, bad customer."

She likened her life as a prostitute to being in a bad relationship. "It's like if you like a person. Even if other people say he's no good, if you don't think so, you're still going to want to be with them."

Still, there was a payoff. Li Lan's favorite place to go dancing was then known as the Dai-Ichi Hotel (it's now called the Fiesta and is owned by Willie Tan). Every Thursday night the Dai-Ichi presented a Filipino band named the Big Beats. The night was known as TGIT— Thank God It's Thursday.

The Dai-Ichi on TGIT nights was one of the most democratic social spots on Saipan. The two or three times I checked it out, I saw a mixture of two or three hundred Chinese, Thai, Filipino, local, and mainland men and women enjoying themselves, dancing to loud music under strobe lights. The Big Beats played on a stage with a Miller Lite banner behind them. To the rear, a fog machine blew out fake smoke. Like Filipino house bands around the world, the Big Beats churned out uncannily faithful if somewhat cheesy cover tunes from the global Top 200 playlist. On one of my visits to TGIT, I sat through "Jack and Diane" by John Cougar Mellencamp; "Bring Me to Life" by Evanescence, which seemed to be a hit with Filipino house bands that year; Queen's "We Will Rock You"; the Romantics' "What I Like About You"; the Knack's "My Sharona"; and last but never least, Gloria Gaynor's "I Will Survive."

One Blondie medley into the show ("I'm gonna getcha getcha betcha betcha"), I felt like I'd had enough. But I hadn't grown up in a small village, swatting flies and sharing village gossip, working in the fields. For the garment workers and prostitutes, escaping the village, coming to Saipan, heading out to TGIT, and treating themselves to a few Heaven Hill vodkas must have been a rush equivalent to what Midwesterner F. Scott Fitzgerald felt hitting Paris in the twenties.

Li Lan loved TGIT. She loved dancing. This was her favorite place to go on Saipan, and her favorite thing to do. She loved Western music, particularly disco. For her and other prostitutes I met, Saipan was fun. As one woman articulated, Saipan was fun because for once in your life, no one in your family was watching you. No one knew what you were doing. Women who came to Saipan could relax. She said that when she first came to the island, "my thoughts changed dramatically. The very way I think is more free. American lifestyle is more bright." Back in her village, she explained, life was stifling. "China, everybody follow. They go like one. In China, you do something special, other people attention you. Other people talking, talking, talking." If you did anything strange, wore sexy clothes or became too friendly with a man besides your husband, she said, the gossip began, and socially "you are very outside."

She said, "Me, when small, always want to be special. I thinking, 'I want different. I want different. I not to be just like everybody.' " In Saipan, despite the sordidness of her profession, she had found freedom. It might be sad to me or you, and it was obviously sad to her as well. But still, she'd made a choice she felt was worth defending. "Freedom is very important. If you want to do something and someone won't let you do it, you're always going to be upset." The words don't do justice to the emotion in her voice as she spoke.

On the night of April 10, 2002, four gentlemen came to the Yellow House. A deal for sex was brokered, but unfortunately for Ding, Li Lan, and the other prostitutes who worked there, the would-be customers happened to be police officers. In short order, every female present was arrested, cuffed, and on her way to jail.

Ding received excellent legal advice. She delayed her hearings for as long as possible, during which time she got pregnant and became an exceptionally devout member of the Assemblies of God. She promptly filed for asylum on the grounds that if she was deported, she and her unborn child would be persecuted for her religious beliefs. Her case is likely to take years to resolve, and she is free to stay in the CNMI for the duration.

Most of the prostitutes arrested with Ding were advised by their lawyers to plead not guilty. Their attorneys argued that the arresting officers had never spoken directly with their clients. Their clients spoke Mandarin. The arresting officers spoke English. There had been no translator present. What evidence existed that there had been any communication between their clients and the arresting officers about sex or anything else? Their cases were dismissed.

Li Lan, relying on the advice of a busy, court-appointed public attorney, was advised to plead guilty. Unfortunately for her, between her arrest and her sentencing, Saipan had decided to make a much-promoted push to reduce prostitution. As part of the initiative, prostitution had been declared a "crime of moral turpitude."

Since sex—for free, for trade, for love, for fun, and for sale—permeated every level of social and business life on Saipan, the idea that anyone on the entire island had the gumption to make a big deal about prostitution struck me as laughably hypocritical. And yet, according to a straight-faced white public defender I interviewed, the CNMI government was getting its act together. "Saipan is part of the United States," she insisted. "We want to be taken seriously." The result of the new policy was that a foreigner convicted in the CNMI of violent crimes could usually manage to stay; a foreigner caught once for selling herself was subject to immediate deportation.

L i Lan's deportation hearing took place in mid-December 2003 in the CNMI Superior Court. She showed up wearing jeans and an imitation-silk batik-print shirt, with no lawyer. Her hair looked newly straightened and dyed. She took a seat next to the court-appointed translator.

At the bench, Judge David A. Wiseman sifted through his papers, looking for her case file. After several increasingly embarrassing moments, during which he appeared unable to locate it, he muttered something about recommending a week's continuance. The prosecutor politely indicated that he had the defendant with him in court, and that the government of the Commonwealth of the Northern Mariana Islands was entirely ready to proceed. Just in time, the judge found the file, collected himself, and lurched into business, asking, with a heavy Massachusetts accent, "What's the case numba?"

After asking Li Lan if she was ready to proceed, he intoned sonorously, "As you know, the government believes you're here illegally. That you don't have any legal right to stay heah. This is a hearing set at which time you can show that the government is wrong, or they made a mistake and that you do have a legal right to be heah."

Li Lan said that she had two pending labor cases. As mentioned before, many guest workers on Saipan filed labor cases to delay returning to their home countries. In Li Lan's case, however, it was a particularly underwhelming hand to play. The judge deemed her cases too old to be relevant.

He asked Li Lan if she had anything else to say in her defense. In a move described by an observing attorney as "pretty spunky, for a Chinese girl," Li Lan took the opportunity to ask why her court-appointed attorney had advised her to plead guilty in the first place. There was an infinitesimal pause in the workings of the courtroom before Judge Wiseman, again, not without sympathy, responded, "That's something you have to take up with your lawyah."

The government called its one and only witness, Erwin T. Flores of the CNMI Immigration Department. Flores identified Li Lan and stated that she had been arrested for prostitution. Did Flores know of any reason why she should be legally entitled to stay in the CNMI? No, he replied, he did not. The government rested.

A few minutes later the judge issued his ruling. "If any alien is convicted of any crime of moral turpitude, it's one of the grounds for deportation. Based on the court's findings, the court hereby orders the respondent deported. The Immigration will stahhht processing the depahhchaah."


On the way back to her hotel, Li Lan tried to put on a good face. While she was furious with her court-appointed lawyer, she had no argument with the judge. "I believe what the judge said—that his judgment is right."

We drove, and she realized it was her birthday. She and my translator broke into peals of laughter at the irony. I asked her what her Chinese zodiac sign was. She paused to calculate—born 1976 . . . Dragon! Again, more irony. "It's supposed to be lucky!" Yet here she was, being deported as a common whore—on her birthday. "Look at me!" She laughed.

We pulled in to the dumpy parking lot of the San Jose Hotel, two blocks off Beach Road. Across the street was an open yard littered with enormous satellite dishes. On either side were a few dilapidated islander homes with rotting porches and propped-up roofs. Kids, parents, and grandparents loafed around, chewing betel nut, occasionally blasting out arcs of rust-colored spit. Boony dogs scratched fleas and chickens pecked at the gravel in the potholed parking lot. Wary Chinese men slunk out of the building, eyeing us suspiciously. Off to the right of the San Jose's concierge desk was a library with hundreds of Chinese porno movies.

In the driveway, Li Lan toyed with the idea of hiring a lawyer to fight her deportation. She discussed it with my translator. There had to be some remaining legal option to explore. Wasn't there always? "I don't understand government," she complained. "None of us do." Trying to figure out one's rights on Saipan, she said, was "like going to the Bank of Saipan." Referring to a local bank that had been defrauded in one of Saipan's many scams, resulting in many small investors' losses, Li Lan said, "You deposit money, and then a few months later it's been deducted. I had eighteen hundred dollars deposited there, and now there's eleven hundred! And now I'm leaving!"

Li Lan's good-bye party consisted of Ding (the newly Christian *mama-san*) and a half dozen or so young women from the San Jose Hotel. When I arrived, their flip-flops were arrayed around the welcome mat outside Li Lan's fourteen-by-fourteen-foot room. Under the dim fluorescent lights, three or four women sat on the bed, chatting. Two of them stood, passing Ding's new baby back and forth, cooing, "Doi doi doi doi."

Li Lan had already packed her bag. I remembered her story about arriving with two enormous bags, heavily laden with food. Now she had just one, and it was light. Wasn't she bringing back any gifts or mementoes after three years in the United States? I asked. She shrugged halfheartedly. "Maybe I'll go to Duty-Free and buy a name-brand belt."

The night of Li Lan's deportation, I met her at her hotel. Her attitude was the same mixture of stoic *tian,* or sweet obedience, as it had been—sad but accepting. She wore skin-tight jeans, folded up at the cuff about four inches, tennis shoes, and a tight orange T-shirt with fluorescent metallic embossed letters splashed across the chest: HOTTIE.

By the time she had had her papers processed at the Department of

Detention and proceeded to the airport, it was about twelve-thirty at night. We sat in a group—Li Lan, my translator, an officer from the CNMI immigration detention unit named Martin Cepeda, and a Chinese woman named Dong Dong, who was being deported for overstaying her visa. We took seats on some benches outside the airport. Thirty feet away was the door to the airport proper.

It felt chilly for Saipan, perhaps somewhere in the mid-seventies. Cepeda smoked cigarettes while the women shivered, talking quietly and lapsing into silences, thinking, no doubt, of what it would be like to return to their families and to village life. With the moon peeking in and out from behind the clouds, it was easy to imagine the breezes blowing in from thousands of miles away, bouncing across the waves, up the hill, and past our faces, clean and fresh. Dong Dong, who ten minutes before had been apoplectically engaged with two hulking Transportation Security Administration guys trying to search her bags, had relaxed. Breaking into a grin, she chirped, "Bye-bye, Saipan," and handed Cepeda a piece of Wrigley's spearmint gum. Both women agreed that Cepeda seemed like a nice guy.

I asked Li Lan where she'd be if she could be anywhere on Saipan instead of there that night, being deported. She realized that it was a Thursday—TGIT night! "At the dancing place!" she said. She beamed and grabbed an imaginary microphone, then shyly shimmied from side to side, imitating the lead singer from the Big Beats. Switching to English, she said, "She lady, velly nice, a-sing a song."

She sighed and told me for the fourth time that she was resigned about leaving Saipan. But she wasn't sad. "If I had stayed in China," she said, "there would have been absolutely nothing exciting in my life." She wanted to know if my translator or I thought she'd ever be allowed to return to Saipan. In Mandarin, she told me she felt like she might cry. Switching to English, she said with a sigh, "I love Saipan. Maybe I come back someday."

# Conclusion

My stepmother's second husband, Charlie, is about seventy years old. He's one of the most engaged, lively men I've met of his—or any—age. Currently, he chairs the Business Department at Minnesota's Northwestern College. He's been there for eighteen years, teaching corporate finance, corporate strategy, management, and economics, both macro and micro. Before that, he worked as a fusion scientist at Lawrence Livermore National Laboratory at the University of California, Berkeley, one of the most respected research institutions in the world.

Charlie is an ardent fan of "the free market." Politically, he describes himself as "one hundred percent libertarian." We often argue for hours. He's fun to argue with because he's smart, and because he doesn't take things personally.

The other day Charlie asked me what my book was about. He knew the subject was contemporary slavery in America. What he meant was "What's it *really* about?" I told him that if I could sum it up, the meaning of the book was this: We all seek control. Control equals power.

Power corrupts. Corruption makes us blind, tyrannical, and desperate to justify our behavior. I state this with less judgment than the words may suggest. I think human nature has both lovely and evil aspects. But let's agree that the evil ones aren't pretty.

About two years into writing this book, I stumbled across a passage that helped me understand slavery in a way I hadn't before. It was the wistful recollection of a North Florida man named George Gillett Keen, a poor white allowed into the company of some wealthier slave owners on a hunting trip in the 1840s:

> When the day's hunt was over, supper eaten and all seated around the fire, the subject of farming was introduced. One would say, "I've got the best overseer I ever had"; another would say, "My overseer is a worthless fellow"; a third would say, "I am pretty well satisfied with my overseer," and so on.
>
> I would sit there like a bump on a log. You bet I never wanted anything worse in my life than I wanted a plantation of niggers so I could talk about my overseer. . . . I wanted niggers. How to get them was the question.

I feel this man speaks for every human being today who wants an iPod, a cell phone, a flat-screen TV, a new SUV. It is part of our nature to want—please, dear God—not to be perceived as a loser. To be asked to the dance. To *not* have the dumb haircut or the lame, uncool tennis shoes. To *not* be the person at the 2008 high school reunion driving a 1990 Civic. I get it. I identify. A hunger for status dwells in every human being, rich or poor.

Unfortunately, however, like a design flaw, our hunger for status overrides our concern for others' dignity. The modern extension of this disregard is the willingness today of First World people to buy things from a global system of production that, we well know, is based on someone, somewhere, getting a raw deal. And so if we no longer hunger to own "niggers," we just as badly want to own stuff that happens to be produced by "niggers." But since we don't like using words like *nigger,* or thinking of ourselves as slave owners, well, we don't really get into the details so much. To quote Isaac Mizrahi again: "I don't know. And I don't want to know."

There are so many ways we deliberately and accidentally don't know. Factories where modern stuff is made are far away. They're in other countries. We don't see the labor conditions. We hear about them sometimes. But we dismiss it. "Oh, China's going through its industrial revolution, just like we went through ours." So it's okay if their workers suffer.

The virtues of free trade as extolled by my step-stepfather, Charlie, are by now pretty familiar. Free trade and globalization make the world a freer, richer place. Free trade is the most efficient way to allocate our natural and human resources. Charlie cites the fact that two hundred million Chinese people have been lifted out of poverty. He attests that for every job lost by an American to a foreign worker, a new, better job awaits. When I cite statistics suggesting that maybe that's not happening, that lower-class Americans are getting poorer, being paid less, and that most Americans being downsized are getting Starbucks-type jobs or opting out of the depressing low-end job market altogether, he pooh-poohs my fears. If things are so bad, why is the United States still the richest country in the world? As long as our economy grows, and as long as the world economy grows, poor people everywhere will have "a shot" at improving their lives. After all, he says, quoting John F. Kennedy, "a rising tide lifts all boats."

For guys like Charlie, the name of the game is progress. "If you show me something in the last hundred years," he argues, "where somehow the human condition has gotten worse, I'd say, 'Okay, you have a point.' But if you look back, since the development of what we call modern science, from, say, the year zero to the year 1700, well, instead of everyone being controlled by religion or by our feelings, or by some tradition, we now have science, and the ability to cure diseases—what would you rather have? All of us sitting around in candles and lamps, and the smoke of the fireplace? Or would you rather live in a place like you're living in or I'm living in, with an air conditioner, where, if we wanna eat steak, or fish, or whatever, we can get it?" It's a persuasive argument in many ways. And maybe, in the end, Charlie's right.

But one of the problems I have with elderly white guys like Charlie from the richest country on earth, who have already socked away savings for retirement, bought some stocks and real estate, and have a pretty nice life, is that they don't tend to go out to the fields, villages, and slums of Third World countries, learn the language of the local peasantry, and talk *to* the supposedly free people they're talking *about* when they talk about free trade.

Thomas Friedman becomes an expert on globalization when he goes and chats with a handful of Bangalore's sixty thousand software engineers about what a neat evolution they're part of, but I don't gather he spent as much time consulting with Bangalore's ninety thousand street kids. That doesn't stop him—or the guys at the WTO meetings, or the leaders at the G8 summits, and so on—from unilaterally making proclamations and decisions that affect the lives of 95 percent of the planet, convinced that they're all part of the same program.

People like Friedman and many world and business leaders might honestly believe in freedom and justice as much as anyone else. They just have the benefit of not having to know what the hell they're talking about. They can talk about "freedom" and "democracy" and use whatever terms they want. But the fact is, if they—or you or I or any literate, First World, educated person—tried to take a nighttime stroll through most large cities in the world, anywhere away from the heavily policed tourist areas, they'd suddenly realize—probably after being mugged—that the world has not moved past such antiquated, vulgar, outmoded concepts as Marx's "class struggle." We've just decided to believe there's no such thing.

American citizens live in an awesome information vacuum. A study from 2001 parsed everything that was shown on ABC's *World News Tonight,* CBS's *Evening News,* and NBC's *Nightly News,* and broke down sources into racial, gender, and political categories. What emerged is that 92 percent of all "news sources" interviewed were white, 85 percent were male, and, where party affiliation was identifiable, 75 percent were Republican. I'm sorry, but where in this mix is Juan—and Juanita—Valdez? Where are the millions of Chinese people who are supposed to be so thrilled about participating in the new, globalized world? We haven't included them. And as a result, we really don't know what goes on in the world.

As we learned before, Chinese workers, by the dozens and dozens of millions, are forced to work seventy-hour weeks and to live in company housing, which they seldom have time or permission to leave. They are forbidden to form meaningful unions, and those who dare to protest face the armed weight of the police state. They are not free to gather, speak their minds, access a free press, or vote for anything but the one-party state. In virtually every respect taken for granted by Americans, Chinese workers are not free. How, exactly, does buying stuff from such unfree people fit into any meaningful concept of "free trade"?

This is not the time or the place to mount a rousing, solid argument against free trade as it's currently practiced and defined. My own feeling is that it's a neat idea, as are communism, free love, and Santa Claus. But if free-market capitalism was ever a meaningful concept within the United States alone, it does not work as a concept in the "globalized" world, with so many powerful, well-defended players pitted against so many utterly destitute ones with hardly any rights at all.

Like any economic system, free trade is not a force of nature, controlled by God or science. It is designed and controlled by men and women, who, as we've seen throughout this book, have rather predictable, deluded, and self-serving responses to power.

For years, free-trade advocates were pitted against politicians and pundits who argued for "protectionism," that is, providing legal incentives for U.S. companies to stay at home and employ American workers for the American products that Americans would buy. One of the strongest arguments made by the free-trade proponents is that free trade will bring freedom to people oppressed by repressive governments around the world. If this has happened, I haven't noticed. I did notice, however, that recently the Chinese government, in an attempt to help its people, made noises about lifting its minimum wage and enhancing workers' currently feeble rights to form labor unions. The reaction of the U.S. Chamber of Commerce in China was to oppose the government's initiative. So much for freedom's march.

The last generation has seen two billion low-wage workers added to the international labor pool. It is a massive transformation of the worker-employer playing field. But to put it ever so obliquely, in the words of Nobel Prize–winning economist Joseph Stiglitz, "Economic globalization has outpaced political globalization."

There is no question that the free market and the global economy are helping to foster "growth." But what I would suggest is willfully, systematically, or stupidly being overlooked are the ways this growth is transforming the world into new—and radically divided—classes of people, and the ways in which this transformation may haunt us beyond our ability to control it.

At the time of the Western industrial revolution, the difference in per capita income between citizens of rich nations and those of poor nations was negligible. In 2002, the difference was that people in the richest countries of the world earned approximately thirty thousand dollars per person per year, while those in the poorest earned about three hundred per year. To put it slightly differently, two hundred years ago, the income gap per capita between rich countries and poor ones was three to one. A hundred years ago, it had risen to ten to one. It currently stands at sixty to one and rising. (Ironically, this growth in income disparity came about at precisely the same time that slavery was being largely abolished throughout the world, thus freeing up workers' productive capacities.)

When free-trade enthusiasts mention that $x$ million Chinese and $y$ million Indians and anyone else from poor countries have been "lifted" out of poverty, what is seldom addressed is that they have been forced to join the world economy against their will. No one ever asked them if they wanted to sign up. The issue is seldom framed this way. Prior to their joining the modern world and the global economy, most had lived on small subsistence farms, growing the bulk of the food they needed, earning precious little hard cash but staying alive and self-sufficient.

Current global-trade policies, however, led by American and European subsidy-driven food production, have resulted in food being sold abroad below cost, which in turn has forced dozens of millions of Third World peasants off their land. So as these hundreds of millions of people around the world have been "lifted" up from self-sustaining subsistence poverty, they have also been "lifted" off their land, "lifted" away from their extended families, "lifted" out of their traditional way of life, and herded into slums.

According to social historian Mike Davis's *Planet of Slums,* in 1950 there were 86 cities in the world with a population over one million; today there are 400. By 2015, there will be at least 550. Cities will account for virtually *all* future world population growth, which is expected to peak at about ten billion in 2050. In the least developed countries, 78 percent of urban residents will dwell in slums. Worldwide, one-third of all city dwellers will live in slums. At least half of all slum residents are under the age of twenty.

As Davis aptly expressed the difference between rural poverty and modern slum poverty: "Urban space is never free. A place on the pavement, the rental of a rickshaw, a day's labor on a construction site, or a domestic's reference to a new employer: all of these require patronage or membership in some closed network, often an ethnic militia or street gang." There's no such thing as workplace rights because there's no such thing as law, employers, or sustained work opportunities. The "informal sector" of the slums, as Davis noted, "is the absence of formal contracts, rights, regulations, and bargaining power. In the absence of enforced labor rights is a semifeudal realm of kickbacks, bribes, tribal loyalties, and ethnic exclusion. Petty exploitation (endlessly franchised) is its essence."

Odds are irresistible that a few lucky individuals born into slums will somehow become real estate moguls and software engineers—or, as Charlie puts it, "the next Bill Gateses and Michael Dells." But, as Davis noted, the vast majority will work their entire degraded, uneducated lives as "piece-workers, liquor sellers, street vendors, cleaners, washers, ragpickers, nannies, and prostitutes." Or maybe they'll get jobs as lottery-ticket sellers, hairdressers, sewing machine operators working fourteen hours a day for some multinational corporation. But hey, they'll be free. And for most of the millions of peasants around the world, this, then, will be the miracle of globalization.

For U.S. workers, as far as I can tell, the miracle will be how slowly we join them in this globalized lifestyle. So far, most of the discussion about declining wages in the United States has concerned lower-level, unskilled workers. But the numbers of American jobs that can be exported is nearly infinite. It has been predicted by technology and business consultant Forrester Research that between now and 2015, some 3.3 million white-collar jobs will shift from the United States to low-cost countries. Other jobs vulnerable to outsourcing include six-figure Wall Street positions. Lehman Brothers and Bear Stearns have already contracted with Indian financial analysts for number-crunching work. America's 10 million or so IT workers, such as software engineers and designers; customer-service help-desk staff; reservation agents with hotels, car-rental agencies, and airlines; accountants; and radiologists are also losing jobs to overseas labor markets.

For advocates of free trade, this process is proof of the "creative destruction" of the free market. As Harvard Business School economists Michael C. Jensen and Perry Fagan predict, things will indeed get hairy for U.S. workers. Wages for some "will fall dramatically over the coming two or three decades, perhaps as much as fifty percent in some sectors"—but for those with the guts to stick it out while the world is remade in the name of efficiency and free trade, "a wonderfully optimistic future" awaits.

Okay.

So this brings me back to the quote from Justice Brandeis, who said that you can have either a great disparity between rich and poor or you can have democracy, but you can't have both. Will we revert back to a world in which slavery once again becomes an accepted practice?

I don't imagine we will. Far more profitable and productive—on the face of it—is to keep trying to convince every worker and every poor person in the world that he or she is an "entrepreneur," and that he or she simply needs to "buy in" and "get skills" and become a productive member of a modern, global, capitalist society. Such citizens can look forward to a future of political "freedom" in a world that just happens to have a tremendous disparity between rich and poor. I'm thinking of such countries as Brazil and the Philippines. These are nations with some of the greatest economic inequality in the world, yet they offer political rights comparable to those offered by the United States. Maybe life won't be so bad in this kind of a world. But I'm not so sure I want to find out.

What strikes me about contemporary slavery, as well as all other forms of labor abuse observed in this book, is the centrality of irrationality. In the past, people enslaved one another because they didn't know any better. I'd find it difficult to proffer such an excuse today.

As mentioned earlier, it would cost each American household about fifty dollars a year to double the wages of poor Hispanic farmworkers. New York University professor of American studies Andrew Ross cites a study of garment production in Mexico estimating that to raise workers' wages 100 percent would require a retail hike of only 2 to 6 percent. Similar estimates can be found and applied to most miserable sectors of the world: to improve the lot of the world's most wretched would simply not cost much.

Americans have already experimented with myriad ways to improve the lot of the working and lower classes: minimum wage, the right to form unions, workplace safety standards and guaranteed compensation for workers injured on the job, forty-hour workweeks, minimum guaranteed vacation time, a free universal education. While we're at it, we could include standards for sanitation and utilities systems; purity of water, air, medicines, and foods; transportation, parks, Social Security, and so on. As resented as they are, these are the laws that made the habits, and these are the habits produced by the laws, that brought the West out of the medieval world and into the modern age.

Why, one wonders, is it so hard to imagine that some combination of these approaches couldn't or shouldn't be encouraged in the Third World? Instead of a race backward—a race back through time to the days of mass misery for the benefit of a few—the next period of human history could just as easily emerge as a race to equality and justice. It might be tedious. And it might be difficult. But there really isn't much of an alternative.

Plenty of legal approaches could nudge a grudging world toward this fairer place. First and foremost among them would be the establishment of global labor and environmental standards. A worldwide minimum wage would be a complicated creature to engineer: it would have to be pegged per country, according to cost of living and so on. Opponents of such an idea will seize upon how complicated it is. Such opponents might be reminded that there was once a time when the idea of building a modern airplane was also considered complicated. It could then be reemphasized that in a world where free people trade with less-free people, where free countries trade with corrupt countries, and in which there are simply more people than jobs, without such protection, wages paid to workers around the world will simply fall and fall. And fall. And that that falling will one day lead us somewhere we probably don't want to go.

As George Orwell once noted, "Economic injustice will stop the moment we want it to stop, and no sooner, and if we genuinely want it to stop the method adopted hardly matters." And he's right. There are many ways of making the world a fairer place, but the time for hand-wringing over such issues cannot go on for another century or two. If the planet is to survive, we cannot afford to have half or two-thirds of the population living in abject filth and misery.

With a shift in perspective, equality and social justice could come to be viewed as the environment has. In the same way that it is becoming unacceptable to sacrifice environmental well-being for economic gain, we could insist on a world where it is unacceptable to force quite so much misery upon those whose productive labor provides our freedom and comfort. As we are seeing with global warming and the threats of increased temperatures, storm velocities, and ocean levels, we may, in time, come to see social pandemics as equally menacing—if predictable—threats. The issue will then become one of self-preservation more than justice. Never mind the question "Are you fine with your comfort relying on the misery of billions?" The question would be "Do you want them to come kill you?"

In May 2006, *O Globo,* one of Brazil's leading newspapers, published an anonymous interview with an anonymous subject said to be a prisoner housed in one of the country's notoriously hellish prisons. Many readers credited the source as Marcos Williams Herbas Camacho, also known as "Playboy," the leader of the PCC, one of the nation's largest prison gangs.

Reigning from prison, the outfit has killed scores of people in the last year and has staged more than three hundred attacks on police, bus stations, and public forums, humiliating farcical government attempts to maintain order. I don't know if these words were made up or came from Playboy or anyone else from the slums. All I know is that they sound pretty credibly like what a person might sound like after being born in one. Before becoming famous for crime, said the interviewee,

> I was poor and invisible. For decades, you never bothered to look at me. People only heard about us when the slums collapsed, or from romantic music about "the *favelas* at sunset," stuff like that. Now we're rich, thanks to the multinational cocaine trade. And you guys are scared to death. We are the late blooming of your social conscience.
>
> We're at the core of what is beyond solution . . . we're a new species, a wholly different animal from you . . . there's no more proletariat, no pitiful or exploited masses. There's a third thing growing out there, cultivated from the mud, schooled on absolute illiteracy, graduating from the prisons, like an alien monster hidden in the cities' cracks.
>
> We're on the edge of a postmisery that has begotten a new murderous culture, propped up by technology, satellites, cell phones, the Internet, modern weapons. It's shit with chips and megabytes. My soldiers are a mutated social species, they're the fungus growing on a big dirty mistake.
>
> We're on the attack. You are on the defensive. You are obsessed with human rights. We are cruel and merciless.

The solution? he was asked.
There isn't one. It's too late.
I have a hunch this interview isn't real. I've conducted many interviews, and the words just sound too pretty. But it doesn't matter. Because the sentiment they contain sounds very, very real.

Osama bin Laden, to my thinking, is just another name for Osama bin jobs, Osama bin minimum wage, Osama bin social justice. The poor will find ways to revenge themselves on the rich. And the ideology that provides the most comfort and justice to the largest number of people will prevail. If the revenge motive of brand Osama holds greater appeal than brand Freedom, well, I guess that means brand Freedom didn't do such a great job of delivering on its promises.

"The precondition," states artist and writer John Berger, "for thinking politically on a global scale is to see the unity of the unnecessary suffering taking place." Indeed. Because while in a world of several million people, or several hundred million people, slavery was fine, mass injustice in a world of seven billion equals pain, equals misery, equals desperation. Add TV and the Internet and it equals blowback. It doesn't matter if you think you're a liberal or a conservative. If you can read this page, you are on top of the world and billions of people are beneath you. Your ignorance and your lack of a program will likely equal the squalor of your grandchildren's existence.

When I first started writing this book, I considered myself a liberal. I thought it was mean that people and corporations with power aren't nicer to people with less power. Now I laugh at that idea. There are so many billions of poor people out there. They are not educated, but they're certainly not stupid, and I very much doubt they can be lied to or angered indefinitely.

But to anyone in this world today who feels compelled to go on TV and talk about freedom or tell us all about the glories of globalization and free trade and democracy—any writer, any politician, any corporate advertising person invoking that stupid word *freedom* over and over again—I have some advice. Go out into this newly globalized world you're profiting from, go visit the people being "lifted" out of poverty, the workers who are making your products. Go live in their huts, eat their rice and plantains, squat on their floors, and listen to their babies cry. Sniff some glue and pray with them. Try to get justice from their police if someone hurts you. And then come back and let's talk about freedom.

# Acknowledgments

This book began life in 2001, with New Yorker editor John Bennet. It would not exist without his patience. I'd also like to warmly thank Bill Clegg, Jin Auh, Daniel Menaker, and Dana Isaacson, who, as agent, agent, editor, and editor, lent tremendous amounts of help and expertise in shaping the material.

The initial lead for the book came from North Carolina labor activist Rosa Saavedra, to whom I'll be eternally grateful. The initial intellectual framework was inspired by the hardworking co-directors of the Coalition of Immokalee Workers. I'd also like to thank my researchers, who provided steady guidance and reality checks throughout: Clancy Nolan, Johnny Dwyer, Bill Hangley, Jr., and, later, Matthew Cole and Julie Tate.

Next come the people and organizations who helped in a wide variety of ways, from Cintra Wilson, who teased a book proposal out of me, to William Betz, Greg Schell, Lisa Butler, Yumei Xie, Jing Zhou, Eric Bozman, Mar-Vic Cagurangan, Charlie Kuivenen, and Dr. Kevin Bales, all of whom assisted in various aspects of the process of reporting and writing this book. I'd also like to acknowledge the critical assistance offered by the Sydney Hillman Award for Journalism, the Richard J. Margolis Award, and the J. Anthony Lukas Work-in-Progress Award; as much as anything or anyone else, their financial help made this book possible.

Finally, I thank my friends and family, and most of all my sister Marisa, for listening during these last few years.

# Bibliography

**GENERAL**

Bales, Kevin. *Disposable People: New Slavery in the Global Economy*. Berkeley: University of California Press, 1999.

Davis, Mike. *Planet of Slums*. London: Verso, 2006.

Drescher, Seymour, and Stanley L. Engerman, eds. *A Historical Guide to World Slavery*. New York: Oxford University Press, 1998.

Ehrenreich, Barbara. *Fear of Falling: The Inner Life of the Middle Class*. New York: Pantheon, 1989.

Finley, M. I. *Ancient Slavery and Modern Ideology*. New York: Viking, 1980.

Fishman, Charles. *The Wal-Mart Effect: How the World's Most Powerful Company Really Works—and How It's Transforming the American Economy*. New York: Penguin, 2006.

Frank, Thomas. *One Market Under God: Extreme Capitalism, Market Populism, and the End of Economic Democracy*. New York: Doubleday, 2000.

Greider, William. *One World, Ready or Not: The Manic Logic of Global Capitalism*. New York: Simon & Schuster, 1997.

McGill, Craig. *Human Traffic: Sex, Slaves and Immigration*. London: Vision Paperbacks, 2003.

Murolo, Priscilla, and A. B. Chitty, with illustrations by Joe Sacco. *From the Folks Who Brought You the Weekend: A Short Illustrated History of Labor in the United States.* New York: New Press, 2001.

Nace, Ted. *Gangs of America: The Rise of Corporate Power and the Disabling of Democracy.* San Francisco: Barrett-Koehler Publishers, 2003.

Patterson, Orlando. *Slavery and Social Death: A Comparative Study.* Cambridge, Mass.: Harvard University Press, 1982.

Ross, Andrew. *Fast Boat to China: Lessons from Shanghai: Corporate Flight and the Consequences of Free Trade.* New York: Pantheon, 2006.

Tonelson, Alan. *The Race to the Bottom: Why a Worldwide Worker Surplus and Uncontrolled Free Trade Are Sinking American Living Standards.* Boulder, Colo.: Westview, 2000.

Winthrop, Jordan D. *White Over Black: American Attitudes Toward the Negro, 1550–1812.* Baltimore: Penguin, 1968.

### FLORIDA

Conover, Ted. *Coyotes: A Journey Through the Secret World of America's Illegal Aliens.* New York: Vintage, 1987.

Kimbrell, Andrew, ed. *The Fatal Harvest Reader: The Tragedy of Industrial Agriculture.* Washington, D.C.: Foundation for Deep Ecology, 2002.

Martínez, Ruben. *Crossing Over: A Mexican Family on the Migrant Trail.* New York: Metropolitan, 2001.

Rothenberg, Daniel. *With These Hands: The Hidden World of Migrant Farmworkers Today.* Berkeley: University of California Press, 2000.

### SAIPAN

Dubose, Lou, and Jan Reid. *The Hammer: Tom DeLay, God, Money, and the Rise of the Republican Congress.* New York: Public Affairs, 2004.

Farrell, Don A. *History of Northern Mariana Islands.* 1st ed. Published by the Public School System of the Commonwealth of the Northern Mariana Islands, 1991.

Kahn, E. J., Jr. *A Reporter in Micronesia.* New York: W. W. Norton, 1965.

Kluge, P. F. *The Edge of Paradise: America in Micronesia.* Honolulu: Kolowalu, 1991.

Willens, Howard P., and Deanne C. Siemer. *An Honorable Accord: The Covenant Between the Northern Mariana Islands and the United States.* Honolulu: University of Hawaii Press, 2001.

————. *National Security and Self-Determination: United States Policy in Micronesia 1961–1972.* Westport, Conn.: Praeger, 2000.

# Notes

Notes have not been included for interviews conducted by the author or sources mentioned explicitly in the text. In many other cases, such as trial transcripts, if the transcript is cited either in the text or below, repeat citations have been omitted.

## INTRODUCTION

xix **"man had no moral view":** Patterson, *Slavery and Social Death,* 154.

xxi **"Do you feel that Negroes":** Hazel Erskine, "The Polls: Negro Employment," *Public Opinion Quarterly* 32, no. 1 (Spring 1968): 132–53.

xxii **In Greece in Homer's day:** Valuations compiled from numerous sources, including Patterson's *Slavery and Social Death* and Eugene D. Genovese, *Roll Jordan Roll: The World the Slaves Made* (New York: Random House, 1974).

## FLORIDA

7 **The fact that few buyers:** See John Kenneth Galbraith, *The Great Crash 1929* (1955; repr., Boston: Mariner Books, 1977), 3–7, for a brief and droll history of the Florida land boom and the larger phenomenon of the boom mentality in general.

7 **But the principal commodities are:** The Florida Farm Bureau compiles various

statistics and other information about Florida's crops and farms. See http://
www.floridafarmbureau.org.

8  **The average migrant has a life:** Facts about migrant workers' income, citizenship status, and other details can be found in U.S. Department of Labor,
Office of the Assistant Secretary for Policy, Office of Programmatic Policy,
*Findings from the National Agricultural Workers Survey 2001–2002: A Demo-
graphic and Employment Profile of United States Farm Workers,* Research Report
no. 9 (Washington, D.C., March 2005).

8  **Twenty thousand farmworkers:** Kimbrell, *Fatal Harvest Reader,* 139.

8  **Nationally, 50 percent of migrants:** *National Agriculture Workers Survey.*

8  **An estimated 80 percent:** Fritz Roka and Dorothy Cook, "Farmworkers in
Southwest Florida: Final Report," September 30, 1998. See http://www.imok
.ufl.edu/economics/labor/final98.pdf.

10 **In Daniel Rothenberg's:** Rothenberg, *With These Hands,* 15–16, 44.

17 **Like half of all illegal migrants:** Karen Schaler, "Border Crossings Hinder
Training of Arizona Bases," *Boston Globe,* April 7, 2005.

21 **Other prosecutors I spoke to:** Many Justice Department officials are forbidden to speak on the record about past or current cases.

23 **Nearly all:** Many activists and farmworker advocates declined to voice criti-
cism of law enforcement officials on the record for fear of straining their close
working relationships.

24 **There are many groups:** Greg Schell, managing attorney of Florida Legal
Services' Migrant Farmworker Justice Project, typifies a different approach.
Schell's twenty-five-year career in Florida has centered on legal approaches to
advancing farmworker justice. Holding that use by corporations of labor contractors and other intermediaries is a key problem in the mistreatment of
farmworkers, and that use of such intermediaries has spread far beyond agriculture, Schell has focused primarily on finding ways to hold growers liable as
"joint employers" of the workers brought to their fields by labor contractors.
Thus responsible, such employers become far less able to evade responsibility
for minimum wage and worker protections.

38 **In the Reconstruction-era South:** Michael Browning, "Still Harvesting
Shame," *Palm Beach Post,* December 7, 2003.

38 **In 1880, 36 percent:** Edwin Embree, "Southern Farm Tenancy: The Way Out
of Its Evil," *Survey Graphic* 25, no. 3 (March 1936), 149.

39 **In 1942, farm interests:** Information about the Bracero Program can be found
through the Bracero History Project, a joint effort coordinated by the Smith-

sonian's National Museum of American History, the Center for History and New Media at George Mason University, the Institute of Oral History at the University of Texas at El Paso, and the Center for the Study of Race and Ethnicity in America. See http://echo.gmu.edu/bracero.

39 **World War II proved:** Robert D. Billinger, *Hitler's Soldiers in the Sunshine State: German P.O.W.s in Florida,* Florida History and Culture Series (Gainesville: University Press of Florida, 2000), 79.

39 **In 1945 there were:** Browning, "Still Harvesting Shame."

40 **One such ruse is painstakingly:** Alec Wilkinson, *Big Sugar: Seasons in the Cane Fields of Florida* (New York: Alfred A. Knopf, 1998).

40 **In the 1970s, an executive:** Marie Brenner, "In the Kingdom of Big Sugar," *Vanity Fair,* February 2001.

40 **In the 1980s, a class-action lawsuit:** Ibid.

41 **In the last few years:** Browning, "Still Harvesting Shame."

41 **They were called, appropriately:** Michael J. Ybarra, " 'Crop Failure' Homeless Are Drawn into a Miserable Life on Farm 'Wino Crews,' " *Wall Street Journal,* October 19, 1992.

43 **In 1993, the Bondses:** Matthew Eisley, "Slavery Suspects Surrender," Raleigh *News and Observer,* August 4, 1993.

44 **Finally, however, in June:** Nancy San Martin, "Farm Labor Suppliers Plead Guilty to Charge of Enslaving Workers," Fort Lauderdale *Sun-Sentinel,* May 12, 1997.

45 **Seventy years ago there were nearly:** Kimbrell, *Fatal Harvest Reader,* 17.

46 **While once upon a time:** Michael Pollan, *The Botany of Desire: A Plant's Eye View of the World* (New York: Random House, 2001), 233.

46 **Between 1910 and 1983:** Jason McKenney, "Artificial Fertility: The Environmental Cost of Industrial Fertilizers," in Kimbrell, *Fatal Harvest Reader.*

46 **It now requires ten fossil:** Wes Jackson, "Farming in Nature's Image: Natural Systems Agriculture," in Kimbrell, *Fatal Harvest Reader,* 69.

46 **Between 1945 and 1985:** Ron Kroese, "Industrial Agriculture's War Against Nature," in Kimbrell, *Fatal Harvest Reader,* 103.

46 **In 1980, a ton of fertilizer:** McKenney, "Artificial Fertility," 128.

47 **Since 1960, the United:** Ibid.

48 **In a fascinating:** Fishman, *The Wal-Mart Effect,* 80–81.

50 **As an article from:** Charles Porter, "Big Fast Food Contracts Breaking Tomato Repackers," ThePacker.com, May 16, 2005.

50 **In 1952, farmers:** U.S. Department of Agriculture Economic Research Services,

"Food Marketing and Price Spreads: USDA Market Basket." See http://www.ers.usda.gov/Briefing/FoodPriceSpreads/basket/table2fruit.htm.

50 **In 2000, the last year tracked:** Ibid.

51 **According to various studies:** U.S. Department of Agriculture Economic Research Services, "Agricultural Income and Finance Outlook" (AIS-84, November 2006). See http://usda.mannlib.cornell.edu/usda/current/AIS/AIS-11-30-2006.pdf.

51 **Some companies, in particular:** "The Best and Worst Return on Equity," *Business Week,* March 29, 1999.

51 **In December 2003:** Tracy Roselle, "With f.o.b.s High, Surcharge Catches Only a Little Flack," ThePacker.com, December 2003.

52 **According to the Economic Research Service:** U.S. Department of Agriculture, Economic Research Services, "Food CPI, Prices and Expenditures: Expenditures on Food, by Selected Countries, 2002." See http://www.ers.usda.gov/Briefing/CPIFoodAndExpenditures/Data/table97.htm.

52 **Another interesting statistic:** U.S. Department of Agriculture, Economic Research Services, "Food CPI, Prices and Expenditures: Food Expenditures by Families and Individuals as a Share of Disposable Personal Income." See http://www.ers.usda.gov/Briefing/CPIFoodAndExpenditures/Data/table7.htm.

53 **According to the Center for Responsive:** See http://www.opensecrets.org.

53 **According to the General Accounting Office:** "Embracing Illegals," *Immigration Enforcement: Weaknesses Hinder Employment Verification and Worksite Enforcement Efforts,* Congressional Report, GAO-05-813 (August 2005).

53 **In fact, in 1999:** Eduardo Porter, "The Search for Illegal Immigrants Stops in the Workplace," *New York Times,* March 5, 2006.

53 **The INS, now called:** Ibid.

54 **The Bush administration's proposed:** "2006 Budget Proposal: Agency Breakdown," *Washington Post,* February 7, 2005.

55 **The results of this kind:** Craig Becker, "A Good Job for Everyone," *Legal Times* 27, no. 26 (September 6, 2004), Points of View section.

55 **In one instance, in 1998:** Ned Glascock, "Foreign Labor on Home Soil," Raleigh *News & Observer,* August 29, 1999.

55 **In a complicated case:** *Hoffman Plastic Compounds, Inc. v. National Labor Relations Board* (00-1595) 535 U.S. 137 (2002).

56 **In 2000, the Department of Justice:** "Victims of Trafficking and Violence Protection Act of 2000," Public Law 106-386, 106th Cong. (October 28, 2000).

72 **In March 2005, Yum! Brands:** Brett Barrouquere, "Taco Bell Agrees to Pay Extra Penny for Tomatoes," *Associated Press,* March 9, 2005.

73 **McDonald's responded:** Lisa Jennings, "Concern over McD Tomato Policy Grows," *Nation's Restaurant News,* December 12, 2005.

73 **Unfortunately for McDonald's:** Jordan Buckley and Katie Shepherd, "Slavery Beneath the Golden Arches?" *Wire Tap Magazine,* January 21, 2006.

74 **As Eric Schlosser, author:** Eric Schlosser, "A Side Order of Human Rights," *New York Times,* April 6, 2005.

## TULSA

91 **In 1972, John Pickle:** "John Pickle Company Trainees Report," April 13, 2002, 3.

91 **Sales reached $15 million:** Ibid., 3.

91 **Pickle had watched the domestic oil:** See http://www.tulsalibrary.org/research/artdeco/artdecointulsa.htm.

92 **The company signed an agreement:** See http://www.forbes.com/lists/2006/10/U38U.html.

93 **(The Kuwaiti economy):** The CIA World Factbook website notes that as of 2006, an estimated 80 percent of the 1,136,000-person workforce was non-Kuwaiti. See https://www.cia.gov/cia/publications/factbook/geos/ku.html.

93 **Murzello, born in Mumbai:** Raymond Murzello, testimony, *Babu Thanu Chellen, et al. and U.S. Equal Employment Opportunity Commission (EEOC) v. John Pickle Company, Inc.,* N.D. Okla., 02-0085 (2006).

94 **As Pickle later:** John Pickle deposition, July 2, 2003, *Chellen et al. v. John Pickle.*

95 **As company literature, written:** "Pickle Company Trainees Report," 6.

101 **per capita income is $720:** World Bank, Statistics, 2005. See http://devdata .worldbank.org/external/CPProfile.asp?PTYPE=CP&CCODE=IND.

101 **(compared with $33,050):** See http://www.fedstats.gov/qf/states/00000.html. FedStats is a website offering official statistical information from a hundred federal agencies on such topics as economic and population trends, crime, education, health care, aviation safety, energy use, farm production, and more.

103 **As Ludbe well knew:** Uday Dattatray Ludbe, affidavit (n.d.), *Chellen et al. v. John Pickle Company.*

106 **As the writer Alexander Cockburn:** Alexander Cockburn, "Friedman's Imaginary India," *Nation,* June 8, 2005.

113 **"Knowing Gulam":** "Re: Flights," e-mail, Ray Murzello to Shari Rumsey, December 14, 2001, 3:10 A.M., exhibit 9, *Chellen et al. v. John Pickle Company.*

118 **Speaking of India, he noted:** Michael Overall, "Workers Allege Abuses; Recruits from India Were Virtual Slaves, Attorneys Say," *Tulsa World,* February 1, 2002.

119 *The Washington Post* **wrote:** "Dream of Coming to America to Work Becomes Nightmare for Workers from India," *NBC Nightly News,* July 17, 2002.

123 **"I have never, and I mean":** John Bowe, Marisa Bowe, and Sabin Streeter, *Gig: Americans Talk About Their Jobs* (New York: Crown, 2001).

127 **his answers to Felty's questions:** Jacon Harbour, deposition, July 10, 2002, *Chellen et al. v. John Pickle Company.*

133 **As it turned out:** EEOC's Proposed Findings of Fact and Conclusions of Law for Phase II Trial Proceedings, *Chellen et al. v. John Pickle Company,* 57.

134 **The U.S. Department of Labor:** *Fair Labor Standards Act,* U.S. Department of Labor's Wage and Hour Division Manual (BNA) 91:416 (1975).

## ANTS

152 **To this day, white American families:** U.S. Bureau of the Census, American FactFinder.

152 **When Frederick Law Olmsted:** Olmsted, *The Cotton Kingdom: A Traveller's Observations on Cotton and Slavery in the American Slave States 1853–1861* (New York: Da Capo, 1996).

## SAIPAN

162 **In a newspaper article, William Tamayo:** Haidee Eugenio, "Feds Note Disturbing Labor Cases in NMI," *Marianas Variety,* November 10, 2005.

163 **half the size of Rhode Island:** Kahn, *Reporter in Micronesia,* 10.

163 **Historically, Micronesians have gotten by:** For a detailed account of Micronesian and Saipanese political development, refer to Willens and Siemer's *Honorable Accord* and *National Security.*

164 **As Henry Kissinger would somewhat:** Willens and Siemer, *National Security,* 148.

164 **"whose geographical dispersion":** Kahn, *Reporter in Micronesia,* 10.

166 **"You could almost see them":** Kluge, *Edge of Paradise,* 69.

166 **Magellan "claimed" the island:** Magellan and his crew, starving and dying of thirst, hit first landfall at Guam. Apparently liking what he saw, Magellan decided to appropriate the Marianas for the Crown. When a local made off with

his skiff, he became piqued and ordered his soldiers to burn a village. After killing a number of natives and failing to conscript others, Magellan and his men left in a huff, and dubbed the islands Las Islas de Ladrones—the Islands of Thieves—a name they would bear for the next 150 years.

167 **After losing the Spanish-American:** For a detailed history of the period following the Spanish-American War in Saipan, see Kahn, *Reporter in Micronesia.*

167 **the first time flamethrower tanks:** Farrell, *Northern Mariana Islands,* 346–83.

167 **In the end, the Japanese:** Ibid., 387.

170 **been joined by about 3,000:** Seth Faison, "Stretching Federal Labor Law Far into South Pacific," *New York Times,* February 20, 1999.

171 **what one congressional report termed:** John Berry, Assistant Secretary of the Interior for Policy, Management and Budget, statement before the House Committee on Resources Subcommittee National Parks and Public Lands, 105th Cong., September 17, 1999.

172 **One man was told:** Terry McCarthy, "Give Me Your Tired, Your Poor . . .," *Time,* February 2, 1998.

172 **While CNMI labor law required:** Wendy Doromal, prepared statement before the Senate Committee on Energy and National Resources, March 31, 1998.

173 **At one South Korean company:** Jennifer Lin, "Your Pricey Clothing Is Their Low-Pay Work," *Philadelphia Inquirer,* February 8, 1998.

173 **cultivated an interest in underaged:** For a description of Hillblom's life and times in Saipan, and the subsequent death and battle over his estate, see Matt Smith, "Cash for Genes," *San Francisco Weekly,* April 5, 2000.

174 **in late March 1999:** Ron Harris, "OSHA: Massive Food Poisoning Outbreak at Saipan Garment Factory," Associated Press, April 7, 1999.

177 **As Allen Stayman, assistant secretary:** Robert Collier, *San Francisco Chronicle,* January 20, 1999.

178 **"the island way," Abramoff explained:** Juliet Eilperin, "A 'Petri Dish' in the Pacific," *Washington Post,* July 26, 2000.

178 **As DeLay, meeting with a group:** Brian Ross, *20/20,* ABC, May 24, 1999.

178 **Later, discussing Saipan in an interview:** Eilperin, " 'Petri Dish.' "

178 **Tan would show up donating:** See the Center for Responsive Politics website, www.opensecrets.org, for a database of campaign contributions connected to Tan.

180 **would also be rewarded with such:** Eamon Javers, *Business Week Online,* December 16, 2005.

180 **One such taxpayer-funded mission:** *Marianas Variety,* 1999.

185  **one cable-television company, five:**  Liberty Dones, "Economy Took a Beating in '05," *Saipan Tribune,* February 21, 2006.

187  **The writer E. J. Kahn:**  Kahn, *Reporter in Micronesia,* 247.

214  **At the top of Saipan's pecking:**  Compiled from e-mails with a Tan spokesperson and the Tan website, www.tanholdings.com.

227  **Chinese citizens were required to live:**  For a more detailed description of Chinese labor laws and practices, see Andrew Ross, *Fast Boat to China: Corporate Flight and the Consequences of Free Trade: Lessons from Shanghai* (New York: Pantheon, 2006); Anita Chan, "Race to the Bottom," *China Perspectives* 46 (March–April 2003), and "Culture of Survival: Lives of Migrant Workers Through the Prism of Private Letters," in *Popular China,* ed. Perry Link, Richard Madsen, and Paul Pickowic (Boulder, Colo.: Rowman & Littlefield, 2002), 163–88; and Anita Chan and Robert J. S. Ross, "Racing to the Bottom: Industrial Trade Without a Social Clause," *Third World Quarterly* 24, no. 6 (2003), 1011–28. See also the Section 301 Petition of American Federation of Labor and Congress of Industrial Organizations Before the Office of the United States Trade Representative, submitted June 8, 2006, at http://www .aflcio.org/issues/jobseconomy/globaleconomy/upload/china_petition.pdf.

228  **Australia-based expert on Chinese labor:**  Chan, "Culture of Survival."

235  **fewer than a quarter:**  Moneth G. Deposa, "Inos: Less Than 25 Percent of 8th Grade Students Earn Bachelor's Degree," *Marianas Variety,* December 15, 2005.

235  **According to a recent survey:**  Ibid.

236  **In 1993, Commonwealth Health Center:**  Statistics provided to author by CNMI Department of Public Health, compiled February 27, 2006.

239  **Between 2004 and 2005, garment sales:**  Dones, "Economy Took a Beating."

244  **"If they do not listen to me":**  Gemma Q. Casas, "Governor Says Miller Bill 'Genocidal,' " *Marianas Variety,* June 20, 2006.

252  **a young freelance reporter:**  *Ms.,* Spring 2006.

261  **On the night of April 10, 2002:**  CNMI criminal case no. 02-117A.

## CONCLUSION

268  **It was the wistful recollection:**  In James M. Denham and Canter J. Brown, Jr., eds., *Cracker Times and Pioneer Lives: The Florida Reminiscences of George Gillett Keen and Sarah Pamela Williams* (Columbia: University of South Carolina Press, 2003), 46.

270  **A study from 2001 parsed:**  2001 Fairness and Accuracy in Reporting Survey.

# Index

labor conditions on, 172–73, 174–77,
181, 186, 202, 205, 206, 211, 213,
214, 219–26, 228, 229, 236, 243,
246, 251–52, 257–58

male promiscuity on, 246–48, 249,
251–52

poverty level on, 171, 197, 239

quality of life on, 190–195, 197–98,
199, 200, 208, 226–27, 229–30,
231, 232–37, 239, 244, 251, 256,
260, 261

sex trades on, 161–62, 173–74, 175,
181, 189–90, 198–99, 205, 245–46,
254–55, 258–65

slavery on, xv, 157, 161–63, 204, 206,
231

substance abuse on, 173, 188, 195,
200

"Third World" atmosphere of,
185–86, 187–88, 197, 263–64

tourism on, 170, 189–90, 191, 215,
239, 246, 258

tropical beauty of, 183–84, 187, 200

as two-tiered society, 186–87, 244,
251–52

World War II and, 167–68

See also Carolinian people;
Chamorro people; Common-
wealth of the Northern Mariana
Islands (CNMI); garment industry; Micronesia; Northern Marianas; Rota; Tinian

Saipan Garment Manufacturers Association, 178, 199, 239

Salii, Lazarus, 165

Sánchez, Mario (pseud.), 16–21, 61,
63–64, 71, 75–77

Sartin, Sharon, 111, 125

Scanlon, Michael, 240, 243

Schell, Greg, 45, 73

Schlosser, Eric, 74

Schwartz, Rhonda, 176

segregation, efforts to end, 36–37, 75

September 11, 2001, terrorist attacks,
108, 111, 191

sexual trafficking
on Saipan, 161–62, 173–74, 175, 181,
189–90, 205
in Thailand, xxii
in the U.S., xviii, xx, 56, 57

sharecropping, 38–39, 90

Sinclair, Upton, 155

Skinner, Jim, 74

slavery
abolition of, xiii–xiv, 272
among ants, 156–57
coercion and, xviii, 137
as corrupting social force, 152–53,
157
essential characteristics of, 80
exploitive labor environments and,
36–37, 138, 162, 172
historical attitudes and, xix–xxii,
79–80, 82–84, 134, 155–56, 275,
278
as manifestation of owner's power
hunger, 151, 153–55, 267–68
in modern U.S., xiii–xv, xvii–xix,
xxii, 56, 151
monetary values and, xxii, 153
prosecution of court cases against,
21–24, 30, 32, 35, 40–41, 55, 57,
64–72, 73–74, 138–41
public indifference to, xiv–xv

### ABOUT THE AUTHOR

JOHN BOWE has contributed to *The New Yorker, The New York Times Magazine, GQ, The American Prospect, McSweeney's,* National Public Radio's *This American Life,* and more. He is the co-editor of *Gig: Americans Talk About Their Jobs* and co-writer of the film *Basquiat.* He has received the J. Anthony Lukas Work-in-Progress Award, the Sydney Hillman Award for Journalism, and the Richard J. Margolis Award. He currently lives in New York City.

A B O U T   T H E   T Y P E

This book was set in Granjon, a modern recutting of a typeface produced under the direction of George W. Jones, who based Granjon's
design on the letter forms of Claude Garamond (1480–1561). The
name was given to the typeface as a tribute to the typographic
designer Robert Granjon.